Gullah Culture
in America

JOHN F. BLAIR PUBLISHER
Winston-Salem, North Carolina

Gullah Culture
in America

by Wilbur Cross

Foreword by Emory Shaw Campbell

Published by

JOHN F. BLAIR
PUBLISHER
1406 Plaza Drive
Winston-Salem, North Carolina 27103
www.blairpub.com

PUBLISHING HISTORY
2012 John F. Blair, Publisher, trade paperback edition
Copyright © 2008 by Wilbur Cross

COVER ART
Two Baskets, 2000
Oil on Linen, 16" x 20" © Jonathan Green
The Collection of Margaret and Jeffrey Lofgren

Library of Congress Cataloging-in-Publication Data

Cross, Wilbur.
  Gullah culture in America / by Wilbur Cross ; foreword by Emory Shaw Campbell.
    p. cm.
  Includes bibliographical references and index.
  ISBN 978-0-89587-573-0 (pbk. : alk. paper) 1. Gullahs—History. 2. Gullahs—Social life and customs. I. Title.
  E185.93.S7C76 2012
  975'.00496073—dc23
                        2011039031

Design by Debra Long Hampton

10 9 8 7 6 5 4 3 2 1

Contents

Dr. Emory Campbell leading a group from Kenya on a tour of Penn Center on St. Helena Island, South Carolina
COURTESY OF JACK ALDERMAN

%⁄∖∖∖⁄%

Going Home
How a Long-Lost Culture
Is Rising from Oblivion

Since long before America's independence, the nation has had hidden pockets of a bygone African culture, rich in native history, with a language of its own, and long endowed with beguiling talents in its traditions, language, design, medicine, agriculture, fishing, hunting, weaving, and arts. Although thousands of articles and hundreds of books have been written on discoveries of Native American cultures and Indian lore, the Gullah/Geechee culture has been almost totally overlooked. It is known only to a handful of North Americans, mainly professional historians whose findings have been published in specialized journals and scholarly books. This book, authored by a longtime historian, explores what very few yet know as a direct link to the African continent, an almost lost culture that exists in the Sea Islands of the United States, along a corridor stretching from the northeast coast of Florida along the Georgia and South Carolina coastal shores to the Wilmington, North Carolina, area, and little more than 50 miles inland at any point.

The first published evidence of this culture went almost unnoticed until the 1860s, when northern missionaries made their way south, even as the Civil War was at its height, to the Sea Islands of South Carolina, where they established a small school to help former slaves learn how to read and write and make a living in a world of upheaval and distress. One of these schools evolved into the distinguished Penn School. There they noticed that most of the native island blacks spoke a language that was only part English, tempered with expressions and idioms, often spoken in a melodious, euphonic manner. Yet this was the barest beginning, for the language carried over into other forms of communication and expressiveness, ranging from body movements and the use of hand and head movements to the rituals of religion, work, dancing, greetings, and the arts.

The homogeneity, richness, and consistency of this culture were made possible by the fortunate fact that these peoples maintained a solidarity over the generations because they were isolated from other peoples and cultures. Thus they were able to maintain their heritage, language, and traditions, unlike other peoples of African and foreign lineage who came to America's shores and over the years blended in with other cultures, as they did in the northern or southern cities and the more heavily populated upper regions of Georgia, South Carolina, and North Carolina. Even today there are more than 300,000 Gullah-speaking people living in the remoter areas of the Sea Islands, such as St. Helena, Edisto, Coosaw, Ossabaw, Sapelo, Daufuskie, and Cumberland.

Part of this book focuses on the engrossing story of sea islanders of Gullah descent who traveled in groups to the region in 1989, 1998, and 2005 to trace their origins and ancestry, later exploring Sierra Leone and other parts of West Africa. I was fortunate enough to have been involved with the research into these West African origins, along with one of the most noted authorities in this field, Joseph Opala, an anthropologist who had made some remarkable studies about Bunce Island, in the harbor of Freetown, Sierra Leone, where in the 18th century thousands of captured Africans were held temporarily to be boarded on ships bound for South Carolina and Georgia.

Many subjects of pertinent interest are included, beginning with a brief introduction to the Gullah heritage and culture in America, its roots, the location and extent of its peoples, its current history and beliefs, and most importantly its exuberance, imagery, color, and contributions to the world we live in. One of the most unusual accounts describes the way in which a young black American linguist, Lorenzo Dow Turner, ventured into the remotest reaches of the Sea Islands of Georgia and the Carolinas in the early 1930s to begin the first scientific investigation of the Gullah peoples and culture. Astonishingly—unlike Native American cultures, which were studied many generations ago by sociologists—the Gullah history and heritage were virtually unknown, even in the Southeast, until the Turner studies were made. Even then, his work faded from public knowledge, and the Gullah culture lapsed again, almost into oblivion, until a slow revival began in the last quarter of the 20th century.

One book alone, covering an entire culture, cannot do more than give its readers a broad panorama of the subject. Yet, remarkably, the chapters in the Gullah history also present a wealth of detail that allows readers to experience the drama, the color, the romance, and the vitality of Gullah, and in effect "meet" many of the personalities who have played a part—past and present—in making it what it is today. The author, using personal and historical research, recounts interviews with Gullah people who have described what it was like to grow up in the old traditions. He takes the reader on a tour of "praise houses," where enslaved Africans and their descendants practiced religion, not only with the familiar spirituals, but with expressions of faith, joy, hardship, hope, and repentance in "shouts," which begin slowly with the shuffling of feet and the clapping of hands, followed by louder and louder expressions of reverence. He introduces the reader to one of the most bewitching aspects of the Gullah culture: its practices of healing and folk medicine. Though originating hundreds of years ago, in many cases these practices have been proven to be scientifically effective and some are the forerunners of medications developed in the present century.

As one who is recognized today for my fluency in the Gullah language and my many assignments to translate it, I was particularly pleased to see the chapter on our speech, which takes the reader on a rewarding and effective road to discovery of the origins and usages of words, phrases, and idiom. And I recommend to you the joys of reading about Gullah foods and recipes, festivals and celebrations, music, song, and dance, and the unbelievable origins of that side of the culture that brings joy to the heart. In retrospect, it is difficult to realize that so many of the uplifting aspects of this unique culture were born in the darkest days—of slavery and inhumanity and torture and discrimination. How Gullah people rose from the ashes to revive and live their culture in the most positive of ways is truly a fascinating and inspiring story.

I can state without reservation that you will reach the end of the chapters with a sense of great human accomplishment, and you will want to pass the book along to others to let them know what the human body, spirit, and soul can accomplish under even the greatest duress.

Emory Shaw Campbell
Executive Director Emeritus, Penn Center,
St. Helena Island, South Carolina

Acknowledgments

This book could never have been written without going to many key institutions and organizations that have been for many years compiling information about the Gullah culture and peoples. Most pertinent among these because of its specific attention to this subject is the *Low Country Gullah Culture Special Resource Study*. This is far and away the most comprehensive, updated, and accurate resource available. It is the result of research by the National Park Service over a period of more than five years in the Southeast. Within its structure it also provides multitudes of references to valuable sources.

A close second for my research was the Beaufort County (South Carolina) Library. The main county library in the historic town of Beaufort has one of the South's largest collections of materials on the Gullah language and the Sea Island culture, including many illustrations and documents. The Hilton Head Island branch library was also a source of solid information and personal assistance. Much of my original research, even before I ever embarked on the Gullah story, was conducted at Penn Center on St. Helena Island, the institution that was founded in 1862 as a school to teach freed slaves and that is now a center for the study of the Gullah culture and language. Back in the 1990s, I served on its Advisory Board for eight years and was inducted into the study of African American affairs. There I "discovered" the absorbing information about the Gullah culture, language, and peoples.

Other institutions that have been invaluable for research have been the South Carolina Historical Society, in Charleston, The Avery Research Center, and the South Carolina State Museum, which has a key department devoted to African American culture and research, including major entries on the Gullah language and history in the South. Also invaluable were the Institute for African American Studies at the University of Georgia, the Penn Center collection at the University of North Carolina, and the extensive collections relating to the Gullah/Geechee culture that have been established at many other universities, including Hampton University, Fisk University, the University of South Carolina, James Madison University, South Carolina State University, Savannah College of Art and Design, Duke University, Yale, the University of Virginia, and the Technical College of the Low Country (South Carolina).

On a personal level, I am deeply indebted to Dr. Emory Shaw Campbell, who has been my chief mentor on this subject for the past 15 years, who wrote the foreword for this book, and who is frequently mentioned herein for his continuing devotion to, and work on behalf of, the Gullah/Geechee people, both today and in the past. Close behind him in my gratitude for assistance is Dr. Joseph Opala, who stands at the top of the list of scholars researching the Gullah culture and its roots in West Africa. He is mentioned and quoted many times in this text, and he is responsible for much vital material that otherwise would never have become part of our story.

Among others who have provided valuable information and/or assistance have been Grace Morris Cordial, South Carolina Resources Coordinator of the Beaufort County Public Library System; Dr. Julius Scott, who not only helped in providing information but also helped keep up my morale during some trying times; Marquetta Goodwine, commonly known as "Queen of the Gullah/Geechee Nation," an exuberant voice for Gullah, a frequent publisher, and the hostess of many broadcasting programs in this field; Walter Greer, a good friend and noted artist who started his career depicting remote Gullah neighborhoods and structures; Veronica Gerald, a specialist in Gullah history, foods, and cooking; and the Honorable James Clyburn of South Carolina, who wrote the preface for a history of Penn Center that I am coauthoring with Dr. Campbell, and who made possible the vital Gullah/Geechee Heritage Corridor bill to help preserve and protect the Gullah culture in America.

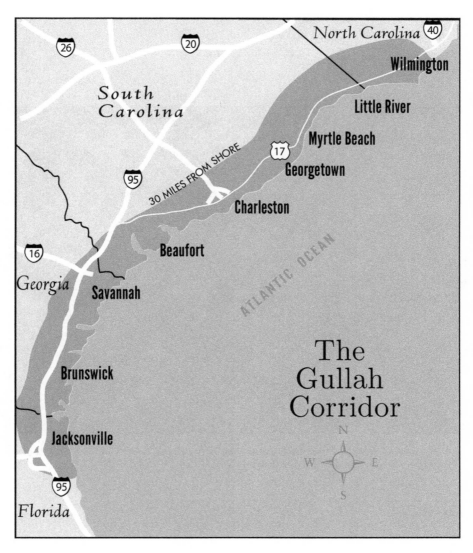

The Gullah Corridor is an area stretching from the southern border of North Carolina down to the Florida line and 30 miles inland.

Sweet potato planting on Hopkinson's Plantation, Edisto Island, South Carolina, circa 1862
Courtesy of the Library of Congress

CHAPTER I

Welcome
Home!

This exceptional and exhilarating story opens in 1989 with the recounting of the trip taken by 14 African Americans, including Emory Campbell, one of the organizers and author of the foreword of this book, to Sierra Leone in West Africa. Campbell was motivated by research evidence that slaves from Sierra Leone had been shipped in large numbers to the Gullah region in South Carolina and Georgia. Surprisingly, some of the descendants of those slaves made their way to what is now Oklahoma. These were the Black Seminoles who waged a war of liberation in Florida with their comrades, the Seminole Indians. The participants in the first "Gullah Homecoming" to Sierra Leone were greeted at the airport by hundreds of citizens, many in traditional dress, and by drummers and dancers. Later, as they toured Freetown, the capital city, and villages of this West African nation, they were astonished to find that they felt right at home because the music, dances, food, dress, and customs were a mirror of the ones back home.

As one student of the Gullah heritage put it, "It has been said that those hapless occupants of slave ships carried nothing with them on their involuntary voyages from West Africa to the New World. This is not true. Though they were stripped of everything but their names, they carried indelible memories of their culture—music, folklore, language, art, and religion—to the Sea Islands." Now their descendants are making voluntary voyages back to their roots in West Africa and embracing once again the land their ancestors were forced to leave behind so long ago.

This chapter focuses on the three "Gullah Homecomings" to Sierra Leone that have taken place in recent years. Sierra Leone lies at the heart of West Africa's "Rice Coast," the region where African farmers have been cultivating rice for thousands of years and the area from which many of the Gullahs' ancestors were taken. For the past 30 years, scholars have focused a great deal of attention on Sierra Leone and its links to the Gullah people. Responding to the new historical findings, Sierra Leone government officials and Gullah community leaders have reached out to one another to restore the family ties that were severed by the slave trade two centuries ago.

O n a November day in 1989 that was unusually brisk for the Low Country and Sea Islands, a group of 14 African Americans gathered in Savannah, Georgia, for a trip that would be more meaningful than any other in their lives. Although they could not be distinguished in any way from other groups of travelers, these passengers were unique—they were going backward in time to West Africa, to seek their ancestral origins, much as Alex Haley had done two decades earlier in his noted *Roots* journey.

Journey Home

It was an exciting time for Emory Campbell when he and 13 other African Americans learned that arrangements had been completed for them to travel across the ocean to Sierra Leone, the place where many of their ancestors had been captured as slaves and brought to America in the 18th century. The trip would cap decades of research on both sides of the Atlantic to pinpoint the origins of slaves, their points of departure and shipping dates during the 18th century, and thousands of details about people, places, transportation, and other reference data. It was not known at first whether the origin of the Gullah (or Geechee) people in coastal South Carolina and Georgia could be traced to specific locations in Africa. But an African American linguist named Lorenzo Turner published an important book in 1949. Turner's *Africanisms in the Gullah Dialect* showed conclusively that the Gullah language contains thousands of names and words from African languages and that many of these can be traced to specific languages. Later, in 1974, a historian named Peter Wood published *Black Majority*, which proved that many of the Gullahs' ancestors came from the Rice Coast of West Africa, the area stretching from Senegal and Gambia to Sierra Leone and Liberia.

In 1986 Campbell received a letter from Joseph Opala, an American historian who had lived in Sierra Leone for many years teaching African studies at Fourah Bay College and doing research on the Sierra Leone–Gullah connection. Sierra Leone is one of the smallest African nations, slightly larger than South Carolina and with a population of about 5 million. It was founded by the British at the end of the 18th century as a settlement for freed slaves brought from England, North America, and Jamaica. Later, "liberated Africans" rescued from slave ships by the British Navy were also brought to Freetown, where their chains were broken.

Opala began his research in Sierra Leone in the 1970s with a study of Bunce Island, a British slave castle that operated between 1670 and 1807, long before Britain's humanitarian role began in Sierra Leone. Located on a tiny island in the Freetown harbor about 15 miles from the capital, the Bunce Island castle is now in ruins. But visitors can see the "factory house" where the slave traders lived, the cannons they used to defend the fort, and the slave yards used to imprison the African captives who were bought and then shipped to America. Opala discovered that Bunce Island sent many of its captives to South Carolina and Georgia in the 18th century. He also found that the language and culture of the Gullah people in those states have many strong connections to languages and cultures in Sierra Leone. Sierra Leoneans were fascinated by Opala's findings—which he shared with the public via local radio and newspaper interviews and public lectures. The local press dubbed Opala's discoveries the "Gullah Connection," and many Sierra Leoneans asked Opala when they could meet their "Gullah cousins" in America.

In January 1987 Opala flew back to America and at Emory Campbell's invitation gave a lecture to more than 100 islanders gathered at Penn Center on St. Helena Island, South Carolina. Penn Center had been established in 1862, at the height of the Civil War, to teach reading, writing, and manual skills to freed slaves. He cited Peter Wood's discovery that many Africans from the Rice Coast had been captured and shipped to South Carolina and Georgia because of their skills at cultivating rice. But he argued on the basis of his own research that among the African countries of the Rice Coast, Sierra Leone is particularly important for the Gullahs. This made sense to Campbell because Claude and Pat Sharpe, a missionary couple who have been translating the Bible into the Gullah language, had already told him how similar Sierra Leone's Krio language is to Gullah. The Sharpes were using the Krio Bible as a guide while translating the Gullah Bible.

Opala surprised Campbell and the other islanders once again when he told them about an off-shoot of the Gullah people living in such far-flung areas as the Bahamas, Oklahoma, Texas, and Mexico. These were the Black Seminoles whose ancestors escaped from South Carolina and Georgia rice plantations in the 18th and 19th centuries and fled to the Florida wilderness. Later, after the Second Seminole War (1834–42), they were forced to move west on the Trail of Tears. Opala, who grew up in Oklahoma and did research in Black Seminole communities in his native state, reported that the Black Seminoles still speak Gullah and eat rice dishes similar to those prepared in the Low Country. The islanders were as amazed to learn about the long-lost family in the American West as they were about their links to Sierra Leone.

In October 1988 the president of Sierra Leone, the late Joseph Saidu Momoh, visited Penn Center. Having heard so much about the Gullahs, the president wanted to see if their culture was as similar to Sierra Leone's as he had heard. Momoh was astonished at the similarities between Gullah and Krio, the English-based Creole language spoken in his own country. He was also amazed at the antique rice-processing implements in Penn Center's museum. The mortars and pestles and fanner baskets are almost identical to farm tools in Sierra Leone today. He was also impressed with the meal served up by the community. The president was heard to say that Gullah rice dishes were just like the food back home in Sierra Leone.

President Momoh was so enthusiastic about the cultural similarities he witnessed that he invited Emory Campbell, then Executive Director of Penn Center, to lead a "Gullah Homecoming" to Sierra Leone the following year. The result was their flight in November 1989 from Savannah, Georgia, to Freetown, Sierra Leone, where they were greeted at the airport by cabinet members and other government officials and hundreds of other people with dances, songs, rhythmic drumming, and banners to make them know that they had come home. When it was discovered that the airline had misplaced their bags, President Momoh presented every member of the homecoming group with a set of traditional clothes. The president joked that "your ancestors left here without their clothes and now you've come back without them!" The Gullah visitors enjoyed the joke, and one could see that dressed in their new African clothes they felt at home instantly.

As they traveled around the country, they were astonished to find many of the activities and idioms of speech that were so familiar to them back home. "It was as though the community in which I was brought up back on St. Helena Island, South Carolina, had been lifted up and transported to Africa," said a member of the group. "I listened to several youngsters chatting with each other; I heard songs and watched dancing; I looked at baskets and clothing in a market place; I ate gumbo and hoppin' john at a luncheon in our honor; and, do you know, they were all Gullah—the Gullah I had known since earliest childhood back home."

One of the ladies in the group sent a postcard to her pastor saying that when she had attended a church service in a village, she knew all the hymns and the words, and could even understand the preacher when he spoke in Krio. "Everywhere we went, we were greeted with Gullah words, often accompanied by gestures that were as familiar to us as 'How are you?' or 'Have a good day' might be back in the States. They simply rolled off the tongues of our hosts and into our ears as though we were longtime neighbors: '*Wi gladi foh si una*' ['We're happy to see y'all']; '*Au una du?*' ['How y'all doing?']. Equally meaningful, we saw fine examples of a common [practice] that Gullahs don't just speak, they use body language, so what they have to say is doubly communicated. There were those same subtle movements and gestures that we were brought up with as children—a twinkle in the eye, a thrust of the chin, a nod of the head, a lift of the eyebrows, and of course, movements of the hands and fingers."

Every one of the 14 people who was privileged to enjoy this unique and very moving experience had stories to tell about his or her encounters with the native peoples of Sierra Leone as they moved about the streets of the capital, Freetown, or in the Mende village of Taiama in the interior, where they went to take part in the rice harvest and to witness traditional dances and ceremonies. In every aspect of life in Sierra Leone, whether relating to religion, medicine and health, foods, cooking, traditions, beliefs, or family matters, they saw parallels to their own experiences back home. As one visitor commented, "Once a Gullah, always a Gullah."

"The people of Sierra Leone were magnificent," wrote Emory Campbell in an article about his own experience. "Like Gullah islanders in the Carolinas, they are proud, friendly, and industrious. We were warmed by their smiles, spoke to them in our common language, Gullah and Krio, which are similar, and were thrilled to see examples of their skills in the market place—so much like ours back home—where hundreds of entrepreneurs displayed and peddled baskets, carvings, musical instruments, paintings, weaving, produce, and cooked foods almost exactly like those in native markets in our own islands back home. And everywhere we went, we saw signs saying, or people greeting us with, 'We glad fo see oonah,' or 'Tun roun ya le mi see who yo da,' or other common expressions in the Gullah tongue. From village to village, children had been kept out of school to see us ('fa see we'), and they kept us for hours, reluctant to have us move on, showing us their rice paddies, their dances, their weaving, and their neat, miniature homes, and gladdening our ears with their glorious singing.

"We met hundreds of men, women, and children as we toured the countryside, and we saw the place from which our ancestors had been taken from their beloved homeland: Bunce Island, with its slave quarters, fortress, jetty, and cannons still standing that had been used to prevent theft of the captured Africans before they were boarded on the slave vessels. In a sacred libation ceremony, we experienced the most emotional moments of our visit, realizing that we were standing on the exact spot where our ancestors had begun their miserable trek into slavery far, far from their native land.

"On our final day, we visited the Regent Community, established by Africans who had escaped from slavery, where we went to church. The people joined heartily with the choir, singing songs familiar to our ears, such as 'Swing Low, Sweet Chariot,' 'Steal Away,' and 'Old Time Religion.' And we listened patiently to a lengthy sermon in which the pastor admonished Africans in the Diaspora against complacency. In effect, he warned us that 'freedom is not free.'

"It was a fitting message to leave with us as we departed for home, where so often his warning was more true than false.

"You can now call me *Gullah*, for I have gone home."

Journey to the Past

It was sultry that June of 1756 in Charleston, South Carolina, and representatives from the plantations were fewer than usual on the south quay, despite the fact that the sloop *Hare* had arrived with what a newspaper advertisement described as "Likely and Healthy Slaves, to be sold upon easy Terms" by merchants Austin & Laurens. The ship was arriving from Sierra Leone, where rice was the Africans' staple crop, and that meant that all the captive Africans aboard were skilled at its cultivation. All the planters who came were rice-growers, and one satisfied purchaser was Elias Ball II, a wealthy planter on the Cooper River. Ball made an entry that day in the "blanket book" he used to record the expenses he incurred for his slaves. The book is still preserved in the South Carolina Historical Society, where Ball's original entry can be seen:

> I bought 4 boys and 2 girls—their ages near as I can judge: Sancho, 9 years old, Peter, 7, Brutus, 7, Harry, 6, Belinda, 10, Priscilla, 10, for £600.

The last mentioned, 10-year-old Priscilla, was taken to Ball's Comingtee Plantation. She would live out her life there and at other Ball family plantations and die about 1811.

In July 2004 Joseph Opala was on a fellowship at Yale when he made a rare and startling discovery about Priscilla's life. In the archives of the New York Historical Society, he found the original records of the *Hare*, the slave ship that took Priscilla from Sierra Leone to Charleston in 1756. He found letters from the slave ship captain describing his slaving activities on the African coast and, amazingly, the original records of the sale of the *Hare*'s slaves prepared by the firm Austin & Laurens. Running his finger down the list of buyers, he saw that Elias Ball purchased "2 girls." Sitting in the ornate reading room of the New York Historical Society, he pointed to the "2" on the page and said quietly to himself, "One of these girls is Priscilla."

Opala was following up on pioneering research already done by Edward Ball, author of *Slaves in the Family*. A descendant of generations of South Carolina rice planters and slave owners, Ball decided to write a book on the Africans his family had enslaved. While researching his prize-winning book, Ball discovered the entry Elias Ball II made on his purchase of Priscilla and the other children in 1756. Later, to his own amazement, Ball was able to link Priscilla to one of her modern descendants, a Charleston man named Thomas Martin. One of the most moving parts of Ball's book is the moment he shows Martin the family tree he created linking him and his family back to a 10-year-old girl brought from Sierra Leone 250 years ago.

Joseph Opala realized that between the plantation records Ball had found in South Carolina and the slave ship and auction records he discovered in New York, they had found something that had probably never been seen before: an unbroken document trail for an African American family stretching from Africa all the way to the present day. Opala immediately thought of Sierra Leone and what this discovery would mean there. Sierra Leoneans had been excited by the Gullah Homecoming in 1989 and the SCETV documentary *Family Across the Sea* based on it. But they pushed Opala to aim his research at finding "more specific" links to their country. They enjoyed meeting Emory Campbell and the other Gullah leaders who had come with him, but they wanted Opala to find individual Gullah people with a *provable* family connection to Sierra Leone.

In 1997 Opala organized the "Moran Family Homecoming." Led by Mary Moran, the family matriarch, they possessed an ancient song in the Mende language of Sierra Leone that had been passed down in their family from mother to daughter for at least 200 years. Lorenzo Turner, the pioneering linguist, recorded Mary's mother, Amelia Dawley, singing the song when he visited her in

Harris Neck, Georgia, in 1931. After seeing the song in Turner's book, Opala organized a search for it in Sierra Leone. In 1990 he and two colleagues—Cynthia Schmidt, an American ethnomusicologist, and Tazieff Koroma, an African linguist—found the song in the tiny Mende village of Senehun Ngola in southern Sierra Leone. Later Opala and Schmidt went to Georgia, where they were able to locate Mary Moran. When the Morans finally came to Sierra Leone in 1997, the public responded enthusiastically to their homecoming. Sierra Leoneans also loved the documentary video based on the Moran Family Homecoming, called *The Language You Cry In*.

But even after Opala found a Gullah family with a provable link to their country, Sierra Leoneans were still not satisfied. Many were disappointed when Opala could not provide the name of the Mende person who took the song to America. "We want a name," they told him. "We want the name of a Sierra Leonean taken away as a slave, and we want to meet his Gullah family in America today." Opala thought their request was impossible at first, but after helping uncover an unbroken document trail for the Martin family leading back 250 years to a slave ship that brought a little girl from Sierra Leone to Charleston in 1756, he realized that he had a name, and he could not wait to take it back and announce it in Sierra Leone. The name was Priscilla.

Opala joined forces with Jacque Metz, a Charleston filmmaker, to organize "Priscilla's Homecoming." They wanted to bring Thomas Martin, Priscilla's modern descendant, to Sierra Leone and make a documentary film of his trip. But Opala and Metz learned that Martin had passed away, and when they went to Africa to make plans for the homecoming, they proposed to the Sierra Leone government that Thomalind Martin Polite, Mr. Martin's daughter, lead the homecoming visit. They later returned to Charleston with an official invitation for Polite. A 31-year-old primary school speech therapist with a soft voice and a contemplative manner, Polite immediately agreed. To Opala and Metz's relief, she was excited to go to Sierra Leone.

Before the homecoming could take place, there was a new wrinkle, though, that had to be considered. Edward Ball had concluded in his book that the *Hare*, the ship that took Priscilla to America, was a British vessel owned by the London-based proprietors of Bunce Island. But the records Opala found at the New York Historical Society indicated that the *Hare* was actually an

American slave ship sailing out of Newport, Rhode Island. Newport was the largest slave trading port in North America, and the ship was owned by Samuel and William Vernon, two of the richest merchants in colonial Rhode Island.

Recent publicity about Rhode Island's role in the Atlantic slave trade came as a shock to many northerners, and especially to New Englanders, who grew up equating slavery strictly with the South. In point of fact, however, Rhode Island was almost as active as Charleston in the slave trade, except that it sent slave ships to Africa rather than receive them. Over the years, Newport vessels made almost 1,000 voyages to Africa, carrying some 100,000 slaves to the New World. Most of these slaves ended up in the West Indies and the southern colonies, but in Colonial times, Rhode Island had more slaves than any other northern colony. Before the Revolution, almost 20 percent of Newport's population was black, and it was said that one-third of the families in the region owned at least one slave, and many of them owned two or three slaves. It was common to see advertisements in the *Newport Gazette* with large black headlines:

NEW SHIPMENT: SLAVES FROM THE GOLD COAST— MEN, WOMEN, AND YOUTHS. IN GOOD HEALTH AND WELL TRAINED FOR WORK IN THE HOME OR FIELDS. TRADING AT PIER TWO SATURDAY AT NOON.

Armed with these facts, Opala traveled to Rhode Island, where he was able to get historians and community activists interested in the state's past to raise funds to bring Thomalind Martin Polite to Rhode Island after she returned from her trip to Sierra Leone. As he saw it, the documentary film recording her journey would have an interesting and unexpected twist—it would not just link Sierra Leoneans and Gullahs, but it would also link Gullahs to the Rhode Island community. Thomalind would later lay a wreath in the water in Newport at the very spot local historians believe the *Hare* sailed from on its fateful voyage to Sierra Leone in 1756. Sierra Leoneans living in the United States stood beside her, saying prayers to their ancestors.

Across the Waters

What makes Priscilla's story unique is the fact that most of the Africans sold into slavery were anonymous, their names unrecorded and fates unknown. Even more surprising, hers is a record that goes back not just to the Civil War, when more and more became known about slavery, but for two and a half centuries. What few people, even many students of history, realize is that from the beginning of the 18th century until the Civil War, more than half a million slaves were brought to North America, and almost half of this number came through the port of Charleston.

How did Priscilla come to be captured? No account of this has been found, but judging from existing records of the slave trade in West Africa, she was taken when her village in the interior was raided by African slave traders who profited by kidnapping people—especially those from rival kingdoms—and selling them to European slave traders. In Sierra Leone the African slave traders were often Fula, Mandingo, and Susu people, and the European traders were mostly British. The dragnet caught those who were kidnapped, prisoners of war, people who were convicted of crimes, and some whose families were forced to sell them to pay off debts. In each case, people were sold for guns, gunpowder, cloth, rum, metal goods, and various trinkets.

European slave traders established some 40 major slave castles, or fortified trading posts, along the West African coast. Bunce Island, the largest British slave trading base in Sierra Leone, had about 60 employees and was the only major British castle along the Rice Coast. The African slave traders transported their captives to these trading centers, where they sold them to European traders like cattle at auction. Indeed the white traders sometimes branded the slaves before loading them onto ships to the West Indies and North America. Remains of trading posts invariably indicate that they were equipped with cannons because they were constantly threatened by pirates or rival European powers, who found that the slaves they seized by force could be just as valuable a bounty as silver and gold.

An ardent researcher, Opala was aided by the fact that he had lived in Sierra Leone for so many years. Not only did he study the ruins on Bunce Island and examine them minutely for evidence, he also did oral history research with elders on the nearby islands. Opala's objective was to obtain oral accounts of what had happened on that island, to complement early written descriptions. As in so many traditional villages around the world, the elders passed verbal historical accounts down to each new generation, and these were an invaluable adjunct to written records. But one elder had quite an incorrect view of the slave trade. Alimamy Rakka, an old chief in Sangbulima village on neighboring Tasso Island, told him that the white people had taken his people away to Europe, where they had all "died of the cold." "No," Opala said in Krio, "they didn't take them to Europe. They took them to America, and many of their descendants are still alive there today." The elder spoke up, wide-eyed. "America. That is a rich country, yes?" and after Opala had nodded in the affirmative, he remarked with a broad smile, "That means I have family in a rich country. That is good news."

The little girl who would become known as Priscilla was one of those who did survive all the terrors of the slave trade in Africa and the middle passage to America. She was likely marched, naked or in rags, with hands tied, for many miles in searing heat along dirt trails from the inland to the coast. The fate of any particular slave was a ghastly matter of human roulette. Typically about 15 percent of those chained below deck on overpacked vessels died at sea and were thrown overboard to the sharks; others reached far-off shores only to succumb to dysentery, malaria, or other diseases before they could even be sold on the auction blocks; and a large percentage were purchased by masters who treated them so cruelly that their lifespan on the plantation was very short. This was particularly true in Brazil and the West Indies, where the average life expectancy after arrival was only four to seven years.

Those like Priscilla who were purchased by rice planters in South Carolina were more fortunate. As historian Daniel Littlefield points out in his book, *Rice and Slaves*, South Carolina rice plantations were noted for a patriarchal system of slavery and for the fact that their owners paid premium prices for slaves from the Rice Coast of West Africa, where people had been growing rice for hundreds of years and were experts in its cultivation. These Africans were highly valued for their technical skills, and it was estimated that about five years would elapse before a slave had, in effect, "paid off" his or her purchase price. It was good business, therefore, to keep them healthy and physically able to undertake long hours of work, often in tropical heat. As Littlefield notes, it was not unusual for slaves on South Carolina rice plantations to live a full lifetime. Priscilla herself was reported to have lived into her mid-60s, quite normal for working adults in the early 19th century.

The records of the slave ship *Hare* show that when the slave girl Priscilla was herded off the ship with the other survivors of the miserable voyage, the wharf to which the vessel tied up was on Sullivan's Island. Located just off the south shore of Charleston, this was the place where slaves were debarked and required to stay in quarantine in a "pest house" for a minimum of 10 days. The purpose, of course, was to prevent the importation of diseases, particularly smallpox and yellow fever, which could devastate the population if an epidemic were to result.

Edward Ball's book, *Slaves in the Family*, won the 1998 National Book Award. Ball spent four years researching his ancestors, who were among the original Charles Town colonists and, eventually, among the wealthiest. As a review of this book stated, "The Ball family are 'old Charleston' personified. They comprised an elite group of planters, patriots, and statesmen of rare accomplishment. And, like others of this class, they owned slaves. From the late 17th century until 1865, the Ball family owned 25 plantations worked by some 4,000 slaves.

"By Edward Ball's educated estimate, there are now between 75,000 and 100,000 people descended from Ball family slaves. He was able to reconstruct the genealogies of these slave families, from the first African captives down to the present."

Ball also traveled to Sierra Leone, where he saw the ruins of Bunce Island with Joseph Opala and interviewed Sierra Leoneans whose ancestors were involved in the procurement of slaves. "I wanted to tell a black and white story—not a black story, not a white one—but a shared tale," Ball explains, describing how he traveled all over the United States to meet descendants of Ball slaves. "I met with about 100 people whose ancestors lived on Ball plantations. They are the people I wrote about. They belong to about 15 families and are middle-class and wage workers, educated and illiterate, light- and dark-skinned, Christian and Atheist—a true cross-section of black Americans."[1]

As it turned out, Thomas Martin was the first person Ball interviewed.

"Mr. Martin was a very dignified, soft-spoken man . . . intensely curious about his history," says Ball. "He knew about his family's life after emancipation, but he knew nothing about his family in slavery. I knew about his family in slavery and nothing about his family after slavery. So we had something to share. That exchange characterized the encounters I had with all the black families."[2] But in the case of Thomas Martin, the exchange led to something extraordinary—the discovery of Priscilla.

Ball discovered that the *Hare*'s arrival had been frustrating for Austin & Laurens, the South Carolina slave dealers. As they described it, the unwilling passengers brought ashore in chains were "a most scabby flock," suffering from skin diseases, semiblindness, stomach "complaints," and various other infirmities. Three of the lot died within days of coming ashore, and the rest were so pitiful that barely half of them tempted any buyers. Priscilla had been lucky to survive the voyage from Sierra Leone.

Within 10 years of arriving at Comingtee Plantation, Priscilla fell in love with a slave named Jeffrey and shared his quarters. By 1770, she had three children, and upon her death in about 1811, she had 30 grandchildren. Her descendants lived on Ball family plantations until early 1865, when Charleston was taken by Federal troops and an officer assembled the slaves and told them they were free. One of Priscilla's descendants, Henry, was among those freed from William Ball's Limerick Plantation on the Cooper River's east branch. He took the name Martin and then began the slow, painful process of trying to become an independent citizen.

Completing the Journey

According to an article in the Charleston *Post and Courier*, Thomalind Martin Polite is "a cheerful woman with hardly a trace of a Southern drawl, much less 'Charlestonese' or Gullah."[3] In fact she readily admits that she hasn't even heard much "true" Gullah, nor can she speak it. Her introduction to the language of her ancestors was through hearing storytellers at the library as a child. She now has a master's degree in speech pathology and audiology and works with the Charleston County School District. She is following in the family footsteps; education is in the Martin family blood.

Teaching as a career for the Martins began shortly after the Limerick slave, Henry, was emancipated. In 1866 Henry, now remembered as Peter Henry Robards Martin, received his first formal education in the one-room Nazareth Church School in Pinopolis, South Carolina. He himself would teach there before moving to Charleston, marrying, working as a carpenter, and finally answering the call to become a preacher. In the latter part of his life, he moved back to the country, where he built a church and taught his parishioners' children until his death in 1931.

With his wife, Anna Cruz, Martin had 10 children. Son Peter Henry Jr., born in 1886, prospered as a roofer. Peter Henry Jr.'s son, Thomas P. Martin, born in 1933, was the soft-spoken man Edward Ball met. A career educator who taught English, Thomas Martin, Thomalind's father, eventually became assistant principal of Charleston High School before he retired, but unfortunately he died before his daughter was selected for the journey back to West Africa.

In the late winter of 2005, Thomalind, bright, talented, and energetic, was almost overcome by the expectations of what it would be like to return to the land of her ancestors. "I can hardly describe it," she exclaimed in an interview about her upcoming trip. "I'm ecstatic. I feel fortunate to be the one chosen to go. I wish my father was still alive, because he should have been the one to go. But with Priscilla at the beginning of the family line and me at the end, I guess it's only fitting." She paused for a moment and added thoughtfully: "Still, it's not as though I'm just taking a vacation to see a foreign land. I'm actually going back to where Priscilla was born—something few African Americans today have ever experienced. How else can I say it? I'll be *going home.*"

For most African Americans, there is a genealogical void in their family history, a line severed by slavery. The Martin family's ability to trace their ancestry to a particular African ancestor via an unbroken document trail that goes all the way back to Africa is such a rarity that it is a truly historic event. To add to the excitement, it was reported that, for the people of Sierra Leone, Thomalind's anticipated arrival—"Priscilla's Homecoming"—was cause for national celebration. The letter Opala and Metz brought from the Sierra Leone government read, "Your visit will promote a greater understanding of the family ties that link the Gullah people of South Carolina and all Sierra Leoneans and help further the bonds of friendship between Americans and Africans in general. I can assure you that your visit will be well-publicized here before you arrive and that thousands of our people will be anxious to greet you, their long-lost family come home from South Carolina."

This was by no means an exaggeration. A year before it happened, Joseph Opala gave a speech on Priscilla's Homecoming at the U.S. Embassy. "I spoke to a packed house, people from the arts, education, the government—all areas of the community," he reported. "In my speech I said, 'We know that this little girl lost her family. She thought of her family every day. And she thought of her home every day until she died.' After I said that, the audience was completely silent. I looked up to see everybody nodding their heads in agreement, 'Of course, of course.' Because, you see, in Sierra Leone, family is everything. Home is everything. They lost people. Hundreds of thousands of their ancestors were taken away by slavery. To have Priscilla's descendant come back is almost like Priscilla herself returning. To the people of Sierra Leone, this is considered incredibly good fortune—a true blessing. A healing. When Thomalind arrives, she'll be greeted by complete strangers joyously calling to her, '*Pree-SEE-la! Pree-SEE-la!* It will be a very emotional moment. This will be just a beginning, the first door of many to open as all of us, on both sides of the Atlantic, find ways to reconcile with this powerful past."

Origin of the Gullah

The Gullah people are the descendants of African ethnic groups who arrived in America as early as the late 17th century and were forced to work on plantations in South Carolina and later Georgia. They were from many tribes including the Mandingo, Bamana, Wolof, Fula, Temne, Mende, Vai, Akan, Ewe, Bakongo, and Kimbundu. The mixture of languages from Africa, combined with English, resulted in a Creole language that eventually came to be known as Gullah. As Philip D. Morgan, a historian at the College of William & Mary, explained, "The slave owners had to communicate with their slaves, so they made sure the slaves used European words. So in the English colonies of North America, slaves used the English-based Gullah language to communicate with one another."[4]

"Yet down through the centuries," reported historian John H. Tibbetts in an article, "Living Soul of Gullah," in the spring 2000 issue of *Coastal Heritage* magazine, of which he is the editor, "the Gullah people managed to retain extensive African sources in their speech and folklore. The grammar of Gullah is African, and many aspects of Gullah culture—religious beliefs, arts and crafts, stories, songs, and proverbs—are also derived from African sources. The Gullah people have preserved more of their African cultural history than any other large group of blacks in the United States . . . a re-creation of Africa within the new world."[5]

The Gullah people live in the Low Country, the distinctive low-lying semi-tropical lands of the coastal plain of South Carolina and Georgia and the Sea Islands that border the coastline. As Tibbetts pointed out, although many people think of the Gullah culture in terms of major Sea Islands such as St. Helena, James, John, Edisto, and Wadmalaw, "the classic Gullah culture actually existed most notably on the mainland tidal areas, along rivers for 30 miles inland known as the *rice coast.*"[6] Many Gullahs live in rural areas. According to Dr. Lawrence Roland, a historian at the University of South Carolina, "They maintained a separateness. Gullah people were marginalized economically and socially."[7]

Joseph Opala has written: "The Gullah people are the descendants of the slaves who worked on the rice plantations in South Carolina and Georgia. They still live in rural communities in the coastal region and on the Sea Islands of those two states, and they still retain many elements of African language and culture. Anyone interested in the Gullah must ask how they have managed to keep their special identity and so much more of their African cultural heritage than has any other group of black Americans. The answer is to be found in the warm, semitropical climate of coastal South Carolina and Georgia, in the system of rice agriculture adopted there in the 1700s, and in a disease environment imported unintentionally from Africa. These factors combined almost three hundred years ago to produce an atmosphere of geographical and social isolation among the Gullah, which has lasted to some extent up until the present day.

"The climate of coastal South Carolina and Georgia was excellent for the cultivation of rice, but it proved equally suitable for the spread of tropical diseases. The African slaves brought malaria and yellow fever, which thrived on the swampy coastal plain and especially around the flooded rice plantations. The slaves had some inherited resistance to these tropical diseases, but their masters were extremely vulnerable. The white planters moved their houses away from the rice fields and adopted the custom of leaving their farms altogether during the rainy summer and autumn months, when fever ran rampant. The plantations were run on a day-to-day basis by a few white managers, assisted quite often by certain talented and trusted slaves working as foremen or 'drivers.' The white population in the region stayed relatively low, but the importation of African slaves increased as the rice plantation system expanded and generated more and more profits."[8]

Opala explains that the Gullah slaves faced a very different situation from that of slaves in other North American colonies, living in isolated communities and having little contact with whites. Their numerical strength and isolation made it possible for them to preserve African cultural and communal traditions and resist changes. As far back as the early 1700s, Gullah slaves were solidifying not only a distinctive language, but customs, rituals, music, crafts, and diet. Their native cultures were so ingrained in their minds and hearts that, although they had been entirely stripped of clothing, utensils, and belongings before being thrust into the holds of slave ships, it was impossible for their masters to strip them of their memories.

Two vital factors in the preservation of the Gullahs were: (1) the fact that a high proportion of the slaves brought to South Carolina and Georgia were from West and Central Africa as compared to the West Indies, and (2) the fact that they were isolated from outsiders because they lived in a disease environment hostile to white settlers. "The isolation of the Gullah community lasted throughout the period of slavery," says Opala, "and continued even after the Civil War and the emancipation period."

By the turn of the century, with rice and cotton plantations being abandoned and the land sold off, the Gullah people found themselves more and more secluded in what is one of the most geographically remote areas of the United States. Many lived on islands without bridges or in hamlets without roads, and with absolutely no communication with the outside world. Only today have some of these tiny outbacks of cultural preservation been fully appreciated and their irreplaceable values understood.

Until recent years Gullah culture has been orally transmitted—not written—passed down from generation to generation by word of mouth and through the habits of work, worship, and the making of crafts. "Without a written language," wrote Tibbetts, "the passing of knowledge within a culture can quickly break down. An oral culture is transmitted primarily through families, and when there is a break—even of just 30 years or so—the loss often cannot be regained."[9] All too frequently such a break occurs when family members in younger generations become ashamed of their background, thinking it inferior and breaking away from the old traditions and manners of expression. They venture out into another world—one that seems to them to be more sophisticated, and offering opportunities to make a better living and live in a more affluent society.

Marquetta L. Goodwine, an African American resident of St. Helena Island, South Carolina, and founder of the Gullah/Geechee Sea Island Coalition, has long pointed out the difficulties of convincing her people that they should be proud of their culture and their language. "For years, we were told that our language is broken," she writes. "A generation of people were told, 'You'll never get through life talking like that,'"[10] pointing out that black city dwellers, in particular, tended to ridicule those in the rural areas, whom they considered to be inferior.

Gullah culture has, indeed, been under threat for years from both out- and in-migration. Beginning at the turn of the 20th century, many Gullahs left the rural areas to migrate north to cities on the eastern seaboard, scuttling their old ways of speech, dress, and manners in order to fit into their new environment. The chance that Gullah culture would be lost was also increased by the influx of outsiders moving to the Low Country and Sea Islands to establish resorts and vacation homes, buying up farmland and sometimes entire villages from people whose families had resided there for generations. In many cases Gullah people living near these new developments could no longer afford the increasing taxes and rising cost of living.

Fortunately, though, times are changing. One pioneering effort has greatly enhanced the status of the Gullah language: the publication of the New Testament in Gullah, an effort of more than 25 years on the part of Christian missionaries, Gullah community leaders, and others who dedicated their time and talents to what has been described as "an effort of genius." The introduction to *De Nyew Testament* states, "While in the past Gullah was mistakenly characterized as poor English, today it is recognized as a distinct language. It is an English creole, born several hundred years ago out of a contact situation where Africans were taken from various nations and language groups to grow rice in the marshy low country area along the Southeastern coast of the American colony."

Popular demand for the Gullah New Testament outpaced its supply immediately after publication. There is now widespread interest in the Gullah language and culture, and visitors to South Carolina and Georgia now expect to be exposed to Gullah culture, particularly music, art, crafts, and food. In effect, the situation parallels that of many years ago when readers young and old were first "discovering" the culture of the American Indians and their arts and crafts. Long-time residents of the Low County find it amusing to note that more and more first-time visitors are asking not just about beaches and sightseeing boats, but where they can buy Gullah sweetgrass baskets and paintings, listen to the "hallelujah-type" singers, sign up for Gullah tours, and visit restaurants serving hoppin' john, fried green tomatoes, watermelon tea, and neck bones 'n gravy.

The Gullah Today

Only a few years ago observers were warning that Gullah was a dying culture. More than one specialist in this field estimated that there was little chance that this culture could long survive because of the rapid growth of the urban areas, the decline of farming and rural communities, and the influx of outsiders whose interest was mainly in vacationing, leisure homes, and commercial development. The isolation of Gullah communities was steadily breaking down, sparked by young people finding jobs in the cities and older people dying off. But then something happened. Instead of the culture dying as one magazine article after another warned in the direst terms, activists rose up in the community to extol their culture. These activists pointed to the danger of their cultural roots dying, to be sure, but they also highlighted the community's continuing vibrance.

Twenty years ago Joseph Opala pointed out that "the Gullah still hold to their special identity, and they still take pride in their common heritage. Those who have moved away often return for family gatherings to expose their children to grandparents, to Gullah lore, and to the local life." He noted, "The Gullah are also showing an increasing spirit of community service and self-help," citing Penn Center and its programs that host year-round public events so that people of all races, ages, and denominations can learn more about the Gullah culture, heritage, and language, as well as meet with and talk to modern-day Gullahs as friends and neighbors. Specialists generally estimate that there are as many as 100,000 speakers of Gullah today in the South Carolina and Georgia Low Country region.

As Dr. Emory Campbell, former Executive Director of Penn Center, has pointed out, people of Gullah descent are as commonplace in the Low Country and Sea Islands as those of any other ancestry. "Although the use of the land is changing, and more people are working away from the land," he said, "we still have a number of people who raise part of their own food and who fish the waters and hunt in the forests. Even looking at it from a purely residential standpoint, owning and keeping one's land is still important. It provides that sense of place so central to holding families together—that family compound which provides the physical connection so vitally important to this culture." Campbell has spent his life earnestly working to preserve his own Gullah heritage, combining an innate interest in African American affairs with a strong professional knowledge of health problems, social sciences, public education, and community service.

He also attributes the strength of the Gullah heritage—through slavery, the Civil War, the turmoil of Reconstruction, and the manacles of segregation—to the bond between the people and the land. "People cannot maintain their culture," he reminds us, "without a land base. One of the reasons that sea islanders have preserved their close heritage is because they had an early opportunity to own land and stabilize their families." He speaks also of the human connection, "the value of a child getting to know his or her heritage, of finding self-worth, of putting more value in family and the way they live. The connection requires an educational focus, both on *this* side of the sea, here in America, and *that* side of the sea, in Africa. Here we must work to ensure that our own children, as well as the adults, understand their culture and heritage."

Campbell has devoted much of his time in recent years to establishing a better link between the Gullah community and West Africa, so that people can personally experience that sense of connection and what it means. "But there is still much to do," he warns. "It's not just the Sea Islands and the African lands across the sea. I see it as America *recognizing* the connection between the two. You see, the African American culture is one which permeates almost every segment of American society. Yet unfortunately many tend to think of this as a culture developed only on this side of the ocean—after slavery. When we can all understand and respect the origins and adaptations of this remarkable culture, then we can truly bring the connection full circle."

During his time as Executive Director of Penn Center on St. Helena Island, South Carolina, Campbell maintained that preserving this heritage was the mission of the center, one of the oldest and most historically significant African American institutions. Founded in 1862 as a part of the Port Royal Experiment, it was originally designed to help former slaves make the difficult transition from slavery to freedom. At the same time—though not yet realized at the time of its founding—it was to be one of the means by which the Gullah culture could protect itself from annihilation, preserve itself, and flourish. As the 1990 documentary *Family Across the Sea* put it, "Penn Center is a place where the connection between the African past and the American present is vibrantly explored."

The Slave Population

Few people today appreciate the size and extent of the movement of slaves from Africa to North America during the period of the Atlantic slave trade. Charleston was the chief slave trading port on the Atlantic seaboard, where records showed that some 120,000 slaves were legally brought and purchased by plantation owners from the late 18th century to the early 19th century. There are estimates of thousands more brought in "off the record," to avoid import duties and other costs. "Throughout the colonial era, Carolina slave holders showed a preference for people from the rice-growing areas of Africa—the Windward Coast, including Senegambia and Sierra Leone," according to an article, "Living Soul of Gullah," in the spring 2000 issue of *Coastal Heritage* magazine, one of the South's most prominent periodicals in the field of Sea Islands history. These slaves were so skilled in the cultivation of rice from generations of farming in their native villages that rice became one of the staples of the southern economy in the Carolinas—referred to, in fact, as "the driving force of the South Carolina coast's slave-based economy for more than 150 years."[11]

Joseph Opala, recognized as one of the top scholars in this field, says that Sierra Leone is even more important for the Gullah than the other African nations on what was once called the Rice Coast of Africa. Opala says that Sierra Leone is the only Rice Coast nation with a *two-way* connection to the Gullah. Many slaves were taken from Sierra Leone to the Low Country, but Gullahs also returned to Sierra Leone. Some of the freed slaves the British landed in Freetown were Gullahs from South Carolina and Georgia. Indeed, the founder of Sierra Leone's famous Fourah Bay College was Edward Jones from Charleston. So it was that when Emory Campbell and his group visited Sierra Leone in 1989, followed by similar groups ever since, they were in effect exploring the very heart of the Gullah culture and its origins and impact on the world. Opala cites the example of a woman from Sierra Leone who was doing graduate studies at the University of South Carolina, and who chanced to meet some Gullah people while on a vacation trip to the Sea Islands. After returning to Sierra Leone, she told Opala with delight, "They speak our language!"

Gullah father and son opening oysters on their wooden scows in 1904
NEGATIVE/TRANSPARENCY NO. 478150. (PHOTO BY JULIAN DIMOCK.)
COURTESY OF THE AMERICAN MUSEUM OF NATURAL HISTORY LIBRARY.

CHAPTER 2

Catching the Learning

The scene moves to Pennsylvania, to the Friends' Freedman's Association of Philadelphia and the work of Laura M. Towne. At the age of 37, Laura, a dedicated abolitionist, decides that her mission as a nurse and teacher is to travel to the Sea Islands and render badly needed instruction and assistance to the black inhabitants. Her decision seems remarkable, even to our progressive contemporaries, because she will have to defy convention as a white woman living and working among former slaves. Arriving on St. Helena Island in April 1862 with her lifelong friend and fellow teacher, Ellen Murray, she begins her mission of attending to the medical needs of the freedmen.

In July of that same year, she opens the first school for freed slaves. Her first class consists of nine students, with the school operating out of the back room of a plantation house. It will soon become known as Penn School, in recognition of William Penn and the founders' origins. Towne and Murray will operate the school for the next 40 years. They will spend a great deal of time on language, and they will become very interested in the speech of their students and in the families around them on the island—but they will have no realization that they are working in a culture that will one day be recognized as the Gullah heritage.

T he scene is Philadelphia in the year 1862. The spotlight is on a young lady of 37, Laura Matilda Towne, who was born on May 3, 1825, and raised in Salem, Massachusetts. She was educated as a homeopathic physician, in a system of medical treatment based on the use of minute quantities of remedies that in large doses produce effects similar to those of the disease being treated. This radical new approach to healing was based on the theory that "like cures like," and that the symptoms of an illness were identical to the symptoms experienced by a healthy individual who had been given a drug that could treat that illness.

Laura was also educated as a teacher and had all the attributes for becoming a person of importance in the years ahead. She was well recognized for her devoted volunteer work, teaching underprivileged children in "charity" schools. Moreover, after moving to Philadelphia in 1840, she moved in "socially progressive circles," and she therefore developed a very positive "in" with families and individuals who counted in a society considered to be one of the most exclusive in the East. She was also, however, an avid follower of William Lloyd Garrison, editor of the antislavery newspaper *The Liberator* and one of the most outspoken and influential leaders in the battle for freedom. As a dedicated Garrisonian abolitionist, however, she was frustrated in her attempts to take any kind of positive action in Philadelphia, mainly because women were discouraged from such "unfeminine" crusades.

Described by a contemporary as "pragmatic, down-to-earth, and strong-minded—a born administrator," Laura soon added the role of missionary to her calling. She followed dramatic news reports that Federal naval forces had achieved a strategic victory in a battle in Port Royal Sound, South Carolina, and thus, with the help of the Union Army, had freed the town of Beaufort and several of the adjoining Sea Islands, including St. Helena. The most important fact was that St. Helena was the site of numerous cotton plantations whose owners had fled inland and westward, away from advancing Union forces, thus abandoning hundreds of slaves who were now without any means of support or knowledge about how to survive without supervision and instruction. Realizing full well that they desperately needed guidance, training, and leadership, Laura announced that she was going to travel by steamboat down the coast to South Carolina to establish a school to teach these freed slaves how to fend for themselves and survive when faced with circumstances far beyond their comprehension or lifetime experience. Laura based her plans not entirely on personal impulse, but on several programs that were still in the raw stages of planning—the goal being to help educate black individuals and families whose lives had been thrust into turmoil by recent events in the war-torn regions of the South and, most specifically, on St. Helena Island.

One of the notable courses of action was a Federal program later named the Port Royal Experiment, described as "a dress rehearsal for Reconstruction." This program ultimately recruited more than 50 abolitionists, many of them young and fascinated by the adventurous nature of the campaign "to tutor the freemen out of slavery and into freedom."[1] Thus, in early April 1862, Laura Matilda Towne found herself, along with some 20 other abolitionists, mostly of her own age, on board the *Oriental*, a steam-and-sail vessel of such antiquity that it had been all but scrapped as of no practical use to the Federal Navy. Rough weather, the condition of the vessel, and the presence of young passengers who were not accustomed to life at sea all contributed to making the voyage a fearful one for most of those on board. To add to the doubts of the passengers, several members of the crew took delight in faking terror as the old ship pitched and rolled, saying in loud voices they were not sure whether it could withstand the high seas without capsizing.

Despite the discomforts and gloomy anticipations, the *Oriental* arrived alongside the quay in the picturesque port of Beaufort, South Carolina, one of the largest natural harbors on the Atlantic coast, framed by waving palms and stately oaks, permitting its passengers to disembark in a setting far more civilized than they had imagined. Rich in history, Beaufort was one of the oldest settlements in America, having been discovered by the Spanish in 1514 and chartered by the British in 1711 as a center of indigo and rice plantations. The town, long known for its charm as the "Queen of the South Carolina Islands," attracted the newcomers. Among them was also a band of Gideonites, mainly young people from Boston and New York, who, like Laura, had high hopes of being able to ease the trials and tribulations of the freed slaves and guide them on the road to true emancipation and independence. But for those, including Laura Towne, who were committed to the far plantations, the pilgrimage had just begun, and it was fraught with unseen difficulties and frustrations, not the least of which was *communication*.

By April 16, Laura was temporarily situated at the Beaufort home of Caroline Forbes, a typical Sea Island lady who lived in a fine home with an expansive sea wall on three sides, abutting the Beaufort River, Brickyard Creek, and the bay, with luxuriant shade trees and brilliant blankets of flowers. There she experienced the amenities of southern living, but not for long. During her first walk down the road into the town, she was pained by the desertion and desolation, and somewhat unnerved by the presence of Union troops, some of whom galloped past on horseback in a reckless manner, and others who lounged idly on street corners in dirty uniforms staring in an unfriendly manner. She discovered that there were two Pennsylvania regiments stationed in the area, mostly in an artillery encampment.

Walking down the street with Caroline, she experienced her first glimpse of southern black children, whom she described later as "the most odd creatures—dirty and ragged, with a mode of speaking that was not very intelligible." (It was some time before she realized that when they referred to "befit" they meant Beaufort.) But she also had kind words to say about the children, who "tumbled about at all hours" on the front porch and in the main hall of the house where she was staying—"all very civil, but full of mischief and fun."[2]

Laura also had a chance to visit two of the local schools, where she observed "little darkies" learning their letters, which were primarily the pronunciation and meaning of one-syllable words. When she asked why there were so few children in the schools, she was told that most black women and children had been sent to the plantations to keep them away from the soldiers, and that many of the men had been conscripted into the Union Army or were given jobs at nearby encampments. She observed that some of the black children were very light in color, that two of them actually had red hair, and that one had "straight hair and a head like Andrew Jackson." Although the children seemed happy enough in school, there seemed to be no system in their education, and only a modicum of concentration. It was easy to see that the education of freed slaves required helping them learn how to undertake even the most rudimentary methods of survival and rehabilitation.

Laura had expected to meet other young people from Philadelphia and Washington, mainly affiliated with freedman's aid societies or Protestant churches, and all committed to emancipation, who had been passengers on an earlier vessel from the North. But she was informed that they had already gone to plantations on St. Helena, Lady's Island, Dataw, and other nearby Sea Islands to begin their task of trying to educate the freed slaves in the areas taken over by the Union troops. It was at this point that she became considerably disturbed by a situation that had never occurred to her or been discussed. The local families and even the Union officers not only tended to overlook the fact that the slaves were free, but led these poor blacks to believe that if they did not continue in service to the white population they might well be transported back to their former owners and once more degraded. As she observed it, the former slaves were still almost like children, and they would listen to their elders, no matter how subservient they were likely to remain if they took no action to change their lowly status.

The Federal government had already instituted a plan whereby freed slaves could work in private homes doing housework or washing, or in the cotton and vegetable fields, or in the few small markets near the waterfront, receiving minuscule wages. Other freedmen, like one referred to as "Uncle Robert," had the initiative and incentive to deliver milk and eggs or churn butter for the white families in residence.

By the end of April, Laura was able to write home with the good news that, having now become fairly well acclimated to the southern climate and community, she was finally beginning at least part of her professional career: tending to the maladies of the blacks on a nearby plantation who had contracted measles and mumps. For this she was rewarded with an invitation to attend a "praise house," a small cabin in the midst of splendid live oaks, hanging with Spanish moss, and was treated to native singing, praying, and reading from a tattered old Bible. Later she also attended a "shout" in one of the larger cabins, lit only by burning logs in a small fireplace. The participants sang a clamorous chorus, with three leaders in front of the group clapping and gesticulating and then leading the rest, shuffling on their heels around the room in a circle, turning occasionally one way and another, bending their knees in a kind of curtsy, and stamping their feet with such vigor that the whole floor vibrated.

By May Laura moved her experiences outward from the town of Beaufort into the countryside, riding to farms and plantations to meet the blacks—mainly women and children—who were trying to cope with the planting, care of livestock, gleaning, and other typical chores that needed immediate and continuing attention. She was quite depressed at their despondency and in some case despair at having no master in charge of their plight, but surprised at the vigor with which they reacted to having a "white lady" come to give them assurance and guidance. She could see that these people had no sense of economics, because they tended to pay far more attention to the edible corn crops keeping them from starvation than to cotton, which was the money-making crop for their future.

During her stay in Beaufort, and while on trips into the surrounding countryside, Laura Towne used her experience as a teacher not only to observe all of the things that were needed to educate the freed slaves, but also to calculate the nature and outlook of individuals, families, and groups to determine what methods and facilities would accomplish the immense undertaking for which she had volunteered. At first it seemed to her that no lone individual such as she could ever hope to cope with the desperate needs of these people, for whom freedom itself was a colossal—and unexpected—obstacle. She could see that just teaching them to read and write and to learn useful crafts was only the beginning, outranked perhaps by the urgency of helping them to develop socially, mentally, and morally.

In a larger sense, Laura was not only an educator but a missionary who would "bring the light of God's truth to people in need of such enlightenment." She did not know how many freedmen would come to rely on her help and that of other educators who would join her, but she had been told that there were in the Sea Islands some 10,000 blacks who had been abandoned, now that their masters had fled from the advancing Union Army. She could see from her initial association with just a few of these unfortunate people, and from the physical desolation on all sides, that the task was Herculean to begin with and would require not months but years and years of sacrifice, patience, and resolution on the part of those who had volunteered to undertake it.

Laura's first assessment of the job ahead of her was that religion would probably be her strongest ally down the road. Most of the freed slaves—at least the adults—relied on God and hymns and prayer meetings to cope with their miserable conditions, bondage, and desperate need for some kind of hope for the future. The most cultured and forward-looking individuals were the religious leaders who—though few had any formal training as ministers—could attract their followers to services of worship in which hope and salvation were themes accepted by those in attendance, regardless of the miseries they might be suffering during the rest of their daily lives.

In a few instances, there were even Sunday schools, which she attended in Beaufort and outlying villages in order to teach letters and cards of words. Somehow it seemed that being in the presence of God made it more possible to communicate to the young and old alike.

Another very important element in this endeavor, known as the Port Royal Experiment, was the unsettling fact that war and all its horrors and adversities were ever present. There were only about 4,000 Union troops in the Beaufort area, but all around them inland were some 20,000 Confederate soldiers, who might at any moment decide to try to rout their enemies. The volunteers from Philadelphia, New York, and New England knew full well that they were sitting on a powder keg. And indeed Laura Towne herself was later to be caught up in several skirmishes that would have fatal outcomes.

In late May, Laura made the decision to move away from Beaufort to an area near the village of Frogmore, some 10 miles to the east in the center of St. Helena Island. Her reasons were threefold: she was getting tired of the petty bureaucracy and the presence of so many military officers who had rules of their own; she found it difficult to try to establish a school, what with so few pupils and other programs already in operation, if poorly; and she had just received some $2,000 worth of clothing, rations, equipment, and other supplies that would make her less dependent on her Beaufort hosts. She had learned, too, that living quarters and rooms for a school were available in one location because the owners of Oaks Plantation had fled and were little likely to return.

Laura regretted the fact that she would no longer be able to administer medical aid to the sick, as she had been doing more and more often, but she reasoned that the presence of the military, with nearby field infirmaries, would suffice for emergencies, and that her treatments had been largely for children for minor aches and ailments. She had also received a number of much-delayed letters from her family and friends in Pennsylvania, two of which had the most welcome news: her good friend and associate Ellen Murray was soon to be on her way south, and she would be joining her as a teacher and partner. So it was time to make a move and aim at her original goal to help the freedmen become capable and independent.

Ellen's arrival was to be a cause for both blessing and lament. Earlier she had twice traveled from Philadelphia to New York to board her expected ship and sail to Beaufort, only to be disappointed. When she was finally embarked on her voyage, the passage was frightening, grim from beginning to end, leaving her in little condition to venture into an unknown wilderness to start teaching others the value and compassion of freedom. She was greatly relieved to meet up with her long-time friend and teaching associate to set out for their new habitat on St. Helena Island, little realizing that this would be their home and career together for almost 50 years.

Off to St. Helena and a Site for the School

On Saturday, June 7, 1862, Laura Towne repacked her steamer trunk, ready for the hot and dusty cart ride over buggy roads and farm paths toward Frogmore. She expressed great consternation and anxiety not only over leaving behind so many children and elderly people whom she had been treating, but also because recent skirmishes between Confederate and Union troops had forced the evacuation of many of the defending soldiers in Beaufort to form battle lines elsewhere, leaving the town virtually undefended, and the freed slaves subject to seizure and assault. Many of those in town were panicky because the bridge had been burned by fleeing infantrymen. She regained her composure somewhat, however, as she journeyed to the east, past farmlands and cotton crops showing much less devastation than those nearer the Beaufort River and Sound. Her apprehension had diminished considerably by the time she reached her destination and temporary quarters in a deserted house on Oaks Plantation. These accommodations were arranged by Edward L. Pierce, a young lawyer from Milton, Massachusetts, who had been assigned to aid the blacks and oversee cotton production in the Sea Islands. Now they encountered groups of blacks of all ages, though mainly women and children, who viewed her with a mixture of curiosity and shy amity, and she welcomed the less feverish ferment of her new surroundings.

Almost before trying to unpack and make living quarters out of semi-vacant rooms with only the vestiges of furniture or furnishings, Laura began planning where they could set up a classroom to entice students to begin lessons. She decided on the former parlor as the most likely schoolroom, with reasonable space, light, and ventilation, and then moved every bench, chair, and stool she could find into position. Her work was interrupted when one of the black ladies living nearby rushed in to announce, "Miss Murray has come!" The news—though so long hoped-for—was so unexpected that she felt faint and had to sit down momentarily before going outside to greet Ellen and hear all the news about her trip down from the North. They had to sleep in padding on the floor that night, having given over the bedroom space to two other young ladies who were relatives of northerners involved in the Port Royal Experiment. Their eagerness kept them awake discussing plans for establishing their new school and for accomplishing their goals to teach their expected pupils. They wanted to start at once, with no more delays or requisitions for additional equipment or help.

It should be pointed out here that Towne and Murray were at the time only partially aware of the fact that, in South Carolina, just by teaching black students how to read or write they were flouting a law whose breaking carried a large fine of up to $100 and/or imprisonment. Yet their plans remained unchanged: they would teach basic literacy skills as the cornerstone of learning at Penn School, including not only reading and writing but multiplication, the alphabet, and the Bible.

Several days went by, however, before they could spread the word about their plans and talk some likely pupils into attending. The potential students were shy and hesitant, if not confused by all the attention they were receiving. On Opening Day, June 18, they had nine pupils, all adults, and most very timid about what would be expected of them. Within a month, the number multiplied tenfold when prospective pupils, motivated by curiosity, learned that there was no imminent risk in attending. From the standpoint of the two green teachers, however, instruction was going to be a challenge. As Laura Towne later recorded in her diaries, speaking of the conduct of the female pupils, "They had no idea of sitting still, of giving attention, of ceasing to talk aloud. They lay down and went to sleep; they scuffled and struck each other; they got up by the dozen and made their curtsies, and walked off to the neighboring fields for blackberries, coming back to their seats when they were ready."[3] At this time she had no problems with male students because there were so few to consider—they all preferred to be in the fields hunting or on the waters fishing to "catching the learning."

Despite the rather disjointed attempt to establish a normal curriculum, Towne and Murray named their fledgling institution Penn School in honor of William Penn. In a solemn ceremony on the grounds, they presented the school with a brass bell inscribed with "Proclaim Liberty," patterned after the large bell in Independence Hall. This seemed like a fitting occasion and symbol for the new school—to teach freed slaves how to turn their new freedom into something productive and meaningful.

In spite of the fact that there were many suddenly abandoned plantation buildings on St. Helena Island and the other Sea Islands, there were no appropriate facilities for education. Thus, in early 1863, after some months of teaching in very limited facilities, Towne and Murray were grateful to receive a three-room frame building with ready-built-in partitions to serve as the first real schoolhouse in the South designed for the instruction of freed slaves. This welcome gift—one of the first "prefabricated" structures in American history—was from the Pennsylvania Freedman's Aid Society, one of the few sources of income over the ensuing years other than what the Towne family and close friends contributed whenever the financial situation became desperate.

Even though they had moved away from the military operations in the Beaufort and Port Royal Sound area, those at Penn School who were trying to establish educational curricula were constantly threatened by hostile skirmishes on St. Helena and even farther out toward Fripp Island and the Coosaw River, where units of the Confederate Army were engaged in intermittent rear guard harassment. At this time, in fact, Laura and Ellen were urged by one of their benefactors from Beaufort to return home at once, even if they had to leave their newfound friends and belongings, not to mention their aspirations, behind. Referring to James McKim, father of a young lady of about their age who transmitted the verdict that they were in a "dangerous situation," Laura wrote in her diary, "Ellen and I are determined not to go, and I think our determination will prevail over his fears, so that he will not order us home, as he has the power, I suppose."[4]

Late in July, the pressure and problems of establishing a school and adequate classrooms increased when General McClellan moved Union troops from their encampments on nearby Edisto Island to other positions. At the same time, this required the evacuation of the freed slaves who were there under their protection—some 1,600 in all—by relocating them to St. Helena. As it was, both Laura and Ellen were now involved in teaching Sunday school lessons as well as their lay classes, and thus had not a single day of rest from one week to the next. Laura was also very committed to using her medical experience, as she was the only person with such training at Penn School or in the entire area. She treated ulcers, injuries, respiratory ailments, measles, mumps, insect and snake bites, and an assortment of other ailments, as well as delivering babies and caring for colic and infant-related maladies. She reported in one letter that she regularly got up at six, ate a hasty breakfast, and then saw three or four patients. Then, by nine o'clock, she was on her way to one or two of five outlying plantations to see other patients. "The roads are horrible," she wrote, "and the horses ditto, so I have a weary time getting around."

One of her antidotes for avoiding the dreariness and monotony of the drive was to read aloud to everyone on the wagon. They "hurried" home by two o'clock in order to "snatch a lunch" and begin their classes. They then spent two hours with the children before going on to the adults, with Ellen bearing the brunt of the classes and Laura alternating between teaching and further doctoring in an area referred to as the "nigger houses," or street of cabins. That activity was followed by dinner and more attention after the meal to patients who were in need of treatment. At one time she was also in charge of a small detachment of freedmen who had been ordered to train as recruits in the event that southern pickets invaded the area in search of supplies and equipment. For this purpose she was given an assortment of muskets and pistols with which to train a ragtag group of defenders. Late afternoons she would run up a small flag, distribute the weapons from a locked cabinet, and drill the men for an hour, after which she would dismiss them and place the weapons back under lock and key. Since neither the leader nor the troops had much knowledge of either weapons or military strategy, it is doubtful that the drills would have proven of much use in the event of an attack by Confederate skirmishers.

Once the military exercises concluded, the ladies would dress for dinner, as was the custom despite the environment, the sparsity of tableware, and the scarcity of customary food supplies. Fortunately meals were not the problem they had expected. "We have nice melons and figs," Laura reported, "pretty good corn, tomatoes now and then, bread rarely, hominy, cornbread, and rice waffles. . . . We have fish nearly every day . . . and now and then turtle soup."[5] Meat of any kind was a scarcity because livestock was rarely raised for that purpose on the island, and the kinds of game—mainly squirrels and possums, caught by only a few hunters—were almost inedible. Despite the demands and constraints of her self-imposed work schedules, she always found time to appreciate and comment about the beauties of the environment. "I wish you could see the wild flowers," she wrote to her friends up north, "the hedges of Adam's needle, with heads of white bells a foot or two through and four feet high; the purple pease with blossoms that look like dog-tooth violets—just the size— climbing up the cotton plant with its yellow flower, and making whole fields purple and gold; the passion flowers in the grass; the swinging palmetto sprays and the crape myrtle in full bloom."[6] Much as she enjoyed the works of nature, she wrote frequently about its pestilence, especially the midges, punkies, fleas, and mosquitoes—the last-mentioned being so prevalent at certain times of the year that they had to sit in their room at night under netting. This restriction was a major aggravation for Laura because she could not write her daily diary or letters in the evening, having twice set the netting on fire from the candle she was using for light while writing notes.

During the first year of Penn School, and on into the second, the work of Towne and Murray was greatly diverted and interrupted by military operations, although the campus, such as it was in its infancy, was far removed from the Union encampments and from the traffic of gun boats and other war vessels on the Beaufort River and in Port Royal Sound. Many disruptions were not of a martial nature but rather of a social and communal imposition. As young ladies from the North, they were constantly receiving invitations to dinners, speeches, entertainment, drills, and other diversions of the military, many of which were difficult for them to decline because they relied so heavily on the officers and troops of the Union for their protection. Although Laura referred to them with due respect, she also intimated in private that they were very time consuming and in some cases demanding on her work and commitments to the cause of teaching those in need.

One of the continuing problems was that among the refugees from Edisto Island there were many able-bodied men who were now living on St. Helena, eating rations being supplied for the villagers by the army and in effect avoiding the military service that was required for males who were healthy enough and of the age for service. In one instance on September 12, a platoon of soldiers suddenly arrived and spread out through the fields and buildings, ultimately seizing some 20 men who were hiding under beds, in closets, and behind farming equipment, and marching them off to Fort Pulaski to serve as laborers. It was disheartening to realize that now there might not be enough able workers to harvest the corn and cotton crops, badly needed for food and income, respectively.

With the refugee men from Edisto gone, and with many of the free slaves conscripted by the army, a further problem was the possibility of forays by Confederate insurgents, or sometimes renegades, seeking food and supplies or just out to kill some Yankees. "Three boats of rebels attempted to land on these islands last night, two at the village and one at Edding's Point," Laura wrote in her diary in late October. "The Negroes with their guns were on picket; they gave the alarm, fired, and drove the rebels off." It was fortunate that she had maintained the muskets in good condition, kept them in a closet under her supervision, and even drilled the irregular soldiers on the grounds outside the schoolrooms.

The tiny school staff was augmented when, in the early fall of 1862, Towne and Murray were joined by Charlotte Forten, age 25, a Philadelphian born into an influential and affluent black family who had started her teaching career in a school in Salem, Massachusetts, the first African American ever hired. Yearning to help her people and be part of what she hoped would be an upward movement out of slavery, she volunteered to be sent to the Sea Islands of South Carolina to join in the educational movement just under way. She almost immediately saw her personal crusade floundering when she found that many of her pupils spoke only the Gullah language, an adaptation of English brought over from Africa, and the lack of the formal school routine she was accustomed to was also very upsetting.

"The first day of school was very trying," she wrote in her diary. "Most of my children are very small, and consequently restless. But after some days of positive, though not severe, treatment, order was brought out of chaos. I never before saw children so eager to learn." Although she enjoyed many periods of accomplishment and satisfaction that she was helping her own race, she was often overcome with doubt about her ability to achieve the starry goals she had dreamed of. Also disturbing were the many instances in which the native blacks had been mistreated, even by some of the northerners who were supposedly helping on the road to freedom. Charlotte "toughed it out" for some two years, however, helping Penn School over its first elemental hurdles, before physical and emotional stress forced her to resign and head back north.

One of the missions of the school was to teach each student a "life skill." While it was all but impossible financially at this early stage to hire teachers to instruct pupils in industry, trades, and agriculture, the teachers could provide solid programs in farming, the main source of income on St. Helena Island and an enterprise that was essential at Penn School itself in order to ensure supplies of produce, meat, and other foods from their own farm. When they began the school, Ellen Murray wrote in a report to Philadelphia, "we had no means of establishing an Agricultural Department, and feeling that the very best thing we could do for our pupils was to keep them on the farm instead of in the cities, we gave time in the morning for all our pupils to work from three to four hours with their parents on the farm and then, commencing at eleven, to give five hours to academic work."[7] This blend proved to be not only economically but academically successful for the budding institution.

That the early Penn School educational curriculum not only survived but continued to expand was astonishing, especially because most of the 50 or so other educational programs that were zealously launched by the government as part of the Port Royal Experiment were short-lived, and they were entirely disbanded within a matter of only a few years. Penn School was successful at least partly because, although it had rudimentary beginnings and demanded a discipline totally unknown in the Sea Islands, it was rooted in a rigorous, no-nonsense curriculum modeled after the principles of schools in New England and Philadelphia. One of the visiting teachers from the North was Sam Philips, who was warmly received when he returned from a visit to his home. "He told us about the North," reported Laura, "and said he was glad to get back to his people. They surrounded him when he came and fairly cried for joy over him, and this touched his good, kind heart. He has accomplished a great deal, and the children at our school are never tired of telling what he has done, or how well he has taught them, and showing the much-prized books and slates he gave them." She was concerned, however, that he was pale and thin and probably should not have returned so soon—if at all. She was particularly apprehensive when, a few days later, the island became "wrapped in the smoke of battle, and the people hear the roll of cannon."[8] The reports were that Fort Pulaski was being attacked by a rebel ship called a ram and was in danger of falling into the hands of the enemy.

Fortunately calm returned a few days later, and Penn School continued along its early pattern of study. By the time the Christmas season arrived, the sounds of war were far away. Laura Towne and Ellen Murray were conditioning their students for both the religious and secular understanding of the meaning of Christmas and the ways in which they would observe it. They tidied and scrubbed every part of the church, draped the pulpit in Spanish moss, and placed a wreath of red holly and palm leaves along the top, from which the moss fell like a gray waterfall. They attached opposite the pulpit a hand-lettered inscription, "HIS PEOPLE ARE FREE," festooned with a cluster of red berries and magnolia leaves, which were also looped between the church's stone pillars. Then, to complete the decorations, they hung circlets of green on the walls, each as a backdrop for one of the flags that had been sent to Penn School for the occasion. As for the participants, all of the teachers were dressed in blue garibaldis (with blue buttons down the shoulders) and black skirts, which they and their female students had spent many hours sewing and bedecking. "The celebration went off grandly," it was reported, including a talk to the pupils of the school by Lieutenant Colonel "Liberty" Billings, an officer in the First

South Carolina Volunteers, a black regiment under the command of Colonel Thomas Wentworth Higginson.[9]

The spirit of the yuletide celebration was manifested in the singing of a hymn written specifically for Penn School that very Christmas by the noted poet of that generation, John Greenleaf Whittier, which joyously proclaimed in part:

> Oh, none in all the world before
> Were ever glad as we!
> We're free on Carolina's shore,
> We're all at home and free.
>
> Thou Friend and Helper of the poor,
> Who suffered for our sake,
> To open every prison door,
> And every yoke to break!

Among the other songs and hymns that were popular at that time among the students, and particularly among the children, were "My Country 'Tis of Thee" and "John Brown's Body," whose tunes were often accompanied by home-made flutes and stringed instruments, and sometimes by drums and tambourines made by the students themselves. It was little short of astonishing that the two young ladies and their compatriots, totally unaccustomed to their new environment or the local population, could draw people of all ages and several races into the spirit of the season—and even supply the wherewithal to do so in a habitat where there were so very few amenities to begin with.

Even more remarkable was their gumption, if not downright courage, in standing up to what today would be considered outright terrorism. Consider for example their plight when in early February 1863 the 178th Regiment, N.Y. Volunteer Infantry, with the alarming name *Les Enfants Perdus* ("The Lost Children") was landed on the island, fresh from the North, supposedly to guard the area against counterattacks by the Confederate Army. Instead, Laura reported, "they are doing all sorts of mischief. They take the people's chickens, shoot and carry off their pigs, and, when the people defend their property, they shoot the men and insult the women." When they went so far as to burn a row of houses near Lands End, the teachers and some of their local military friends took action and succeeded in making the area in and around Penn School off limits to these brigands from New York.

But the Yankees were not the only ones at fault. Many of the male blacks who had been conscripted into the Union Army were ill trained, had inflated ideas about their new "authority," and sometimes terrorized the community. Such was the case on a bleak day in late March when a dozen black soldiers, armed with muskets, suddenly appeared in the church where a Penn School class was in progress. They had been ordered to search for males of recruitment age to be seized and drafted into the Union Army. The pupils were alarmed, but fortunately there were no young men in the classrooms at the time, so the would-be "recruiters" had to leave empty-handed. But the incident both frightened and infuriated Towne, who immediately complained to one of the officers she knew, telling him that it was extremely dangerous to order black soldiers to undertake an assignment they could not handle.

The teachers discovered that they could improve the quality of their classroom curricula if they observed various holidays and made the learning process fun as well as educational. A good example was the Fourth of July, which they observed during the second year of Penn School. In addition to having discussions about the meaning of the Fourth of July and its place in America's history, the pupils made buttons, badges, and other typical tokens of the holiday and learned the verses of "The Star Spangled Banner," which they sang "with great gusto." They also gave their version of the typical religious "shout" on the porch of the school building and distributed watermelon slices to all the guests. Then Charles F. Folsom of Massachusetts, who had arrived on the scene as temporary school superintendent, read the Declaration of Independence, followed by an oration by the black minister from the nearby Methodist church. Among the guests were a number of officers from the 54th Massachusetts Regiment (colored), including Colonel Robert Gould Shaw, who was soon to meet his death so heroically while leading his black troops in battle at Fort Wagner on July 18, where nearly all of the officers of the 54th were killed or wounded.

The war was never far away. "We could hear the guns all day and night," Laura wrote later to her friends up north. And two weeks after the Fourth of July, she was hastily summoned away from her classroom to Beaufort to help nurse the casualties who had been transported down by the hundreds from a battle at Morris Island. The field hospital was inundated with food donations from the farmers, including melons, sweet potatoes, chickens, and other produce, but there was little that could be done for many of the most gravely wounded. The citizens were further stretched to send potatoes and other vegetables to the soldiers on Morris Island, who were suffering from dwindling food supplies as a result of the engagement.

All in all, it was a very demanding fall for the founders of Penn School, and they looked forward to taking a break at Christmas time to sail home on a northward-bound packet, the *Arago*. But Ellen Murray became increasingly ill with a fever that she was unable to shake, even with steady doses of quinine. In addition to this setback that required a change in plans, the new school was threatened again when parishioners declared the brick church where classes were being held off limits as "private property," to be used for religious purposes and not as a school for "coloreds." Even her desperate attempts to send a letter about her undesired change of plans and the dreary thought that "we shall have no Christmas for the school and no school probably" went awry when a fierce winter storm prevented many ships from putting to sea at all.

January 1864 was a low point. "We have no milk, and at times no wood," she wrote in her daily diary, explaining that there was not a single man at the school who was well enough to bring in supplies, and that even the boys and girls were too sick to attend classes. When Laura, herself unwell, made the rounds of the dwellings in the neighborhood to take medicine for the sick, she found the doors latched so that she could not get in and was alarmed that the residents were practicing a native remedy that did more harm than good: washing patients with strong vinegar, salt, and pokeroot, ground from a very poisonous plant.

The increasing need for her help and medical services on St. Helena and in the surrounding regions, as well as a real dread of sea voyages in the small and unseaworthy ships that were available for civilians, finally convinced Laura that she would have to commit herself utterly to the mission she had undertaken— at least until the following summer. She entreated her family to ship down, whenever possible, some carpets, furniture, and other household goods to help improve the low quality of their surroundings. "This is my home, probably for the rest of my days," she wrote, "and I want to be comfortable in it." Her goal was going to take some doing to accomplish because her quarters in St. Helena village after leaving The Oaks were described as "nearly as ill built and open as a rough country stable," with bare boards and wide cracks.

In the summer of 1864, Towne had a brief respite when she took the long journey north, and by the time she returned she found work beginning on a new schoolhouse, whose parts had been prefabricated by the Freeman's Aid Society of Pennsylvania and transported by ship and mule team to Penn School. It is evident that the school was by now beginning to grow quite rapidly because she reported 50 "scholars," 150 more who were taking rudimentary lessons, and three teachers in attendance. Her new school bell was being shipped, and after they hung it in place, it would be greatly admired by the students, a few of whom would be permitted to ring it as a reward for good marks or attendance. Inscribed on the casing, as mentioned earlier in this chapter, were the words "Proclaim Liberty."

The winter of 1865 was nasty and grim on St. Helena, with no stoves, plants frozen stiff, milk icing in the dairy, and the earth a hard ball. For the first time since arriving on the island, Laura was too ill to leave her room for the better part of a week. But many of the school families were not so fortunate. "The children are all emaciated to the last degree," she wrote, "and have such violent coughs and dysenteries that few survive. It is frightening to see such suffering among children." One of the problems was that the intense cold found very few families with blankets, and many children died of the cold before the government finally distributed blankets to the neediest homes. It was devastating to Laura, whose early training in homeopathic medicine made her realize what the problem was and how it could be alleviated, but left her without the means of taking any counteractions to prevent widespread tragedy. Even after the freezing winter waned and spring approached, the disaster had only partially abated. In the school area alone, there were about 100 "almost naked and entirely filthy" people, most of whom were deathly ill, still awaiting boxes of supplies that had been promised but were endlessly delayed. "The people come to our yard and stand mute in their misery," she reported, unable to find even scraps of clothing, and with no room to take many inside a building for relief.[10] To compound the problem, the intense cold and freezing rains had destroyed the small winter crops, made fishing almost impossible, and sent what small game there might have been in the forests into hibernation, leaving the populace starving. The Penn School teachers did what they could to obtain grits and rice from Beaufort and the military bases, but these rations were far too skimpy to meet the overwhelming need.

The coming of spring brought increasing relief both in the matter of clothing and food, but it also brought a great anguish for the freed slaves. On April 14, 1865, several from Penn School traveled to Charleston to see the United States flag raised on Fort Sumter by Union General Robert Anderson, who had been compelled to surrender the same fort four years earlier. On April 23, a town crier in the village of St. Helena announced that Abraham Lincoln had been assassinated—ironically, just at the time that the troops were celebrating the recapture of the fort. Many of the blacks had considered Lincoln to be a saint and their savior, and they went into a long period of mourning, conducting religious services and praying that the assassination had not taken place and that their president was only wounded and would recover. At Penn School, the children draped the classrooms in what pieces of black cloth they could find, and some pinned scraps of the cloth to their shirts or hats to show their sorrow.

Oddly there is no record that the school children, teachers, or residents of St. Helena actively celebrated the end of the Civil War. There was simply too much disruption during this period among the troops—both Union and Confederate—and too little news that could be readily comprehended by isolated people. In point of fact, there was very little to celebrate in the Sea Islands. The 12-year period of Reconstruction that was about to begin in the South was to bring more bane than blessing to most of the blacks, brimming as it would be with a scurrilous tide of carpetbaggers and scalawags. Although the teachers and students at Penn School and the citizens of St. Helena Island were, because of their remoteness, largely bypassed by individuals and groups bringing economic devastation to the South, they suffered the backlash of discontent and turmoil that affected towns such as Beaufort and Charleston. As a result, Laura Towne and Ellen Murray found it increasingly difficult to cut through the shattered communications network to order badly needed supplies and equipment. To make matters worse, most of the Union officers they knew who had been stationed in the Beaufort area and who had helped them greatly in times of need had been transferred or relieved of duty.

In January 1869, Laura Towne and Ellen Murray moved to the nearby village of Frogmore with the expectation that a shipment was soon to arrive from Philadelphia including not only school supplies but badly needed furniture. A two-story house was being built for them by one of the local carpenters, and for once, after seven years of living in the most makeshift surroundings, they would have what could be called a home. On the education front, classes at Penn School had increased steadily in size and content. On the home front, however, the situation became grave when, in the late spring, a drought combined with unusually hot weather all but decimated the corn crop, threatened the cotton crop, and seriously affected the vegetables, especially potatoes, which were the mainstay of most native diets. With wells going dry and very little water available from streams, many of the classes in farming and agriculture had to be curtailed. To offset these difficult circumstances, the teachers enlarged the classes in such subjects as carpentry, shoemaking, metalworking, and the arts.

Crop problems of this kind had been, and always would be, one of the biggest concerns of Towne, Murray, and others associated with Penn School during the next 30 years. Yet it is remarkable that in every case of agricultural disaster, they managed to take courses of action to keep the school functioning and in some cases even to use pestilence and blight as part of the down-to-earth training programs of young pupils who would have to face such setbacks all of their lives. Penn School had been founded, after all, not simply to acquaint students with the arts and letters but to alert them to, and train them in, the ways of living against all odds. On May 7, 1871, Laura Towne wrote a note in her diary: "Just think, forty-six years of age! Almost half a century and with so much history in it too!" She later added, "I do not ever intend to leave this 'heathen country.' I intend to spend my days here."[11]

Little did she realize that her work was not only helping a few tiny communities on a remote island, but that she was laying the groundwork for programs that over the next century would help to save an entire culture from slow extinction. That culture, though almost unknown in her time by any specific name, was the Gullah culture.

Slave quarters on a plantation at Port Royal Island, South Carolina, circa 1862
COURTESY OF THE LIBRARY OF CONGRESS

CHAPTER 3

A Quantum Leap

We jump from the 19th century to St. Helena Island in 1989, when the Gullah contingent left their Sea Island shores to explore their ancestry in West Africa and see some remarkable truths. Although neighboring islands such as Hilton Head, Edisto, and Kiawah have changed abruptly, St. Helena has remained as it was because it was isolated, with no bridge to the mainland until the middle of the 20th century. (The lack of bridges to most of the Sea Islands, especially the smaller ones, is one important reason why the Gullah culture was able to maintain its integrity throughout so many generations.) This is, in effect, a naturalist's dream of an island, long noted for its remoteness, untouched beauty, thick pine forests, swaying legions of bright green palmetto, kaleidoscopes of flora and fauna, Spanish moss, marshlands with ever-changing colors, tidal inlets, estuaries and creeks, archaeological shell rings, tabby ruins, and the abundance of surrounding sea life which is so vital to the survival of the coastal families. We see this pearl of the Sea Islands through the eyes of key figures in its 18th- and 19th-century history, particularly Laura Towne, George

Washington Carver, W. E. B. Du Bois, Martin Luther King Jr., and, more recently, southern novelists and poets. This island might well be called "land of
the Gullahs" because it is one of the few Sea Islands that has resisted an influx
of tourists and development. Consequently, its peoples have been more isolated
than in many areas of the Carolinas and Georgia.

I n his classic and widely commended book, *Haunted by God: The Cultural
and Religious Experience of the South*, author James McBride Dabbs focuses
strong attention on the spiritual values of the Sea Islands. The Sea Islands
of the Atlantic form a slender, subtropical line along the American coastline
from the Carolinas to the northern tip of Florida. They are rich in history and
noted for their natural beauty, composed of a conglomerate of pine and oak forests, fertile lowlands, and salt marshes, interlaced with broad rivers, tidal creeks,
inlets, and broad savannahs. One of them, St. Helena, South Carolina, is a vital
and pivotal setting in the history of the Gullah culture in America. Originally
named St. Elena by the Spanish explorer Pedro de Quexos in 1525, it is one
of the largest islands in the Carolinas and has the kind of natural harbor and
habitable land that encouraged exploration by the Spanish, French, and English. The Warto and Yamasee Indian tribes remained in the area now known
as Beaufort County until about 1715, when the remaining Indian peoples were
driven across the Savannah and all the way south to what is today St. Augus-
tine. St. Helena was isolated from the mainland by tidal creeks and the Atlantic
Ocean during the 19th century and remained so until 1927, when the first
bridge was constructed linking the island to the mainland. For this reason, even
during slavery days, self-sufficiency was embedded in the island culture. In fact,
the topography has sometimes been referred to as similar to the West African
coast where the slaves originated; it is a network of working waterways and
tidal creeks that supported a traditional African and Low Country way of life.
Certain degrees of freedom were afforded for fishing, crabbing, and hunting
to supplement the diet and create income for the Gullah. Agricultural cultivation of family plots outside the slave quarters provided needed vegetables, such
as tomatoes, okra, and greens. Game was hunted on adjacent Hunting Island,

which had traditionally been a game reserve since the English habitation of the Sea Islands.

St. Helena is noted for the fact that it embodies much of African American heritage and culture, which is unusually well preserved in the historical compound of Penn Center, founded in 1862 as Penn School to educate freed slaves. It is also the home base of many studies about Gullah history and the Gullah Institute, which was founded there in 2005.

Over the past several decades, the predominantly African American community of St. Helena Island, like many island communities on the southern part of the Atlantic coast, has experienced the rapid transitions of aggressive and often carelessly planned development. The result is a profound sense of displacement among the indigenous population, a separation from a way of life that evolved out of slavery, through emancipation and then Reconstruction, and into the 20th century. The rapid expansion of luxury residential complexes, commercial businesses, resort and tourist attractions, and the infrastructure to support them has drastically changed the once idyllic rural farming communities of the islands. Although St. Helena is not as totally transformed as some of the neighboring islands, the people of the island are fully aware of the fact that vigilance is now a way of life they must maintain to guard against further displacement. Undoubtedly the beauty of the island, its warm climate, and the possibilities for recreational activities have attracted the new development.

St. Helena Island is located in Beaufort County among the tidal rivers, saltwater bays, and marshes that cover much of the South Carolina coast. Jutting into the Atlantic Ocean, it is 53 square miles of developed land, open spaces, and wooded areas. A bridge connects the island to the county seat of Beaufort. The two-lane highway through it is the access route to the smaller islands of Fripp, Harbor, and Huntington. Across Port Royal Sound are the Parris Island Marine Corps installation in one direction and the luxury "plantations" and condominiums of Hilton Head and Bluffton in the other. In 1970 the population of St. Helena was only 3,500—much smaller than today. With few exceptions, its residents were the descendants of Africans who were once slaves there and who purchased small parcels of land after emancipation. In the isolation of the remote island, the Gullah culture was given birth from African and European cultures and remained intact until the invasion of modern development.

On St. Helena and other islands, Gullah stands as one of the oldest cultures in the United States. Among its attributes is a strong relationship to the land and the way families and communities use the land. Therefore mass development and the influx of large numbers of new residents threaten the very survival of the culture. On St. Helena the population has increased by nearly 5,000 in the last generation.

The story of St. Helena Island raises questions about how development should occur in the southern coastal states and the importance of honoring environmental and cultural characteristics of communities. Equally so, it points out the dilemma of development without the inclusion of the voices of those at whose expense it takes place and of the public policies that determine who will benefit from development. During the bitter years of slavery, the main inhabitants of St. Helena and other islands of the South Carolina coast were the thousands of enslaved Africans brought there to work the rice, cotton, and indigo fields. Finding the hot, marshy islands undesirable, the white plantation owners chose to build their family homes in the more comfortable settings of Charleston and other historic communities. In their relative social and geographical isolation, the enslaved Africans evolved their own culture—the Gullah culture—which was a worldview and way of life based on retained Africanisms and the Eurocentric customs of their masters. Key to Gullah culture is a complex but intimate relationship to the land upon which they labored and which gave them the basics of their survival. After emancipation, many of the former slaves purchased small parcels of island land upon which to make their new lives. Across the islands they fashioned compounds reminiscent of the family complexes of African villages. The generations that have followed have inherited not only the land itself but also a way of relating to the environment and the way families live and work on the land.

In his book *The Abundant Life Prevails*, recognized as one of the finest tributes to St. Helena Island and its religious traditions, author Michael C. Wolfe wrote, "I know an island off the South Carolina coast where the Spanish moss hangs from ancient twisted live oak trees and at night the moonlight casts eerie shadows on the narrow oyster shell roads. It is an old place. A European settlement flourished in this area long before the Jamestown or Plymouth colonies. It is a small place, only fifteen miles long and five miles wide, formed by the ocean's ferocity. Through the centuries, tidal erosion and battering hurricanes have broken the Carolina coast into these small islands separated by rivers and tidal inlets."[1]

As Wolfe reports, the island residents came here long ago as "unwilling immigrants" from a tiny island named Bunce, in Sierra Leone, West Africa. Even so, they love their island home on the Carolina coast. Many authors, both local and national, have written about St. Helena Island, and increasingly about this unique culture called Gullah. Many, like James McBride Dabbs, have noted the spirituality of the island and its residents. A good example is Margaret Creel, who has done groundbreaking work on antebellum Sea Island religion, tracing the religious life of the enslaved from colonial times through the Civil War. In her book *A Peculiar People: Slave Religion and Community-Culture Among the Gullahs*, she examines the components of community, religion, and fortitude that provided this population with its cultural autonomy and sense of consciousness. The culture in her account has been described as relating to "one of the most singular groups and stirring stories in all of American history."[2]

"But what happened to these islanders after the war?" asks Michael Wolfe, to which he answers:

> In 1861 two religious traditions collided on Saint Helena Island. Already firmly entrenched on the island, the slaves' religion represented a mixture of Southern evangelicalism and African practices. The other, newer tradition would be an imported faith found primarily at the Penn School established for the islanders by Northern missionaries whose Protestantism emphasized citizenship, character development, service, and self-discipline. Saint Helena Island and the Penn School are historically important because they served as a stage on which a "rehearsal for reconstruction" transpired when the area around Beaufort, South Carolina, fell into Union Army hands in November 1861. Seeking to prove to a skeptical America—North and South—that newly freed men and women could be good, responsible citizens, Northern missionaries funded by the federal government traveled to South Carolina to labor among the newly freed African Americans.[3]

Despite the fact that what was known as the Port Royal Experiment failed in its ambitious mission to educate enslaved peoples and help them learn skills and trades to support themselves, Penn School survived, though often on the fringe of disaster. In 1900 when the school faced financial and leadership problems, the Hampton Institute in Virginia saved the day, bringing in educators from the North to conduct what was initially called an "experiment" in educational salvation. Focusing on "character development" among the African American islanders, Penn School "linked hands with a worldwide network of Christian organizations, progressive educators, and government agencies." Somehow the school managed to face what were often severe, changing circumstances and crises, particularly after World War II when the South was plagued by interracial strife and when Penn Center became one of the most important focal points of the civil rights movement.

"Through the years," reported Wolfe, "Penn evolved into much more than a local private school. Its leaders embraced that most ancient of American Puritan dreams, 'the shining city on the hill,' and these missionaries came to believe that from their lonely island outpost, led and empowered by God, they could change the world. . . . Furthermore, the Penn School's history sheds enormous light on American ideals of social progressivism and the religious motivations of those ideals. Like so many other social progressives in American history, Penn's leaders were not merely building a better society, they were dreaming of the Kingdom of God on earth."[4]

As discussed previously, during the early 20th century, the American Protestant dream shifted dramatically, and missionaries who arrived on St. Helena were certain that they knew all the answers to the islanders' problems. They came to pursue their own objectives and to proclaim a particular message about religion. As the years passed, however, these teachers learned to listen to the islanders and to appreciate the local culture, "discovering that God spoke in a variety of languages and traditions,"[5] when a larger, dominant society tried to interact with a smaller, local culture. Although the "outside world" was focusing on St. Helena and the Sea Islands, the African American islanders went about their own lives, practicing their religion and seeking God through visions and ecstatic rituals. Thus the story of St. Helena is somewhat a case history to show how two vastly different traditions, missionary and islander, "emerged from their own environments, how each sought particular goals for the island, and how they eventually merged into a living faith community."[6]

The Hardships of Nature

Despite the abundance of positive factors about the island environment, such as fertile soil, valuable timberlands, glorious foliage, plentiful foods from the rivers, inlets, and shores, and some six months of the year when the climate is attractive to visitors, the year-round residents, until recent times, had to endure periods of debilitating heat, pestilence, and storms. Most notable in this last category was the Sea Islands hurricane of 1893, when, on the night of August 27, the storm made its way from the Gulf of Mexico and, instead of following the Gulf Stream, veered inland in a curve like an archer's bow, not only with hurricane-force winds but also with a tidal wave that averaged almost 10 feet high and in many places much more, ravaging the land and drowning many of the occupants. The "tide of death," as it was referred to, made landfall just south of Beaufort, South Carolina, and claimed almost 3,000 lives (one-tenth of the population on St. Helena) in a single night. But that was only the beginning. The gaunt figure of famine silently stole across the land because all vegetable growth was destroyed, livestock was swept away, and fresh water was turned to salt. The noted founder of the American Red Cross, Clara Barton, directed a 10-month relief effort, conscripting what few boats were still intact or could be brought in to transport survivors to the mainland. However, it took almost a month from the time the governor was able to get his urgent message to Washington, D.C., until help actually arrived, and hundreds of people died from injuries, storm-related disease, or starvation. As was later determined, this outrageous delay was to a great extent caused by the fact that African American segments of the population were deemed to be more accustomed to suffering and less in need of help than their white brothers and sisters.

The great storm brought out the best in many of the residents in that they labored together to bring back their ravaged land, digging drainage ditches to carry away stagnant, mosquito-breeding waters, planting seeds supplied by state and federal governments and the Red Cross, and building emergency shelters from lumber supplied by relief agencies, private citizens, and church congregations in some of the inland towns not devastated by the hurricane. Looking back on the great hurricane of 1893 and other natural disasters that have beset St. Helena in the past, Emory Campbell attributes the intense and almost heroic sense of survival on the part of the population to the fact that such a large percentage of those affected were the descendants of the enslaved families and later freedmen whose very lives were day-to-day studies in survival and reliance on family members and neighbors rather than outside groups or organizations. So even though 30 days elapsed before any assistance came from beyond the island's shores, the people were taking positive steps, often strengthened by strong religious faith. At the core of this kind of inner strength was Penn School, which, being far from the shore and whose buildings remained more or less intact, served as a center of hope. With a teaching staff and pupils whose very goals were aimed at individual subsistence and development and whose objective was to be supportive to one's neighbors, Penn was able to put into practice what it had long preached, as will be seen in following chapters describing the role of the school in the community.

History shows, too, that the islanders in general were more attuned to survival than, say, the town- and city-dwellers on the mainland. Until well into the mid-1900s, the small farms and saltwater creeks and streams that flow nearby gave the people of St. Helena Island most of what they needed to be self-sufficient. The rest was up to their own hard work and ingenuity and the strong sense of interdependence that was fostered among them since Reconstruction and even before. Families and extended families worked the fields, fished the waters, and shared and exchanged goods and labor. Everything that went on their tables and most of what their families used came from the natural environment of the island. What cash was needed was earned by taking produce by boat to mainland markets or by working at Penn School, for many years the island's most prominent establishment. Starting in the 1920s when the first bridge connected St. Helena to the mainland, people from Beaufort and other towns came to buy the rich produce of the islands. Local people also began to take seasonal or part-time jobs on the large truck farms or in the seafood industry, oystering, shrimping, crabbing, or working at the mill where the shells of oysters were processed for use in farming and the manufacture of building materials.

With the coming of development in the latter half of the 20th century, the self-sufficient way of life changed for the islanders. Emory Campbell, who for 22 years served as the Executive Director of Penn Center, explains: "The biggest impact has been the need for cash. The old culture known as the Gullah, and just now being recognized as a major heritage, had existed without the need for cash. Everything the Gullah people needed was done by them, among them, and you might say, in coordination with the entire community. If you needed a net knitted, you knew where the net knitter was. You shared information. All of a sudden, development and the need for cash comes. Now on the island people have to buy food, look for better ways to fix the roof or equip their homes, but since they don't grow crops or maintain a tool shop, and since they have a job that takes all their time, and hardly ever get to go fishing, they realize they have changed day-to-day occupations and a way of life."[7]

In a story circle, arranged to present an insider view of life in the Sea Islands, three African American islanders, Ursell Holmes, Ethel Green, and Martha Chisholm, recalled how different life was when they were growing up.

> *Holmes:* My grandparents worked mostly in the fields. They tried to support themselves with the fieldwork to grow tomatoes and cucumbers, corn and vegetables, and sometimes okra, beans, and peas. They would take them to Beaufort and sell them. They did not do too much outside work, although sometimes my grandfather worked on the Penn School farm. Everybody had cows and horses that they used to help farm because they had no farming equipment like you have today. At certain times of the year, they did hog killing, and in our community, everyone shared the meat from the hogs. So that's how we lived.

> *Chisholm:* And you had the sweet potatoes, and corn. Folks grew their own corn and ground it, so you got the corn meal, you got your husk, you got your grits. We grew sugar cane and ground it and then made syrup. They also grew rice, and the little children had to shoo the blackbirds out of the field so they would not eat the rice. I cried many a day when the birds would fly over my head and I could not make them go away because the rice was taller than I was. Turkeys, they raised and sold them at Thanksgiving. The marine base at Parris Island was always a good market. Folks would come by and find out what you had and buy it—the city folks who lived in town who weren't able to farm. Or the insurance man and the mailman would say, "Miss So-and-so, I need two quarts of lima beans" or "I need some eggs" or "I need me a chicken for Sunday." You'd supply what was needed and then get paid—usually less than what was charged at local stores.

Green: I lived with my grandmother, I didn't do a lot of fieldwork, I was just there tending my grandmother's garden, but it was a big garden. She had field peas, butter beans, okra, peanuts, greens, corn. During the summer, we had fig trees, peach trees, pear trees, plums, and so forth. So we picked all those fruits, and Granny preserved them in jars and put them aside for the winter. My uncles were the farmers, so when it was time to learn about the crops, I worked on my uncles' farms. My mother was gone a lot of the time because she was a domestic with a U.S. Marine major on nearby Parris Island, and then went with his family when he was transferred to another base at Quantico, Virginia. She sent money back home for my upkeep, to send me to school, and for my clothing. I went out on nearby farms to work. I didn't have to go, but it was a chance to get away from home. That was where the other children of the neighborhood were, so I could have some playmates and enjoy some fun. Those were the farms of the white folks who were able to have costly equipment like tractors and trucks, and that was where you made your money in the summertime.

Chisholm: The river was our "supermarket." The river was always there. Before my grandfather went to work at four o'clock in the morning, he would go in the river, throw his net, and pull up a bucket of fish to bring home. Then we had to get up and clean those fish before we went to school, and lay them out for Grandmother to cook. Whenever there was nothing to eat, they would say, "Go get something." There were always plenty of crabs, oysters, clams, or different kinds of fish. We had a wood-burning stove, and often my grandmother would fry up a batch, so we could always have some that were ready to eat.

Today few families can afford to raise most of the foods they eat, and small farmers are having difficulty competing with large growers in the market. Many islanders still maintain small gardens, but in the end they almost always have to go to a supermarket to supplement their needs, and that can be more costly than they expect. Many islanders who were, or are, farmers believe that the changes that increase the cost of living have been the result of governmental regulations that have favored the corporate farms and other big businesses. Through their Growers Organization, the large farm owners, many of whom live outside the area and even outside the state, have been able to influence legislation and regulatory agencies in ways not to the liking of small farmers. For example, they have changed the way tomatoes are cultivated. As one local grower complained, "All of a sudden, the big farmers were not going to plant the sweet soft tomatoes any longer. The breed they selected was one that was local to Florida—beautiful to look at, but with a skin so tough that if they dropped to the ground they practically bounced back at you. The homegrown variety was more easily bruised, and thus less marketable in bulk, but it is a sweeter and more tender tomato. This new tomato was quite expensive for the small farmers to grow, but they tried and it worked for a while. The next thing the regulators decided was that you had to farm 'stick' tomatoes, which require rows of sticks in much the same way that you would do for climbing roses. Then the requirements specified that growers had to cover the fields with plastic, maintain a certain amount of irrigation under the plastic, and intake gas to kill the weeds. All of these procedures and equipment and labor priced the small farmer right out of the market, as well as ending up with a product that has led to many complaints from consumers."[8]

Walter Mack, an educator and former Penn School student, further explains: "When I was growing up, all the local farmers grew what were called 'hotbeds,' which were small nurseries where they used their own seeds and planted their own seedlings. Lately, it has been required that you have to buy your seedlings. Clemson University states that the hybrid seed is best, but I don't necessarily think that is true, because with the hybrid, you get all kinds of diseases and all types of problems. Right now, if you plant tomatoes, they can't touch the ground and you have to spray almost every other day to keep the diseases away, since the hybrids were developed in greenhouses and were not resistant to local diseases." Mack explains that some years ago, Clemson was one of the many institutions serving as government-supported agricultural agencies and making recommendations for farmers. His complaint is that such agencies focused on the large farmers, whereas the small farmers had to try and adapt the technology as best they could. He says, "Maybe those techniques or practices just were not right for small farmers, but they were good for larger farmers who had the equipment to produce those types of crops using that technology."[9]

Two of the most sizeable tomato farm operations on St. Helena Island were among the largest in the nation. Following the seasons, these corporations transferred the migrant workers to the planting of tomatoes in other states ranging from Florida to New England. Thus the residents of the Sea Islands viewed these temporary and absentee neighbors much as they saw some of the plantation owners of old: people who did not live there and, other than owning the property and reaping its benefits, had no connection to the land or the community.

Fishing also changed because of outside intervention. Whereas people had once fished for food and income, fishing now became just a recreational sport, and even the laws focused more on the regulation of sport fishermen. The State Wildlife Commission designated a 60-day annual season for baiting shrimp and limited the amount of shrimp that could be caught. Indigenous fishermen preferred the old, traditional method of baiting because they believed the approved method polluted the waters. But the waterways were being polluted in other ways, too—by waste runoff from cars, boats, golf courses, homes, and hotels. Developers did not anticipate the effects of the large volume of sewage from septic tanks—more than the land would hold. As a result, yards were often flooded and sewage lines overtaxed, causing seepage into the creeks and streams, and shellfish beds often had to be closed at times because of the heavy pollution.

Many islanders lamented the environmental changes, such as the lack of wild animals that they used to see when they were growing up, including rabbits and deer that would run across the fields or slip into the backyards to nibble cabbage and collard greens in the garden. They were a supply of food for people, too. But now they no longer had any place to go. Even the turtles that would come out of the water to sun on the banks seemed to be fewer and fewer.

Most people on St. Helena still maintained small gardens or did small-scale farming, and the custom of sharing and swapping was still alive and well. "Here, I'll bring a mess of this or a mess of that by the house for you," neighbors would say, and okra, tomatoes, watermelons, cucumbers, squash, and the fixings for a salad or a pot of gumbo still remained standard among islanders. But freezers replaced canning jars for preserving fruits and vegetables for winter use by people who wanted to grow their own vegetables to avoid the fertilizers and chemicals used on commercially grown produce.

Walter Mack was still farming, too. "I'm doing something different, though. I am trying fruit trees, and I want to get into herbs and flowers. People think some fruits don't grow around here, but I don't believe that. I have been very successful in growing apples. Blueberries thrive down here, as well as figs and pears. The muscadine grape is another one that is easily grown because muscadines are indigenous to this area. Growing up, I remember my grandmother had citrus fruit trees—oranges, tangerines, and lemons. I want to try to get back to doing some citrus, because I think they can make it here, you just have to get the right variety."[10] Mack is one of the local farmers who believe that the family farm and the traditions of self-sufficiency that were so important to island families of the past can be adapted to have a place in the 21st century. Some years ago, the Tuskegee Institute introduced local farmers to "u-pick" and other strategies of the modern farm entrepreneur, with the idea that tourists would be attracted to farms not only for the fresh produce but also for the visual appeal of fruits and vegetables that are in their native surroundings. "People love to see things growing in the natural setting," said one of the institute's researchers. "If you ask kids where a tomato comes from, most of them would answer, 'out of the store.' The idea that you can take children to see tomatoes growing is a selling point—almost like going on an outing to a petting zoo."[11] Of the small black farmers in his area, Mack could think of only one who is currently able to make a living from farming as a full-time job. "He has a large u-pick operation. One thing that he started was a greenhouse to grow strawberries year-round. If nothing else, it's a big attraction. He decided that a tour of his farm operation would be successful. Everything is based on the tourist industry, and he is in a good location. He still does some truck farming along with his u-pick. He has truckers coming in from New England buying up loads of produce from him, especially his main crop, which is watermelon."[12]

St. Helena Island was designated by the county as a Rural Agriculture District, a not-so-small feat accomplished through the active participation of local residents who successfully negotiated a plan that excludes the development of golf courses, condominium complexes, waste treatment facilities, and other environmental intrusions on St. Helena. It calls for the island to remain a place where homes, family gardens, small farms, and limited large truck farms can co-exist. Lula Holmes says, "We feel that we want this to remain rural. Let it be rural. Its beauty and the people are rural. For one thing, you get to know your neighbor. You are on speaking terms with people. You look out for one another. You share food, share crops from the field. They send you potatoes, they send greens, and especially to indigent persons."[13]

The challenge of preserving the spirit of interdependency and degree of self-sufficiency that were good for St. Helena in the past will depend on the ability of small farmers to run profitable operations, whether that be u-pick farms, farm tours, trucking to markets, roadside farmers' markets, or other innovative ventures suitable to the 21st century. It will also depend on demonstrating the desirability and profitability of farming to younger generations, to explain just how such an age-old livelihood as farming can fit into the computer age. Equally important, however, it will depend upon public policies that make it possible for small farmers to compete in the marketplace, fair lending practices, and access to relevant information and assistance from government-supported agencies engaged in agricultural research and demonstration projects. The rest, as before, will be up to the hard work and ingenuity of the island people and their centuries-old customs of interdependency.

Speaking about a proposal for an Endangered Communities Act several years ago, Emory Campbell stated:

> I don't know how far it would go, but it would surely be a very important protective measure for communities. It would be based on how a community could sustain itself better if it were protected. We propose many ways of addressing more jobs for more people, yet we never do very much to protect the community itself from destruction. In Beaufort County there are a substantial number of people that have the basic resources for moving into the middle class, and that is *land*. But then we pay no attention to that situation and we tax them right off of that very land, in effect disposing of it at the courthouse steps, just for a few hundred dollars in taxes. Administrations overlook the fact that property is a basic resource for a family to move from poverty up to a higher level. Another instance is where people don't have that kind of land base, but are heads of solid, stable families, who are long-time residents who want to live here, who provide a very important resource to the community through their skills and through their education and knowledge. We've got to find a way of protecting them and keeping them. We've paid a lot

of attention to historic buildings and how to restore and protect them. But not the people themselves. We drive people away because the historic land becomes so expensive and taxable in higher brackets that the very property they have lived on is no longer affordable.

We want to utilize our land as an asset for economic development, and in a way that is in keeping with the culture as nearly as possible. We could provide businesses that are related to the culture that can either be productive on-site, or we can produce items that can be sold away from site. We are looking at ways of really helping people develop their individual businesses that can take advantage of this new economy. We have an organization named the Native Island Community Affairs Association on Hilton Head Island, which instituted a revolving loan fund to help small businesses. We fund tour companies, small landscape businesses, restaurants, all kinds of shops, service and repair facilities, and many other types of operations. So we want to grow small businesses that would utilize the cultural assets as well as the environmental assets that we have.

If there is one element that is inevitable, he says, it is change.

The people of St. Helena always start their story from the viewpoint of the island's history, "the old ways," but they, too, know they live in changing times. It is not that they resist change, but they are concerned about how change has taken place and how it will continue to fluctuate. They believe the best way is through a delicate balance of preservation and development. The right way to do it is to build the community based on what is there and how we can enhance the population and the community, in general, based on how we improve it—what we call "sustainable community development." The indigenous people of St. Helena understand this term to mean building community in a way so that all levels of the community are able to participate and share in the economic benefits derived from the contributions of their labor and their assets. Much of the development in the Sea Islands over the past 30 years has happened at the expense of the indigenous population, without their participation and without concern for its impact on their lives. The result has been a profound sense of displacement from the way they traditionally took care of themselves and earned their livelihoods, from cultural traditions and practices, and from a future they envisioned for themselves.

It all boils down to the land itself. Marquetta Goodwine expressed it as follows:

> For Gullahs, the land is an extension of themselves. Throughout the history of Gullah and Geechee people, land has played a central role in their everyday lives. All aspects of Gullah and Geechee culture are tied to the land, and it serves as a psychological reminder of their connection with the ancestors and their communal plantation life. In their uses of medicinal plants and herbal remedies, their knowledge of the natural environment is essential. Religious sermons of the past and present emphasize strong cultural ties to the land. The land has supplied these populations with nourishment for their bodies, as well as self-sufficiency, since the days of emancipation; and land ownership after emancipation induced autonomy and pride. The use of land and their ties to it, unfortunately, have been forced to change over the years; however, where possible, the Gullah and Geechee people of South Carolina and Georgia remain tied to their land in many ways.[14]

According to Campbell one of the major changes in land ownership really started in the 1950s, when a developer had the bright idea of building an environmentally sound community on Hilton Head.

> But of course, these developers perceived much bigger ideas than satisfying just a few people, and some got greedy with visions of how far they could expand. The case of developing, say, 5,000 acres was replicated not only on one island but then on others, and on the mainland all along the coast from northern Florida on up through North Carolina, and wherever you can find an island. The problem we sea islanders become more and more aware of is that the rapid developments since the 1950s, with the accompanying high-density population it has created, have not taken the course of healthy or natural community growth. As if to add insult to injury, most islanders believe that developers and real estate companies have operated in greed-driven, underhanded ways or have taken unfair advantage of vulnerable situations to get what they want.

This undesirable situation unfortunately was not just local, nor were its extremes of good and bad exaggerated. It was widespread. And yet it did not overwhelm the residents of the Sea Islands, already accustomed to many traumas of both man and nature. As James McBride Dabbs wrote at the conclusion of his book, *Haunted by God*:

> Here is the irony of the whole Southern situation. We have evil and have had evils almost beyond compare; I have never denied this. But somehow we've never ceased being haunted by God. Somehow we've remained human. Somehow the stars of kindliness, of courtesy, of integrity, of courage, and indeed, of a strange kind of humility have never gone out. Somehow, though we've hated too much, we have loved somewhat. Somehow there has been a community, and men have taken some pleasure therein. These are all good things, however limited. It does not matter whether we intended them or whether they came by the lovely or—as Aeschylus said—the awful grace of God. They are here [these many things], and we should thank God for them.

Slaves sitting in front of a building on Elliott's Plantation, Hilton Head Island, South Carolina. In a written inscription on the back of the original photograph, this structure was described as the "nursery" where slave children were cared for.

CHAPTER 4

Growing Up Gullah

This chapter contains narratives by and about African Americans of Gullah descent and how they grew up in the Sea Islands and Low Country of the Carolinas and Georgia. They range from those at the low end of the economic scale in tiny remote villages to individuals who are well known in the South, in America, and even internationally. There is also a personal narrative of a white resident growing up on Myrtle Island on the May River in the town of Bluffton, South Carolina, in the 1960s and 1970s who was "half-Gullah" himself, in that he could speak the native tongue and was familiar with almost everything to do with the aboriginal culture as it existed in his neighborhood. His absorbing account relates how his childhood was one in which his friends and their families were native-oriented to the extent that they spoke more Gullah than English, and still do today. As he says, he "fished the May River, crabbed the coves, chanted the hallelujahs, caught turtles in the lagoons, swung from oaks on the wild grapevines, gathered oysters in their beds, ate hoppin' john with 'lasses, broke my arm playing kickball, and otherwise lived the jubilant and free-flowing life of Gullah kids." In these varied accounts, the reader will get a sense of the many aspects of Gullah life for people in a variety of situations, whether at home with families, at work, at church and other spiritual experiences, suffering illnesses and loss, enjoying music, art, and dancing, and in many other lifetime experiences.

O n Hilton Head Island, South Carolina, there is a common term used by the older generation of African Americans—"before the bridge," referring to the days when the only access to the island was by small boat and a sometimes unpredictable little ferry. Most of the people who lived on the island were African Americans with direct ancestral ties far back to the Gullah culture. Dr. Joseph A. Opala, as one of the foremost scholars in this field, has said the following:

> The Gullah still form a strong, cohesive community in South Carolina and Georgia. It is true that their isolation has been breaking down for the past forty years . . . but the Gullah still hold to their special identity and they take pride in their common heritage. Those who have moved away often return for family gatherings to expose their children to grandparents, to Gullah lore, and to the social life.[1]

Because of their special upbringing and sense of duty, these African Americans also show an increasing spirit of community service and self-help needed to counteract the growing problems in recent years in the Sea Islands, "where land developers have made huge profits constructing tourist resorts, luxury housing, golf courses, and country clubs for wealthy people attracted to the mild climate and island scenery. Land values jumped from a few hundred dollars an acre to many thousands. And some Gullah people who sold their land felt that they had not been paid the fair market value."[2]

Who and what are these people along the stretch of islands, coast, and inland whom we have come to know as Gullahs?

Dr. Emory Shaw Campbell is a native son who left his early environment temporarily and returned not only as a leader but also as a visionary and proponent of constructive policies and programs. He was born on Hilton Head

Island, South Carolina, in October 1941, the sixth of 12 children. His parents were both teachers—as were his paternal grandparents. He attended classes in a tiny one-room schoolhouse. When it came time for further schooling, he had to walk across a narrow swing bridge to the then small village of Bluffton to a segregated school, where he graduated as the class valedictorian. This was followed by a daily 40-mile hitchhiking commute to Savannah State College in Georgia. He later earned his master's and doctorate degrees from Tufts and Bank Street College, respectively.

"'Family values' perfectly explains the remarkable success attained by the Campbell family," says Don McKinney, an editor, author, and book reviewer who himself is a former resident of Hilton Head. "Every one is a success story—African Americans who can trace their roots to the Civil War and beyond.... All but two of the living family members live on a thirty-five-acre tract of land in Spanish Wells, part of an African American community that has flourished for centuries. The Campbells meet once a month to talk about what they are doing, discuss family business, and reinforce the ties that have held them together for so long."[3]

The Campbells are noted in the Sea Islands for their record of service to the community. One brother, for example, is Executive Director of the Boys and Girls Club of Hilton Head, another brother is the Deputy Director for Community Services for Beaufort County, and several other siblings are teachers or administers in local social services programs. One of the reasons that there is so much family participation in community and educational services, reports McKinney, is that, in the strict Gullah tradition, they were all brought up to understand personal values, discipline, learning, family loyalty, traditions, and the importance of church attendance and worship.

"In addition to family loyalty and education, their parents and grandparents insisted on discipline," explained Herb Campbell. "My grandmother, Mama Julia, used to teach in our little schoolhouse, and I'd meet her up at the fork of the road to walk to school in the morning. If I wasn't there, she'd go on without me, and boy did she walk fast! I'd have to run like crazy to catch up with her, because if she got there first and rang that school bell, I was late. And everybody that was late got whipped on the hand with a switch. I learned my lesson." Mama Julia also had a remedy for pupils who complained that another pupil was calling them names and should be punished. "No way," came the reply. "Don't care what somebody else calls you. You know who you are."[4]

Herb's older brother, Emory Campbell, served for more than two decades as Executive Director of Penn Center (the subject of Chapter 2 of this book), where he was responsible for instituting the now much-heralded Heritage Days program. This week-long event has done much to present and enhance the Gullah culture, not only to the public but to many African Americans themselves who were not fully aware of their distinctive heritage. Emory has won many honors, including a Human and Civil Rights Award from the National Education Association, which made the presentation in recognition of his "thirty years as an activist for preserving the Gullah heritage, protecting the environment, and improving his community's living conditions."[5]

Thin, lithe, and about six-foot-three in height, with tousled gray hair and a ready smile, Emory is one of the most familiar faces on Hilton Head Island, St. Helena Island, and locations all up and down the coast. He is constantly on the go, heading up his Gullah Heritage Consulting Services, escorting groups on his Gullah Heritage Trail Tours bus, giving more than 50 speeches and presentations each year, guiding local farm and historical programs, and contributing extensively to newspaper editorials, scholarly publications, documentaries, and television news shows. Yet if a stranger approaches him in a museum, school, or even on the street and requests information, he thinks nothing of spending 15 or 20 minutes of his time to be of help. This is especially true if a teacher with school children in tow asks a question about history or African American affairs. "I was visiting a museum with eight of my pupils," recalls one teacher, "and saw Dr. Campbell and asked him a question about a subject we were studying. Do you know, he spent almost half an hour with us. The children were enthralled with what he had to say. And, best of all, which they appreciated, he himself enjoyed every minute of it and never once gave us the feeling that we had taken him out of his way."[6] And to hear him speak Gullah, which almost everyone who meets him eventually asks him to do, is a real treat—rich and meaningful and melodic in its tone. He readily admits that his appreciation of Gullah needed a bit of a push when he was a child. "When my grandmother spoke to us in Gullah," he recalls, "we used to laugh. We thought it was outmoded. But now we understand that it is our strongest link to the African past.

It is interesting that many of the most ardent supporters of our language and our history are African Americans who moved to the North, found it incompatible, and then came back to the islands."[7] Many people who meet him for the first time would agree with Gary Lee, a *Washington Post* staff writer, who spoke of him as a "fountainhead of information, whose graying hair and thoughtful speech gave him an elegant Old World demeanor."[8]

Vertamae Grosvenor is another prominent Gullah. She is an author, actress, poet, culinary expert, anthropologist, and commentator. For many years she hosted National Public Radio's award-winning documentary series *Horizons*. In the 1980s she was a frequent contributor to that program with a series of documentaries, including "Slave Voices: Things Past Telling" and a special about Daufuskie Island, South Carolina, once populated almost entirely by Gullah residents, which won her a Robert F. Kennedy Award. She was also honored by the National Association of Black Journalists for a segment on "South Africa and the African American Experience," which aired on *All Things Considered.*

Vertamae, a premature twin, was born and raised in Hampton County in the South Carolina Low Country, where her first language was Gullah. Affectionately known as "Kuta," which means turtle in the Gullah language, she weighed only five pounds and barely survived. "My brother weighed, like, a five-pound bag of sugar," she explained on one of her broadcasts. "But he died and I was very, very weak. My maternal grandmamma, Sula, put me in a shoebox and placed the box on the oven door of the wood-burning stove. When folks came to look at the 'shoebox baby,' they exclaimed, 'It looks like a *kuta*.' So the name stuck." Her mother was too infirm herself to nurse her, so she was fed goat's milk.

When Vertamae was 10, her parents moved to Philadelphia. But life was difficult when the kids at school teased and taunted her because of her Gullah accent and manners. This was not all bad because it pushed her into a kind of isolation, where she began reading many books, especially those that guided her to different places and peoples around the globe and sharpened her imagination. Later, during a trip to Europe at the age of 18, she met some of the kinds of people she had read about and began to appreciate the richness of foreign heritages. These included those of Africans and the Gullah/Geechee forebears.

Because of her background, which was always close to the family kitchen and the culinary traditions of the Gullah people, and her continuing association with people from many lands, she became fascinated with cooking, and in effect started and enhanced her career as an author by writing recipes and publishing cookbooks. Her first book, published in 1970, was *Vibration Cooking or the Travel Notes of a Geechee Girl.* The books not only provide recipes but also delve in depth into the cultures and the peoples that created them, hence she describes herself as a "culinary anthropologist." She ingeniously coined the term *vibration* as a method of cooking, spontaneously adding ingredients here and there without measuring them, and she also refers to "making do" with leftovers.

Growing Up on Sapelo Island

Cornelia Walker Bailey, author of *God, Dr. Buzzard, and the Bolito Man,* referred to as "a saltwater Geechee," was born and raised on Sapelo Island, Georgia. She is the kind of native storyteller who, while enjoying life in the present, can relish the experiences of the past, and captures in her writing the spirit of the community, the people she has known there throughout a lifetime of rich experiences, and her love for departed family members and friends. She is of the last generation to be born, raised, and schooled on Sapelo Island.

"I am a Sapelo," she says. "Life goes on much as it does anywhere else, but if you get to really see and feel what's here, you will see the difference. The proud faces as well as the angry walk, the easy smile as well as the hard frown, the easy life as well as the hardship—it's all here, reflected in the faces and stature of each individual. The old who don't want to change and the young who does. But get to know the young ones and you will see tradition and hear pride. We are all proud of our heritage."[9]

She looks back on her life as a young girl and recalls seeing the ladies at such places as Raccoon Bluff, fishing with a drop line and cane pole from a bateau boat "while trusting in the Lord because they couldn't swim."[10] She cannot forget the drama of watching men fishing at night with flambeaus, looking for alligators with a long pole and giant hook. She talks, too, about "the smell and sweat of the men as they walked behind oxen and mules, plowing task after task of fields."[11] Her memory takes her back to so many little things in her Gullah life, such as the taste of fresh-dug sweet potatoes cooked in hot ashes, watching older brothers and sisters dancing the "Buzzard Lope," and observing a group of young men on a Saturday night with their moonshine, playing the guitar, blowing the comb, and trying to do the tap dance or the soft shoe with somewhat hesitant girls, not at all sure of themselves.

One of her favorite characters when growing up Gullah was Grandpa Bryan, a "mysterious fellow" who was one-half Creek and one-half African, who was said to have come from the Okefenokee Swamp in southern Georgia. He was a self-made barber and would use a bowl when cutting men's hair, clipping all around it and then lifting it for a bit of trim so that the neck ended up in a perfectly straight line—which would cause the kids to snicker when they went to church and sat behind one of Grandpa Bryan's customers.

Church holds many memories for Cornelia Walker Bailey, but most especially the music. "The songs we used to sing in church," she says, "we've been singing for years and years. Nobody really goes to the hymn books—they sing from memory. When Grandma used to sing, she had a captivated audience. She'd sing 'When I Get to Heaven' and 'Things I Used to Do.'"[12] Part of the appeal was that Grandma was unusually expressive because she liked to tipple a bit from the bottle before setting off for church—or any other occasion when she might have a chance to vocalize!

Cornelia recalls in great detail many little things about her father when she was growing up on Sapelo Island—how he used to sing around the house, though without such an appealing voice as Grandma's, how he could hold the children spellbound with his stories, and how he showed them how to make fishnets or fox traps. But his prime skill, much appreciated, was his ability to cook hominy grits, which they all considered a real treat. In other ways, she says, "Papa provided for us the best he could. We had alligator dishes, along with pork greens. We had game birds and shore birds—wild turkey and gannet. We had fish of all kinds. We had turtle of all kinds. We had deer, squirrel, rabbit, raccoon, and possum. Some only in season, some by means of poaching. Sometimes nothing at all."[13]

A Gullah Song in Mende

The following song, recorded in Harris Neck, Georgia, in the early 1930s, was first presented by Dr. Lorenzo Turner, the foremost scholar to make a study of the people and their language three-quarters of a century ago. It indicates the transition from an African dialect to modern Gullah.

Gullah scholars today, such as Dr. Emory Campbell, take delight in presenting such songs in a sing-song kind of language to interested students.

A wohkoh, mu mohne; kambei ya le; li leei ka.
Ha sa wuli nggo, sihan; kpangga li lee.
Ha sa wuli nggo; ndeli, ndi, ka.
Ha sa wuli nggo, sihan; huhan ndayia.

Modern Mende
A wa kaka, mu mohne; kambei ya le'i; lii i lei tambee. A wa kaka, mu mohne; kambei ya le'i; lii i lei ka.
So ha a guli wohloh, i sihan; yey kpanggaa a lolohhu lee. So ha a guli wohloh; ndi lei; ndi let, kaka.
So ha a guli wohloh, i sihan; kuhan ma wo ndayia ley.

English
Come quickly, let us work hard; the grave is not yet finished; his heart [the deceased's] is not yet perfectly cool [at peace].
Come quickly, let us work hard; the grave is not yet finished; let his heart be cool at once.
Sudden death cuts down the tress, borrows them; the remains disappear slowly.
Sudden death cuts down the trees; let it [death] be satisfied, let it be satisfied, at once.
Sudden death cuts down the tress, borrows them; a voice speaks from afar.

One of Papa's most unique skills, appreciated by all of his own and the neighborhood's children, was his ability to take the bladder from a fresh-killed hog and make a balloon out of it by rolling it in warm ashes until it was thin and then blowing it up—"our first balloon!" He could also make whistles from spent shotgun shells, or whittle toys to play with, or show everyone where to find the tastiest kumquats and other fruits in the forests, fields, and neighboring orchards.

Much of what Cornelia Walker Bailey remembers as vital parts of her life and family activities growing up Gullah are now only memories. "Our old schools are closed down," she says. "Our churches have only a handful of worshipers left; our neighborhood organizations, such as the Farmer's Alliance, the Eastern Stars, and the Masonics, are no longer; and there are no more praise houses. It is even hard to find the kinds of boys and girls who used to giggle in the dark under the stars, with a chorus of frogs and crickets for company. Even our ghosts don't walk anymore. There is no one for them to scare now. No one walks the road at night. No jack o' lantern leads the weak-minded or drunk-minded away to some dark woods for a night of fright."[14] She is sometimes sad, sometimes even angry, at what has been lost since the time when she was growing up. Still she says she is happy for such fond memories. "For in many ways we are still living in the days of the *Buckra* [name for a white person] house and the *Buckra* fields. I am still in *Massa* fields. I can see and hear traces of the old days, and there in those fields I can also retain my dignity and be myself without undo influences. It's not easy, but I watch the birds and my mind is free, even if the rest of me have committances."[15]

From Small-Town Girl to Stardom

Many a Gullah person has risen from the most humble origins in neighborhoods in the poorer parts of town to successful careers in music, the arts, business, and other callings. One fine example is that of Anita Singleton-Prather, who carried the procedure one step further by actually using her simple beginnings as the theme for her road to success. She was born in the picturesque and historic village of Beaufort, South Carolina, the sixth of eight children of Caesar and Inez Singleton. As Cathy Harley of the *Beaufort Gazette* described her upbringing, "Education was a driving force in the Singleton family, with her mom as a teacher at Broad River Elementary School, who helped prepare children for desegregation, and her dad as a second-generation graduate of Tuskegee Institute."[16] She attended first and second grade at an all-black school but by third grade elected to transfer to Beaufort Elementary under the new "freedom of choice" plan offered to blacks. But she had to sit at the back of the classroom, where she was forced to deal with the "N-word" and where she first heard about "cooties," body lice that the white students claimed all blacks were infected with. But she was outspoken and not to be ridiculed, and she frequently answered lesson questions when the teacher was about to pass her over. "I was very competitive, even with boys," she recalled. "If you were going to play football with me, you were going to get tackled no matter what!"[17]

After receiving her bachelor's degree in psychology from Howard University and her master's in education from the University of South Carolina, she followed in family footsteps as an educator and began teaching in local schools in Beaufort and on nearby Lady's Island. But she showed such talent as a storyteller—in the classroom and out—that she was soon filling requests to appear on stage and radio. And thus began a whole new career, all based on her own upbringing in a Gullah household and her ability to convey the ups and downs, the humor and despair, and the very essence of the individuals and families she had known all her life. Her one-woman show, *Tales from the Land of Gullah*, became a hit nationally on PBS, and she created Gullah Kinfolk, with 25 members from age two to 75, which has produced compact discs and cassettes with such titles as *Songs uv dee Gullah Pee'puls*, *The Gullah Kinfolk Live*, and *A Gullah Kinfolk Christmas*.

Anita Singleton-Prather's most popular effort may be her creation of Aunt Pearlie Sue, so much so that she is referred to by this name as much as by her birth name. The character is based on her grandmother Rosa Singleton, also known as "Ronnie," whom she describes as her mentor and role model. She was "always pleasingly plump, stylish, and her hair always done. Growing up in a large family, everybody had their special person, and my grandmother was my special person when I needed attention." Aunt Pearlie Sue has become so renowned that she is considered a real person in her own right, appearing widely and continuously in broadcasting, on the stage, and at major events, such as Charleston's famous Spoleto Festival. And she always begins with a prayer and a song.

Another good example, in a completely different field of endeavor, is that of Althea Sumpter, who grew up on St. Helena Island, South Carolina, and recalls "running around the grounds of Penn Center so often that I could find my way around blindfold, since my mother and many other family members and friends were graduates of the school." As a Quaker she also finds Penn Center dear to her heart because it was founded by Quakers, and in the beginning and for many years it was closely associated with this denomination. Her background was so strong and influential on the way she thought and where she wanted to head in a career that a large part of her time and efforts have been devoted to researching, writing about, teaching, and promoting the Gullah culture and heritage. Her master's degree from the University of South

Hopes and Fears and Aspirations

"As the ox carts creak and the buggy wheels swish through the sand, a voice may be heard rolling over the marshes," wrote T. J. Woofter Jr., a renowned author and sociologist who, in the 1920s, when only a handful of researchers undertook to study the lives of freed slaves and other African Americans in their native habitats, had much to say about their hopes and fears and aspirations.

Lawd, I wish I had an eagle's wings.
Lawd, I wish I had an eagle's wings. o
Lawd, wish I—O Lawd, wish I, o
Lawd, wish I had an eagle's wings
I would fly all de way to Paradise.
I would fly all de way to Paradise. o
Lawd, fly all—O Lawd, fly all o Lawd,
Fly all de way to Paradise.

Carolina was based on her research and writing on civil rights, and her doctorate, received from Clark Atlanta University, was in African American studies, with a dissertation entitled "Navigating the Gullah Culture Using Multimedia Technology." And today her ongoing research includes the collection of oral histories and multimedia documentation of the Gullah culture on the coast of South Carolina and Georgia. She has also directed media and productions with the Martin Luther King Jr. Center, served on the faculties of several universities, lectured in many capacities, produced films both independently and for television, written and edited extensively, and organized numerous workshops. In almost every instance, the subjects and backgrounds have had roots in her upbringing in the Gullah/Geechee culture and the dedication she has to the understanding of, and interest in, this subject field. One of her most unique achievements, as she describes it, was the way she used a short story she had written on growing up on the Gullah coast in her dissertation for an academic degree. As she explained, "I was able to include that short story in my dissertation as an example of a participant-observer. It was difficult to defend my role in a traditional academic arena. But I was successful."[18]

All along her road to success, she has been able to develop new ways of approaching an ancient culture. As reported in a unique communiqué known as *Stories from the Goosawatchie Gullah Elders*, "Gullah society has often proved difficult to study because it is an insider culture. As an ethnographer and producer with training and experience in both cultural preservation and digital technology, Althea Sumpter is able to document her own culture through her access as a trusted insider. By using digital video, still photography, and audio documentation to create interactive design tools on Gullah culture, she offers a model for other researchers and communities wishing to employ digital technology to document persons and cultures."

The Visible Gullah

With its broad sweep of triumph and tragedy, history and personalities, and elation and despair, the Gullah culture has spawned fine artists of many schools, with works in many galleries in the South, large and small. One such locale is Gallery Chuma in Charleston, South Carolina, where the principal artist on exhibit is Jonathan Green, who is considered to be one of the most important painters of the southern experience and who is preeminent in capturing the traditions, people, and scenes of African American culture. Described as "one of South Carolina's treasures," his work over more than two decades has been exhibited at major national and international venues and published in many periodicals and books.

Green was born in the small Gullah community of Gardens Corner in the Sea Islands of South Carolina, and raised by his grandmother in a matriarchal society that relied heavily on oral traditions. Looking back on his early life, he explains that he was always interested in how crafts of all kinds were studied and created and was curious about the nature and hopes of the people in his family and community. "I had all this stuff in my head," he once explained, "but I didn't have a place for it until I started painting. I know I can't save a whole culture, but as an artist I can help create better awareness perhaps." And that he has done in good measure by helping people all over America and abroad to understand his heritage. "Through the years many African American artists, such as painters Eldzier Cortor and Ellis Wilson, photographer Jeanne Moutoussamy-Ashe, and the late folk artist Sam Doyle, a native to the area, have featured the colorful Low Country and its people in their work," wrote Carroll Greene Jr. in a profile of the artist, "but Green's body of work, about 150 Gullah works, is perhaps the most ambitious artistic expression of Sea Islands culture ever successfully undertaken."[19] Jonathan Green's most vivid memories of Gullah life are culled from the 1960s. "I can remember things as a child, such as hair wrapping, men weaving fishing nets, farming, and hunting. There is very little of these activities going on now. What fishing and hunting that goes on is mainly sport and not out of necessity as before. Food used to be preserved in various ways, drying, canning, and smoking. Now, only gardening seems to continue. Mattresses were made of Spanish moss, and men made furniture for use in the community."[20]

"Within the community, each family was known for providing some specific goods or services. For example, one family would sell seafood, another family would sell produce, and another family moonshine, and so it went. My grandmother was a quilter," Jonathan Green recalls.[21] One must bear in mind that the first bridge connecting the Sea Islands to the U.S. mainland was constructed only after World War II. Indeed many of the island residents had never been on the mainland before that time. Jonathan Green, who was born in 1955, grew up in Gardens Corner, a farming community on the mainland near the South Carolina coastal town of Beaufort, where the Gullahs also live in large numbers. He is the first known artist of Gullah heritage to receive formal training at a professional art school, the Art Institute of Chicago, graduating with a bachelor of fine arts degree in 1982. He readily admits that he did not always have much appreciation for his Gullah heritage. Like many others, he had to leave home and journey to faraway places to comprehend the value of his Gullah roots. Prior to living in Chicago, he served in the Air Force, which took him to North Dakota, Colorado, and Texas. He also traveled through Europe and Mexico. After all of this, he reminisces, "I wanted to go back to my roots. The older people were dying, and I began to see people [the Gullahs] differently. I saw them as a people with a strong link, probably the strongest link with Africa of any of the black American people. I had studied African art, and I began to appreciate a certain uniqueness."[22] Jonathan Green's background provides him with an insider's understanding of the Gullah people and their traditions. For instance, in *Tales*, the artist shows a group of men at the end of the day gathered under a huge live oak listening in varying degrees to the yarns of a storyteller. The scene is a continuation of the strong African oral tradition transplanted to America. Another painting, *Banking Yams*, illustrates an unusual method of storing yams by putting them in little huts made of dried corn stalks and straw. His painting, *Two Baskets*, is featured on the cover of this book.

Through art, at least, such traditions will be preserved. Jonathan Green's Gullah art is a testimonial to harmony of style and content. "Human figures, which have always been the artist's favorite subject, are rendered featureless in the Gullah paintings. The viewer is not permitted past the dark oval faces. At first the figures seem to bar introspection, but these featureless persons are not anonymous beings. In their communities they are recognized by size, shape, stance, and gesture, the way one recognizes a familiar person whose back is turned toward you. The lack of features seems to suggest an archetypical human being and, in this instance, serves to universalize a people in their daily routines and special occasions. Jonathan Green's earlier works showed considerable cubist influence, perhaps Picasso, Cezanne, or others, though his strong interest in the human figure is evident."[23]

The Gate Keeper

The most celebrated ironworker of recent times in Charleston, South Carolina, and most probably in all of the Low Country and Sea Islands, was Philip Simmons who died in 2009. When visitors take tours near the southern areas of Church Street and Bay Street, they are more than likely to marvel at the magnificent iron designs on gates and railings and other decorative and functional metal work. These designs are in the shape of hearts, diamonds, egrets, cranes, turtles, snakes, and many other objects of nature. Many of these are the handiwork of Philip Simmons, who was born on nearby Daniel Island in the summer of 1912 and brought up in the Gullah traditions of thousands of African Americans who lived in Charleston and were considered free in the city even before the advent of the Civil War. Most tourists are surprised to learn that, in fact, as one Gullah guide explained, "nearly everything you see around here, in this historic district, was built by blacks—the houses, the walls, the streets, and sidewalks—and not just by slaves either."[24] Or as he, a Gullah himself, expressed it: "*Dem cyapentas, boat mekkah, iyon wukkah, net mekkah, en pleny mo' is wuk dat de Black people bin doin' ya fuh shree hunnad odd yea.*"

Simmons, who has the honor of being described as a "national treasure" and whose forge was in a ramshackle tin building behind his old house on Blake Street, got started in his profession when he was only 13 years old and long finished with any kind of regular schooling. He was brought up in a family that insisted on continuing work and education. "I used to stand in the door of the blacksmith shop," he said, "and see the sparks flying, and I liked that. The blacksmith let me help out, hold the horse while he was putting the shoe on, turn the hand forge, clean up the shop. And after a while he taught me names of everything. He'd say, 'Boy, hand me the three-inch swage,' and I had to know just what he wanted. I learned that way."

Later, after learning at work and studying everything he could about ironwork in his free time, he took the plunge and started his own business. But it was rocky. "There were blacksmiths all over Charleston," he recalled. "I had many competitors. I was shoeing horses and fixing wagons, but people kept coming to me and warning me that blacksmiths were going out of business, that gasoline trucks were now taking over and there would be no more need for horses and wagons and, of course, blacksmiths to make shoes and harness fixtures. I had to study what I was going to do, to change my kind of work. So, as a start, I turned to iron gates and window guards. I've made more than 200 gates and other iron ornamental work since then—even made gates for the Smithsonian in Washington, the South Carolina State Museum in Columbia, and the Charleston Visitor Center."

His work and decisions paid off well. He said, "I put my children through school. I have given money to my church. I have everything I want. And I am rich in friends." He was also rich in prestige as a result, not only because of his talents but also because of his dedication to the arts and the help he gave to talented young people all throughout his career. In 1982 the National Endowment for the Arts awarded him its National Heritage Fellowship, the highest honor that the United States can bestow on a traditional artist. In 1994 he was inducted into the South Carolina Hall of Fame, and in 2001 he received further recognition from the state for "Lifetime Achievement in the Arts."

The Opposite Side of the Coin

Could a white person "grow up Gullah"?

It's an interesting question. Take the case of Robert Lee, Executive Director of Seabrook, a retirement community near the southern part of Hilton Head Island, South Carolina. Many employees who work with him are African Americans, and a large percentage are of Gullah extraction. Although he is white, he says that he feels right at home because, as he puts it, "I really grew up Gullah." Much of his childhood was spent in Bluffton, South Carolina, which was then a small village on the May River. His grandmother was born in the Huger-Gordon Home, a large wooden house on the river that was built around 1800.

My grandmother's only brother, Percy Huger, with the help of a mule and one worker, built the causeway to Myrtle Island, and my grandparents built their house on the island in 1931, where my uncle still lives. The house is long and thin, so that all the rooms caught a breeze from the river. Each room had a fireplace, and on the second floor there was a screened area called the sleeping porch, to stay cool in the summer.[25]

Lee has great affection for the house and what it meant to his family and to him during the long summer visits.

Other than a brother and sister and some relatives, there were very few other white families. Many of my father's playmates and fishing buddies were from the local black families. It was not long before everyone picked up a thick Gullah accent. When I was young, they would read me Br'er Rabbit stories in Gullah, and I learned native songs, such as "The Beaufort Boat Does Not Come." I was very grateful for my heritage. I love the song-like quality of the language, and moreover, I found that many of the phrases had a great deal of personal meaning in the messages they conveyed so persuasively.[26]

Rob enjoys talking in Gullah and at a moment's notice will pop up with one phrase or another. Some of his favorites are:

"*Dog got four feet but can't walk but one road.*"
"No matter how many things you'd like to do, you can do only one at a time."

"*E teet da dig e grave.*"
"He (or she) is overeating."

"*Fox da watch de henhouse.*"
"A fox (crook) is watching the henhouse (money)."

"*Milk ain't dry off e mout yet.*"
"The person is too young for the assignment."

"Evry frog praise e ownt pond."
"Everyone praises his own family."

"New breom sweeps clean but old breom gets corners."
"To get the job done use someone familiar with it."

"Li 'i pitcher got big ears."
"Be careful what you say around children."

In the Land of the Gullahs

What is it like for a person who is not of Gullah descent and generally unfamiliar with the Sea Islands to visit a Gullah community, attend a local church, and meet native residents who have lived there all their lives? The following is an excerpt from an account by just such a person, Gary Lee, a *Washington Post* staff writer who found his experience to be "refreshing and heartwarming indeed."

When I entered the village church the congregation was in full swing, belting out the day's scripture in what sounded like an African dialect. I did not understand a word, but that didn't matter. As I looked with uncertainty into the faces of the crowd—from a matronly villager with skin the color of cocoa to a burly brother with a '60s Afro—all returned heartfelt smiles. Uplifted by a Sunday morning of African-style worship, I followed the scent of catfish and collard greens to a favored local hangout. Along the wooden porch a couple of women in braids were setting out sweet-grass baskets, a handicraft common in West African markets. Under a sagging willow, a few village elders chewed the fat of the week. Inside, families were digging into bowls of gumbo and platters of rice and okra. In nearly every town along Africa's Gold Coast from Sierra Leone to Senegal, I imagined, similar scenes were taking place.

The catch was, I was not in Africa. I was on St. Helena, an

island off the marshy shores of South Carolina and home to the Gullahs. Descended from slaves brought from Africa to the Georgia and South Carolina coast in the 18th and 19th centuries, the Gullahs have clung passionately to the languages, foods and traditions of their origin. While the rest of America, including much of the African American population, is swept up in a tide of cultural homogeneity marked by Nike shoes, baseball hats and Top 10 hits, the Gullahs have held resolutely to the rice dishes, prayer rituals, rites and chants that their grandfathers' grandfathers brought from the Motherland. Although they probably descend from different African countries and disparate tribes, Gullahs today are identified by their common language. Gullah is a Creolized language composed of words from English and several African tongues. Although some members of an older generation still communicate largely in Gullah, most Gullahs use it as a secondary tongue to chat with one another. For almost all of them, English is the first language.

Gullah country does not refer to a single island or town but a string of communities in the Sea Islands of South Carolina and Georgia. Other Gullah enclaves have been traced as far off as Texas and Oklahoma. An intriguing destination for any traveler, the stretch of the South that many Gullahs call home seems to offer something particularly attractive to Americans descended from slaves. It is a dramatic reminder that, in the vast multicultural forest of the contemporary United States, African Americans have roots as deep as any other ethnic group. My introduction to the world of Gullah came through cinema and literature. The 1991 movie *Daughters of the Dust* depicted a community of Gullahs battling to keep the mores of the New World from subsuming their tight-knit social circles. *Down by the Riverside*, a historical account of life on South Carolina Low Country plantations, gives rich details of how slaves brought from Africa to South Carolina worked to retain aspects of their African heritage, from songs to burial traditions. But neither the book nor film renderings of the Gullah story fully prepared me for my wanderings through the settlements where Gullahs live and gather. To observe the Gullahs is to see a people who have been resolute about preserving their culture on American soil. Their skin tones run from the deep color of coffee beans to the hue of brown sugar. And their features, including full lips and big round eyes, recall the look of many West Africans.

"When we look for partners, we tend to look among our own people," explained Jean Smith, a retired seamstress I met on my Sunday morning stroll through St. Helena. "We don't intermarry much. That's why you see more African features in our looks." Dark skinned and direct, she was clearly proud of her culture and eager to share it.

The Gullahs I met were a fountainhead of inspiration. Among the most memorable was Emory Campbell, whose graying hair and thoughtful speech gave him an elegant Old World demeanor. As a former director of the Penn Center, devoted to the preservation of African culture and to the service of the African American community, Campbell straddles the enclave of Gullahs and the outside world of South Carolina.

Gary Lee, "In the Land of the Gullahs," *Washington Post*, September 20, 1998

The Urgency of Preservation

Many people of Gullah descent living today are greatly concerned when they see the changes taking place in their towns and relentlessly encroaching into their neighborhoods. A good example is that of Phillips, a predominantly African American community with a population of about 400 in unincorporated Charleston County, South Carolina. "It used to be a lot quieter out here," said Richard Habersham, President of the Phillips Community Association, when interviewed by a writer from *Coastal Heritage* magazine.[27] His own family has lived in this neighborhood since Civil War days, when recently freed slaves were able to purchase small plots along Horlbeck Creek, with views of marshes and woodlands and yet not far from Charleston.

The village has been referred to as "a doughnut hole" in the middle of sprawling shopping centers and expensive modern homes. As Habersham explained it, "When they build those high-dollar houses, the value of our prop-erty goes up and affects our increasing taxes."[28] Then when taxes get too high, some residents have to sell out and move away, and the new residents are not likely to have any sense of the old historical values.

A Gullah Passing

"February is alive with the vivid sounds and tastes of the Hilton Head Island Gullah Celebration," wrote David Lauderdale, one of the South's most noted and expressive columnists, on February 11, 2007, "but amid the pageantry, the home-going of Brother William Brown, Jr., during the celebration is a reminder of the foundations of the Gullah culture. Mr. Brown's long life shows both the past and potential future of an abundant culture being squeezed out by modern America. . . .

"Gullah is more than simply the language and name of a people; it encompasses the essence of struggle, spirituality, perseverance, and tradition. Mr. Brown came into this world almost ninety-two years ago on Pinckney Island. Today, Pinckney Island is a blur at sixty miles per hour between the two bridges to Hilton Head."

As Lauderdale explains in his obituary to this Gullah gentleman of the old school, Brown took over his father's store, known as the Mr. Boney Brown Store, on the tiny island, and it became something of a center of learning and manners for the children of the neighborhood. Mr. Brown brooked no deviation from honesty, and if he detected any youngsters with their fingers in the candy jar, or climbing the pear trees outside to steal a little fruit, he gave them an instant—and meaningful—lesson in doing unto others as you would have them do unto yourself.

But those days, says Lauderdale, have vanished forever, to the bad luck of present generations. "Today's Gullah descendants face a harsh business world. Instead of a Mr. Boney Brown Store, we have giants like Publix. The odds of success seem insurmountable. But what do you think the odds looked like the day Mr. Brown was born? What did he lean on? How did he make it? Those odds are worth celebrating this and every year."

Another resident from an old-line Phillips family, Jonathan Ford, added that "people tell us we can just sell out and go somewhere else. For those people, mainly from the North, property is just an investment. But for us, property is *home*. You live, you grow up, you die, and you pass it on. We're just trying to preserve what was passed on to us. Our grandfathers and great-grandfathers had to work and buy property that they handed down to us."[29] Other black communities in the area that have Gullah histories and are facing the same bleak future for the original residents are Hamlin, Scanlonville, Six Mile, Ten Mile, Snowden, and Whitehall Terrace. Interestingly the current land plots in question nearly match the boundaries of the original freedman settlements of the period right after the Civil War. And many of today's 10-acre parcels are identical to the original plots purchased for $63 apiece at that time.

As the *Coastal Heritage* article explained, Dr. John Rutledge, the first physician in this area, was the initial owner of Phillips Plantation, and two of his sons were born there: John, a signer of the Constitution, and Edward, who was the youngest person to sign the Declaration of Independence. Habersham and Ford are justly proud of what the towns meant to South Carolina in the past and have great regret that so many of these historical locations are disappearing. They have hopes, like so many people of their heritage, that the upsurge in interest in the Gullah culture will help to preserve some of them before it is too late.

Heirs' property is a problem for traditional African American communities, says Habersham. "They don't want to put the land in one person's name because that person could go and sell it overnight. They think they're safer with heirs' property. But I think they should have their name on the title and not someone who died in 1890."[30] The term he used, *heirs' property*, is the name given to a parcel of land that was originally deeded to freed slaves by the American government at the end of the Civil War as part of Reconstruction. It was given with the understanding that future generations would have no need for wills, inasmuch as it had been illegal under the Jim Crow laws for slaves to read and write and thus there was no way that they could have had written wills or other pertinent real estate documents.

Gullah people view family land as "sacred," says Daniel Pennick. It's a place of refuge, a place to rest after they've seen the world, served in the military, or worked for decades in the North. For others, it's the place to raise children and grow up knowing aunts and uncles and cousins, the place to spend long summers with grandparents. "Everybody's your cousin here," says Habersham.[31] Even so, Pennick, a Charleston County planner, says that heirs' property may have protected many Gullah communities from development. "Developers don't want to deal with an unclear title."[32] That is understandable in a case where several family members may have jointly inherited a parcel that lacks an up-to-date title and where the original purchaser from the mid-19th century is still named as the owner.

About half of the Phillips parcels are heirs' property, says Habersham, and the problem with heirs' property is that any heir can go before a judge to gain the value of his property. And often the only way to get that value is to sell the entire parcel. Sometimes land speculators buy an interest from an heir and ask a judge to auction the entire parcel. In the past many properties that had been given or sold by the government to freed slaves were protected by their very isolation. Rivers, streams, and tidal inlets, which had no bridges large or small, cut off the Sea Islands from the mainland. Surrounding forests, although not impenetrable, provided shields from the more civilized communities. And poor roads—or in many cases the absence of roads—were additional barriers. Then, too, there was the matter of brutal heat, high humidity, and other natural discouragements to all but the Gullah peoples, including mosquitoes, snakes, rodents, and the threat of tropical storms and even hurricanes.

"The only people who wanted the land were Gullah," says Emory Campbell, former Executive Director of Penn Center and now the President of Gullah Heritage Consulting Services, whose family members have managed to retain a large part of their original land parcel on Hilton Head Island. He estimates that the Gullah lands and traditions first faced their most serious threats along the coast in the 1950s and early 1960s when developers—equipped with many countermeasures, such as air conditioners, mosquito sprays, services to counteract semi-tropical diseases, better roads, and bridges to formerly isolated lands—began making inroads. They also hired publicists and advertising agencies to tout the many blessings and boons that vacation-home buyers could count on in places with fancy plantation-sounding names.

Sociologist T. J. Woofter, who studied African American families in the

1920s and reported his findings in a book, *Black Yeomanry: Life on St. Helena Island*, wrote in specific detail about what it was like to be a member of a black family. His commentaries included the following:

> The religious organization is strong. The church is much more of a factor in the control of the Sea Island communities than in the average modern community. Not only is it the place of worship, and to some extent of recreation, but through its peculiar organization of branch "praise houses," it also settles the disputes of the community. This active control by church committees has held crime at a minimum. [33]

He notes that there are three principal points at which the islanders have not adapted to American standards. The first is that the majority are contented with fewer perks than would satisfy the average American family. "This is a survival," he says, "of the standards of the slave street, where less than twenty dollars a year sufficed to feed and clothe a slave. That such satisfaction is not universal is indicated by the drift of many young people to the city, but for the majority who remain, life is an Oriental pursuit of a calm, unhurried destiny, rather than a drive under the spur of ambition."

Many families also fail to accumulate the kinds of savings that are necessary for future expansion and needs as they grow. "Associated with this relative lack of ambition is the failure of most of the families to accumulate that surplus which is essential to progress. And, as far as the land itself is concerned, the farming is too little for any future growth. Only the most ambitious and energetic farmers, whether white or black," says Woofter, "have much to show for a life of toil beyond the subsistence of their families and the ownership of land. The islanders, like other black belt farmers, have been bound to a system in which the lean years consumed most of the surplus of the fat, and the purchase of a few comforts dissipated the balance."

The third problem, he finds, is the relative laxity of sexual morals and high illegitimacy rate, which disrupts the family, "leaving the women to bear the brunt of the job of rearing the children." Slightly more than half of the families were headed by couples living together, but the rest were headed by single women, yet Woofter saw them all as an "orderly community, a healthy community, one which is fairly stable, but in which breadwinning is difficult."

These families had the best chance for a good life if they were farmers, as he said in a description of a typical farmers' fair, and particularly in light of the fact that "even at the fair the influence of the church is felt, as the preacher opens and closes the event." The fairs were typically enlivened also by the singing of spirituals led by leaders "in whom the spirit was with them." He described one in this manner:

> He mounts the platform, closes his eyes, spreads his arms, and literally draws melody from the audience:
>
> *If you want to get to heaven*
> *I'll tell you how*
> *Jus' wrap yo' hands*
> *Around dat plow.*

Much of any program of this kind, whether in a farming community or elsewhere, was successful only if it focused on "experience." Everyone in attendance was always invited to come forward and describe how they achieved some form of success in their lives—usually little matters like doing things in a better and more satisfying way, such as carpentry, fishing, making quilts, cooking, gardening, planting cotton, sewing nets, or any of the other more common aspects of living and accomplishing something.

Woofter adds, "In the early dusk the crowd disperses to travel homeward over the rutted, winding roads, each couple discussing the means of winning an award of merit at the next fair, and planning the disposal of the money it may bring. The decision may fall upon an added room in the home, the tuition and expenses of sending a boy off to school, or it may mean increased participation in the church and other community activities."[34]

According to Jannette Hypes, in an article titled "Gullah: A Language, a Life, a Living History," "religion is one of the most essential parts of this culture. This social organization is the most important in the community. The doctrine is Christian with some variations. One of the most distinctive of these variations is the three-part division of human beings into body, soul, and spirit. According to many elderly island residents, when one dies, only the soul returns to the Kingdom of God. The body and spirit remain on earth. And, although the soul of the person cannot harm the living, the spirit can, at will, cause another to harm him- or herself."[35]

The African-based spiritual beliefs of the Gullah people provide them with another aspect of culture that is unique in America. The culture has attained many of its traits from Africa and has maintained many of them. The people of the Sea Islands are now faced with losing their culture because of modernization. But it does not seem that the culture will disappear. According to sociologist Joseph Opala, "the Gullah are . . . showing an increasing spirit of community service and self-help. Development of highways and bridges has affected the survival of this culture in different ways. The paving of Highway 17 North in the 1930s contributed to consumer interest in the Gullah basketry. This road made the route to Mt. Pleasant, South Carolina, more convenient. The Gullah basket weavers then set up roadside stands and began to experience an increased interest in their basketry from tourists, museums, and gift shop owners. The roadside stands are still in use by the Gullah women and men today."[36]

Hypes and others have pointed out that bridges are also a factor in the many changes that have taken place because they have made the islands vulnerable to development and ready access by outsiders. They also brought more formal education to the children of the islanders, who previously had no access to anything but loosely knit classes taught by teachers with very little professional training.

Addressing some of the same kinds of problems, Bill Saunders was interviewed by the *Low Country Gullah Culture Special Resource Study* and had some significant remarks to make on the subject. Saunders grew up on Kiawah Island near Charleston, South Carolina, which was a little-populated, off-the-beaten-track barrier island and not of much interest to outsiders. That all changed when, in 1972, Kiawah was purchased by the Kuwaiti government and ultimately developed by the Sea Pines Corporation, which also developed Hilton Head Island, as discussed earlier.

> As a kid growing up on the islands in the thirties and forties, there was really no need for money. A lot of us now in our thirties and forties are realizing we weren't so bad off then. When we were young, we

looked at things as being awful. Now that attitude has changed. When I was a kid, we grew our own rice, we had our own grits grinder, and we made our own mortar and pestle with which to clean our rice. We had our own smokehouse, killed our own meat, and we ate everything that was in the river in season. This time of year now you can go anyplace and buy oysters. People then never ate oysters after April. Crab wasn't eaten in the winter. All of these things replenished themselves during that time. Now we destroy them by eating them all the time. Most of our clothes were made of material from feedbags or things that something had been bought in. We made our own mattresses, pillows, and so forth. My grandfather used to build roofs out of something that now I can't find anyone to make, something called "palin." They had an instrument (a draw shave) they made that, when struck with a wooden mallet, would slice through pine and cut into very thin stripping like paneling, and they would overlap these strips on the roof. You could see right through it, but it wouldn't leak when rain hit it; it would just swell up. We made chimneys out of clay on the islands. We took the clay, grass, and other things and would do coloring with it. We used to make beautiful floors from rubbing colored clay onto church brick. Most people needed to hold on to money for their nickel-and-dime insurance. Most illnesses that came up, someone had a remedy for it; we called it root medicine. They would take roots and things (such as "life-everlasting" for colds) and boil them into a medicine. We would also pack open wounds with sand or sugar. Nowadays you get a little cut, you go to the nearest hospital emergency room. There were so many things to be done, and work was hard. We worked from "can see to can't see," from sunup to sundown. We were more independent and didn't recognize it. We are more dependent now than we have ever been. Most of us my age now are looking at the past and looking at the present and saying maybe we need to go back to some of the things we came through that we didn't like too well.[37]

In his memory, the people he knew in his childhood did not think much about their roots or culture. "They were just real people who showed their heritage. My grandfather and many people I knew never had anything, but they were so independent that they were proud of what they did for themselves. They decided what they were going to do and what they were not going to do. They were just beautiful people."[38] Sadly he concluded that the people on the island gradually lost all that between 1945 and 1960, when changes took place that caused many of the islanders to lose sight of their heritage—and of being proud of it.

When we compare the writings and accounts about the Gullah history and culture of the 1930s with today, we see a marked differential in what it was like to grow up Gullah some three generations ago and what it is today. Consequently the increasing interest in this ancient heritage and the vital studies being undertaken, such as the National Park Service study of the Low Country Gullah/Geechee culture, are none too soon. And one of the most important factors in halting the decline is most certainly the Gullah/Geechee Corridor Bill, signed in 2006 to preserve the culture and to make the public more aware of its value to American history in general and to the Old South in particular.

Obit for a Gullah

A legend of leadership is eulogized in the passing of Leroy Edgar Browne Sr., a proud but humble man who graduated in 1934 from Penn School, the first school for freed slaves, a few hundred yards down the road from the site of his funeral. He also graduated from Hampton Institute in 1940. He was proud of the education, and he turned it into wisdom and a place in history. Browne became the first black elected official in America after Reconstruction, which according to long-time friend Thomas Barnwell Jr. "set the pattern for all of the United States," and was elected to the Beaufort County Board of Directors in 1960, five years before the passage of the historic Voting Rights Act of 1965. Browne rubbed shoulders with luminaries of the civil rights movement, including Dr. Martin Luther King Jr. and members of the Southern Christian Leadership Conference. While he moved among the great men of that era, he never forgot his roots. And he left a legacy of service that has paid dividends to the community. He was a champion of the poor and worked to improve the standard of living for people on the Sea Islands. He pushed for clean water and indoor plumbing, which helped prevent disease among island children. In 1980, the community named the Beaufort-Jasper Comprehensive Health building in his honor.

Browne also was a servant to the community. He was a member of the NAACP, the Low Country Regional Council, the board of directors of the Sea Island Federal Credit Union, the Sea Island Farmers Co-op and the Democratic Party Executive Committee. Many people looked to him for wisdom and leadership. Indeed, all of Beaufort County will miss the 91-year-old leader.

Penn Center Newsletter, St. Helena Island, South Carolina

*The Brick Church in the Penn School Historic District near Frogmore on
St. Helena Island, South Carolina. Construction on this oldest building in the
complex started in 1855; slaves built the church and the pews.*
COURTESY OF THE LIBRARY OF CONGRESS

CHAPTER 5

Hallelujah!

The Gullah heritage is one in which religion plays a profound part, and it is not much different today from what it was centuries ago. This chapter covers captivating and often compelling descriptions of Gullah religious faith in its ebullient renderings of obedience to God and higher beings, though basically in the Christian format rather than a pagan being, as is found in some of the religious histories of the far Pacific islands. We see, and almost hear, the Gullahs as they conduct their services, among which are the following: *praise houses*, which are small buildings, often little more than shacks, in which people gather to sing spirituals, pray aloud, dance in joy to the Lord, and express their feelings of joy, hardship, hope, and repentance; *shouts*, which begin slowly with the shuffling of feet and clapping of hands, followed by louder and louder exclamations of reverence, sometimes to the extent that the shouter becomes possessed and drops to the floor in exhaustion; and *stomping* with the feet, usually accompanied by loud clapping of the hands and shaking of the head, to express belief in the Almighty. Other religious customs are discussed, such as baptizing people in tidal waters, always with the outgoing tide, so the sins of those baptized are carried away, and burying the dead with the face of the deceased looking eastward, to be carried upward into heaven with the rising sun.

An unusual development we relate is the story of the ongoing translation of the New Testament, which was launched in 1979 with a team of 20 volunteers and completed in 2005, so that the chapters could be available to some 125,000 people who read very little English even today and to the 10,000 who speak only Gullah, so that they can worship God in their native tongue. This chapter will contain engaging examples, particularly from *De Nyew Testament* and the Gospel according to Luke, 32,000 copies of which were published and distributed by the American Bible Society in the mid-1990s, entitled *De Good Nyews Bout Jedus Christ Wa Luke Write.*

"**N**o practice is more meaningful in the life of the Sea Island people, better illustrates how the different streams of influence flow together, and better reflects the synthesis of an ancient heritage with the culture imposed by the masters than religion."[1] This statement, from a study of native religions and spiritual matters in the *Low Country Gullah Culture Special Resource Study*, reflects the importance of religious faith and the celebration of God in the Gullah people, not only today but going back to the times when almost every individual and every group in America associated with this rich heritage were slaves. The slow move to freedom, though beset with every imaginable obstacle, including the cruel repression of religion in many instances, did not dim the Gullah belief in God, and most particularly in a Christian God and the ascendancy of Jesus Christ.

Studies showed that around the time of the American Civil War, slaves identified with Jesus because of the tortures and enmities he suffered, not dissimilar to their own. They easily related to the children of Israel and their sufferings, and to the constant efforts to find a homeland that they could settle as their own place in the most hostile of all worlds. This outlook has changed very little down through Gullah generations. Patricia Jones-Jackson, late professor of English at Howard University, expressed it in an essay on the development of the Gullah culture:

The prayers and sermons in contemporary African American Baptist and Methodist churches have changed little over the past 200 years. The speakers change, but the formula for expressing the oral tradition of religious exhortation does not. The prayers contain a fixed arrangement, which helps perpetuate the oral tradition. The formulaic opening begins with a quote from the Bible, a poem, or, more traditionally, a quote from the Lord's Prayer. Generally, the minister selects a member of the congregation to give the opening prayer. The speaker called on by the minister does not know beforehand that he or she will be asked to pray. Thus the quotation serves to give the speaker time to collect his or her thoughts. The speaker is at liberty to alter the quotation to his or her own specification, and often the alteration is more descriptive than the original. But oral tradition does not require that a prayer be invariant or that one remember it exactly like the written version; quite the contrary. The speaker is expected to use poetic license and to add an original touch and creativity.[2]

Thus, with this kind of free-flowing tradition, there can be numerous variations and interpretations. For example, where it is written in the Lord's Prayer, "For thine is the kingdom, the power, and the glory," the speaker might say instead, "Oh, Lord, that thine may be our kingdom, we are expecting your kingdom to be a poor sinner's glory." During the rendering of the prayers, it is fully expected that the members of the congregation may respond aloud with their own personal pleas for mercy or salvation or may acclaim their full acceptance of what is being said. This is referred to as a "call-and-response relationship," which is typical of Gullah worship services down through the ages.

When the minister or a speaker acclaims, for example, "God is the bread of life; God will feed you when you are hungry," responses from individuals in the congregation might be, "O, yes, I know he will," or simply, "All right. Yeah. Amen."

The African American form of Christianity found in these church services in the 19th and 20th centuries is in effect an extension of strong African elements, which may originally have been pagan, that were transferred and kept alive within an evolving framework of religious services.

"Religion and religious ceremony have been among the primary research interests within Gullah/Geechee studies, and with good reason," reported the

National Park Service study. "Religion has played a central role in community life, organization, leadership, and survival within the various Sea Islands of South Carolina and Georgia and continues to be the most powerful force in Gullah communities. Gullah religious belief and practice can be compared to the broader belief systems of African Americans as they pertain to the doctrine of Christianity and worship of God; however, a fair portion of Gullah religiosity remains grounded in African cosmology and worldview. There are many components to this body of research: spiritual beliefs and practices, music and song associated with religion, African cultural retention within Sea Island religiosity, and the role of the church within the community." This central role is vital, but perhaps what is most striking, according to the study, "is how little some aspects have changed over time."

The Praise House

There were a few vital changes, of course, in religious services and observations as the Gullah peoples rose from slavery to a faltering freedom and then to a more steady kind of independence in which the individual was more important than the group. But one of the most important changes—both physical and spiritual—was what became known as the *praise house*.

This had its beginnings in the days prior to the Civil War, when even the most amenable plantation owners would not permit slaves to leave their quarters to go to church. A few enterprising slaves, though spiritually cut off from any kind of service or meeting place, took matters into their own hands and designated whatever unoccupied shack they could find as a space into which they and others could go and praise the Lord. These became known as praise houses, and in some instances plantation owners encouraged their people to erect buildings for this purpose, and even permitted the attendance of a preacher (usually white) to conduct Sunday services. In most instances, the worship services were conducted by black elders who, though without any educational or professional stature, were likely to be much more gifted in exhorting their flocks than were preachers following traditional formats of worship. To this day, there are still such houses in existence throughout the Gullah Corridor, though more as historic relics than active meeting places, equipped with nothing more than rough pine benches.

In his book, *Black Yeomanry*, published in 1930, T. J. Woofter Jr., one of the first to recognize what was later to be understood as the Gullah culture, prophetically described the situation in this manner:

> After the slave laws discouraged the gathering of slaves away from their own plantation, masters allowed their people to worship in plantation groups, usually at the house of one of the older people, sometimes in a special praise house. The leaders of these plantation groups were persons of considerable authority in spiritual matters. They have been described as the lineal descendant of the African medicine man, and they were the forerunners of the present Negro ministers. They presided over meetings, gave spiritual advice, and in some cases officiated at weddings and funerals.[3]

His description of a typical praise house, of which there may have been from one to four on each plantation, shows it to be of small construction, with lamplight shining through crevices as well as board shutters. "There is no doubt as to the antiquity of the building, for it nestles beneath a great oak half-hidden by a screen of cassina bushes such as only time can erect. It is built of log framing, with rough clapboards on the sides and roofed with hand-split shingles. Inside, the oil lamp yellows the small pine pulpit of the leader, but leaves the faces of the audience almost in the dark. The floor is uneven and the handmade benches have no backs."[4] He also explained that the word *praise* could in effect be transferred, so that the leader could "carry" it from the praise house to the bedside of an invalid too sick to attend the service, and thus bring about "complete recovery."

In her fascinating book, *Yankee Missionaries in the South*, about those groups of dedicated people who risked their lives to bring spirituality and a sense of worth to the poorest and most oppressed people in America, Elizabeth Jacoway covers the subject in depth and with the warmth and meaning it deserves. Among other comments, she had this to say:

> At the center of island religious life was the *praise house*, an inheritance from the days of slavery. The old plantations, about forty of them,

still gave geographic definition to the island, and on each of these was located a little tumble-down building with rude benches, where the islanders gathered three nights a week for simple, informal, spontaneous worship. As one observer described a praise house service, "In the prayers and songs the emotional experience of the Islanders takes on a vividness and depth which is hardly to be entered into by a member of another race." Here the old-time spirituals, sung in a minor key with many variations of tone and rhythm, remained unchanged.

Here also were found the prayers, full of poetic imagery, powerful in their simplicity. "*Pray on de knees ob yo' heart,*" the leader directed, and an old woman would pray, "*May de bird ob love be in moo heart an' de Lam ob Christ in moo bosom, an' oh, God, who tuk up de sun in de palm ob yo' han' an' t'rowed her out into de sky to be Queen ob de day, listen to we.*" All through her prayer the murmurs of response could be heard, slowly building into a rhythm and finally breaking forth in the gentle singing of a spiritual. Soon the song would blend with the prayer; and as the singing grew in power, the prayer would fade out and the spiritual go on.

Soon another prayer would rise, and the congregation would join in again: "*Now as we bend our hearts equal to our knees, Lord Jesus, wilt Thou climb up on dat milk-white steed called Victory, an' ride ober de mountains an' t'rough de valleys of our sins an' backslidin's.*" The images were vivid, and there can be little doubt that they were real to these simple folk for whom the Bible gave the only suggestions of life beyond their island.

> *I look all aroun' me*
> *It looks so shine,*
> *I ask muh Lord*
> *Ef all were mine.*
> *Oh, ebery time I feels de spirit*
> *Movin' in-a muh heart*
> *I will pray.*
> *Hallelujah!*[5]

After the Civil War some praise houses became centers of importance to the people in the Sea Islands, not only as religious meeting houses but also as the sites for community meetings and planning sessions. Historical researchers on St. Helena Island, South Carolina, for example, conducted a study of these one-room edifices and discovered that they were being actively used for such purposes until recent times, as well as meeting centers for children and young people who qualified as serious members of their congregations.

Praise houses had another related purpose as the locale for a shared religious occurrence known as the *shout*. This was in effect a ritual—a combination of music, song, and movement with strong religious overtones and meaning that had its origins in America in the 19th century and was occasionally practiced up to the present in some old-line Gullah communities. The shout, usually held in a praise house with the benches removed or pushed aside on a Sunday or special religious day, involved not only voice but also shuffling of the feet, stomping, clapping of the hands, shaking of the head, and arm gyrations. It was often referred to as a "ring shout" because it was common for the participants to move in a counter-clockwise ring, slowly at first and then building gradually into a faster cadence in order to keep time with the hand clapping and other movements. It has been referred to also as a "holy dance" and sometimes described as "a ceremonial activity created by people with roots in central and west Africa, who found themselves in a difficult new land and were faced with the need to remember traditions that could enable them to survive here."[6] It was in effect an attempt to "rejoin" their old world of spirituality, reported the Spirituals Project at the University of Denver in 2004.

Roger Pinckney, in his book *Blue Roots*, adds the fact that the singing "followed tribal 'call-and-response' patterns where an elder, usually a sister with a strong voice, would sing out one line of an impromptu spiritual and the congregation would come back with the response. Such was a call for repentance. The sister would shout, '*Sheep, sheep, don't you know the road?*' or some other question that had meaning to the parishioners. And the congregation would roar back, '*Yes, my Lord, I know the road!*'"[7]

Ring shouts were not always permitted on the plantations and sometimes had to be conducted in secret—not an easy undertaking, judging by the vigor and volume of sound with which they usually took place. "The narratives of former slaves," reported the Project, "mention that a large tin basin was sometimes overturned and raised to the rafters to 'catch the sound' and lessen the likelihood that the gathering would be discovered."[8]

There is no doubt that the praise house and the shout were vital parts of the religion of the freed slaves and the Gullah peoples of that day. But not all historians have treated the subject with the respect it deserves. In his book, *The Abundant Life Prevails: Religious Traditions of Saint Helena Island*, Michael C. Wolfe quotes one writer's reference to a typical shout ritual: " 'Then began one of those scenes, which, when read, seem the exaggerations of a disordered imagination; and when witnessed, leave an impression like the memory of some horrid nightmare—so wild in the torrent of excitement, that, sweeping away reason and sense, tosses men and women upon its waves, mingling the words of religion with the howling of wild beasts, and the ravings of madmen.' "[9]

In Gullah Land, Religion Is Music and Song

Shortly after the Civil War, a New England minister, George Hepworth, visited the South and one Sunday morning attended a village church where former slaves were gathered for a service. He described entering and finding about 100 people gathered there in total silence. "At length, however," he recounted, "a single voice coming from a dark corner of the room, began a low, mournful chant in which the whole assemblage joined by degrees. It was a strange song, with seemingly very little rhythm and was what in music is called a minor, not a psalm nor a real song, with nothing that approached the jubilant in it, but rather a mournful, dirge-like expression of sorrow." At first he was inclined to laugh, and then he felt uncomfortable and was about to leave the church. But then, he said, "as the weird chorus rose a little above, and then fell a little below, the keynote, I was overcome by the real sadness and depression of soul which it seemed to symbolize." In the end, he listened for half an hour and was overcome by the emotional strength of the chorus as "the sound swelled upwards and downwards like waves of the sea."[10]

Spirituals, as a medium of faith, says a report from the Spirituals Project at the University of Denver, "are a transforming and transformational music. A principal aim of the songs, when sung in ceremonial context, has been to invoke the presence of spirit. Like the Reverend Hepworth, other nineteenth and early twentieth century observers remarked at palpable changes in the energy of meetings and churches where spirituals were being sung."[11] Time and again, others in the music world have commented on the hidden force that spirituals have had on individuals and entire congregations, sometimes bringing about almost miraculous changes in the spirituality and beliefs of listeners and singers alike. The same conclusion has been expressed repeatedly in many sections of the book-length *Low Country Gullah Culture Special Resource Study*, which places spirituals "at the heart of Gullah religious beliefs" and vital to the African tradition of call-and-response worship, music, and sacred dance. It is interesting—and probably significant—to note that some experts in the field of religious music see a difference between the African spirituals and those that might be labeled Gullah. Could it be that there is a lighter, less somber tone to spirituals along the Gullah Corridor, which is seashore-oriented, than the Africa of vast plains, high mountains, and impenetrable jungles? Certainly they tend to be sung more in unison, without instrumentation but with rhythmic foot stomping, clapping, and strikes of tambourines or gongs.

An important Gullah publication relating to religious music, and the result of many years of research on Johns Island, South Carolina, is *Ain't You Got a Right to the Tree of Life*, published by the Highlander Institute. This volume presents an oral, musical, and photographic record of the Gullah culture and language in modern times, stretching back to the days of slavery, as depicted on one of the Sea Islands closely associated with this venerable native heritage. When first published in 1966, this work conveyed both the trepidation and the jubilation at the time of the civil rights movement, and continues with newer presentations of stories and songs through the late 1980s. As one reviewer commented, "The words and songs within this collection record an important part of Gullah history straight from the mouths of those who lived it." Among the contents are examples of the *shout* as it would have sounded during services at praise houses, in which the congregation is heard not only singing but also preaching, testifying, shouting, and stomping with great vigor and inspiration.

Another classic presentation, and one of the earliest ever compiled, is *Slave Songs of the United States*, collected on St. Helena Island and other Sea Islands and Low Country sites in 1867 and reprinted in 1965. The 136 songs, largely related to religion and faith, represent important contributions to our knowledge of the Gullah language, specifically the omission of auxiliary verbs, topsy-turvy tense, lack of gender identification, and variations in emphasis. Their content also provides the listener with an insight into the problems of the slaves, their despair, moments of inspiration, religion, faith, and interpersonal relationships. In some instances, songs of faith in the earliest days (as well as in more recent times) were variations of sermons by preachers—not exactly musical, but with many intonations. These were referred to as "chanted sermons" or a "rhythmic, intoned style of extemporaneous preaching."[12]

In *Black Yeomanry*, the aforementioned book about life on a Sea Island that was published in 1930, the author, T. J. Woofter Jr., a well-known student of these subjects at hand, had this to say about preaching and singing in church:

> In their prayers and songs, the emotional experience of the island-ers, which centers around worship, takes on a vividness and depth which is hardly to be entered into by a member of another race. Their reality cannot be doubted by one who observes the earnestness of expression, the postures, the nodding, the exclamations. Often men pray until their voices break and the sweat pours from their faces. When this point is reached the emotions of the audience are also in full sway and they begin softly to sing a spiritual. Soon the song blends with the prayer. As the voices of the congregation swell louder than that of the supplicant, the prayer fades out and the song goes on. The very manner in which religious experience enters the life of a young person is foreign to present American church practices. It reaches back to the beginnings of Protestant worship when candidates for membership were instructed by "class leaders" and tested by dreams and visions. This process, in the Sea Islands, is termed "seeking" and usually begins with adolescence, around the age of thirteen or fourteen. The custom is also reminiscent of the African initiation ceremonies in which the young retire into the bush for a period of testing and are then instructed in the business of life by the older members of the tribe. Instead of beginning religious experience under the emotional sway of a revival or of an eloquent sermon, the seeker begins with a dream or vision, sometimes with conscious effort to induce a dream or vision. Any unusual dream at this period may be interpreted as the beginning of the search for salvation. After the first dream the candidate begins to fast and pray in the woods at night. Soon

an older member of the community is indicated in a dream or vision as the "teacher." If the "teacher" has had a dream or vision which may be interpreted to have some point in common, the older person and the seeker assume the teacher-pupil relationship. One woman said that she had dreamed of a silver leaf and a silver needle and soon a seeker came to her who had dreamed of a silver pot, so they knew she was indicated as the teacher.[13]

Cornelia Walker Bailey gives us, in *God, Dr. Buzzard, and the Bolito Man,* a fine sense of what it was like to be young and vibrant and inspired by a real Gullah church experience. She starts her account on an upswing at *dayclean,* the Gullah word for that precious period of time "just before the rising of the sun, in that brief instant when the night clouds are being cleared away and the first rays of light are streaking across the sky. *Dayclean,* we call this, when the day is new and the world is made fresh again. And what more appropriate than this kind of a Sunday dawn and a chance to be young and alive and looking forward to a day of faith and inspiration!"

"Later, on such a morning, after Sunday School," she writes, "churchgoers would promptly take their seats as one of the deacons walked to the front and began to lead the congregation in what was called 'raising a hymn.' Then appears the second deacon and all is in readiness."

> The second deacon gets down on his knees and leads the congregation in a prayer then, and there would be a song, an uplifting song like "We Are Climbing Jacob's Ladder." That song would bring the spirit into the church, so things would start out lively and the whole service would be lively. Then, after the Lord's Prayer, and that was usually sung, it was time for the minister. When the minister would start to preach, you were ready. We had a minister that sometimes would start off mild. He'd start teaching the text he wanted to get into, and then all of a sudden, he'd start the preaching and the tempo started going up, up, up, and the ladies started tapping their feet, and the men started saying "Amen" and stomping their feet, and hands started to clap, and heads started to nod, and it would keep getting to a higher pitch. And then the minister would cut off, *bam,* and there were still some little old ladies in the back screaming, "Hallelujah! Hallelujah!"

After that, the pianist would start striking up chords and the music would get into full swing and the choir would rise in unison and demonstrate how they had been practicing hard for weeks on end and everybody would rise up in a chorus of one of the vibrant, old-time hymns like "Amazing Grace." Everybody was in the same mood, they knew exactly where to come in, without anybody leading the song, and the whole church was rocking then. The whole church was moving. Even the building seemed like it was swinging gently with you.[14]

The Glorious Land Beyond the Tides

"An important departure from mainstream Christian belief," says a historical report, *Gullah Language and Sea Island Culture*, published by the Beaufort (South Carolina) Public Library, "is the Sea Islanders' belief in multiple souls. The soul leaves the body and returns to God at death, but the 'spirit' stays on earth, still involved in the daily affairs of its living descendants. Funerals are elaborate, and mourners decorate graves with prized possessions of the newly deceased. The spirit of a dead older woman may become a 'hag,' though in a great many of the stories, the hag is not a ghost or a dead spirit, but a living member of the community. A hag will 'ride the chest' (sit on top) of her victims as they sleep. In many of the hag tales, the women are very much alive. They keep their human form during the day, but either leave their bodies or shed their skins at night before they go out to find their victims."[15]

Another graveside tradition, described by Roger Pinckney in his book, *Blue Roots*, relates to the custom of "the passing of young children over the grave." If a parent or loving grandparent, he explains, suffers a painful, accidental, or untimely death, the spirit of the deceased will return to visit the children the departed person loved during his or her lifetime. Evidence of this "return" might be seen in the unusual bedtime restlessness of a child who suffered the loss of a close relative, or in some physical ailment or unusual fretfulness that had no apparent cause. But in the Gullah tradition, all of these undesirable problems could be solved by "placating" the spirit with the simple maneuver of holding up and passing all of the youthful relatives back and forth over the coffin at the burial site.

"Grave decorations were another way to quiet restless spirits," says Pinckney. "In a tradition still practiced in central Africa, the last articles used by the deceased were placed upon the grave in the belief that they bore a strong spiritual imprint. Bottles, pots, and pans were common. In later years, they were augmented by unused medicines, eye glasses, telephones, toasters, electric mixers, even sewing machines and televisions."[16] All of these objects were broken before being placed on the grave, not so much to prevent them from being stolen as to accentuate the belief that the act of breaking and rendering useless was part of the ritual itself, symbolizing the ending of things of this world. Historical research shows that the origins of this practice in Africa often involved more than just a few personal and household items but valuable pieces of furniture, jewelry, painted portraits, clothing, and antique chinaware. To make certain that the spirit of the departed was well protected, it was advised that the grave should be ringed with conch shells. Why? Because as one descendant of a slave from Africa explained it, the shells represent the ocean water that had to be crossed from their homeland, and now the water was the medium for taking dead persons back to the land of their ancestors. "The sea brought us, and the sea shall take us back."

In Gullah funerals it is common—as it is in many religions—for the mourners to throw handfuls of earth on a body before it is placed in a casket or on the casket itself as it is being lowered into the grave. Traditions from West Africa called for some of the dirt to be placed in small containers called *juju bags*, which could then be worn around the neck by surviving family members to bring them good luck.

Rites of Baptism

Historically no Gullah was too little or too young to be brought into the spiritual "house" of the Gullah family. Even before birth, steps were taken by expectant parents to make sure that the mother was not in any situation that would expose her to "haunts" or any forces of evil in nature. Such steps might be the application of evil-warding items of clothing or the placing of an object in the bedroom that had been blessed in the name of the Lord. The same preventive measures were in force to the time of baptism, which was almost always by total immersion. As missionary David Thorpe wrote in a letter in 1863, "They all insist upon immersion. . . . Sprinkling wouldn't do, none at all." As he described it, the candidates, 140 in all, came dressed ready for the waters, in "miserable clothing," with their heads tied up in kerchiefs, and they marched from the church to the nearest local creek, where they entered the water and were pushed down until totally immersed and baptized before being herded back to dry land and off "into the bushes," where they dried themselves and donned "shiny robes," to the accompaniment of song from the surrounding crowd of relatives and friends. There was then "a great difference in their looks when they came into the church a second time" for a long service, after which the sacrament of communion was administered to them and they were considered "full members of society."

When a Gullah church was near the ocean, it was often traditional to conduct baptismal services on a beach or along any of the tidal creeks that ran into the sea. These ceremonies were often all-day affairs, with various related activities pertaining to old and young alike. The baptisms were usually just after high tide. The saltwater immersion meant that their sins would be "washed away" with the outgoing tide. Unfortunately, as several resource studies along the Corridor have revealed, many of the historic ocean sites for Gullah baptisms have disappeared because the valuable ocean properties were acquired for beach resorts, boat landings, marinas, and other commercial developments. On St. Simons Island, Georgia, for example, one of the beaches was used by the Emmanuel Baptist Church for baptisms of its members for generations. But in the mid-1960s, it had to throw in the towel and, like many other rural churches, built an indoor baptismal pool.

Gullah cemeteries have been pathetically prone to the ravages of civilization, sometimes because the communities themselves have gradually disappeared over the generations, leaving the land without care or concern, where it was likely to be overgrown by weeds and desecrated by vandals. The Walker family and relatives had graves in one historic resting ground, Behavior Cemetery, which was sprawling and wooded, with headstones going back to the early part of the 19th century. Cornelia Walker Bailey remembers it well, recalling that when they passed the old iron cemetery gate, they always paused long enough to ask the spirits for permission to enter. During a family funeral for a male in the time of her great-great-great-grandmother Hester, a member of the procession would always stop at the gate and intone, "Family, we have come to put our brother away in mother dust."

But today many such cemeteries have few visible gravestones and barely perceptible mounds where there once were wooden markers, long decayed and turned to dust themselves. In many cases, even the sites have been so decayed and razed that the land has been usurped, whether by right or by seizure, and put to more modern use.

Similar examples of civilization throttling local holdings are increasingly rampant. The same has been true of the church properties, ancient meeting grounds, and public lands in the more scenic sections of many of the vintage Gullah homelands—sold off to developers to help pay taxes, rapidly increasing costs, or long-standing debts.

It is significant that the *Low Country Gullah Culture Special Resource Study* conducted intensive research in this subject area and had to report the following: "As rural populations have become smaller, rural congregations dwindle in size, praise houses fall into disrepair, and access to baptismal and funerary sites becomes more difficult. Schoolhouses, traditional gathering places for children from the community, have fallen victim to the racial integration of school systems. Consequently many Gullah/Geechee community activists within the study area have taken on preservation projects related to these traditional cultural sites. Particularly noteworthy are the Rosenwald schools within the study area, which along with Rosenwald schools across the South were named in 2002 by the National Trust for Historic Preservation (NTHP) as one of America's Most Endangered Historic Sites. As these community institutions are lost, Gullah/Geechee people face yet another blow to their cultural identity."[17]

Gullah Religion in Print

Although many elements of the Gullah culture and tradition have faded and even been threatened with extinction, the religious heritage

ᵢme stronger and stronger in many ways. Often, for example, in at-
by translators and scholars to re-create the Gullah language and determine its origins, samples of translation relating to the Bible or sacred teachings
are used. One of the most common is saying grace, as in the following:

> Gee we da food wa we need dus day yah an eby day. Fagibe we da bad
> ting we da do. Cause we da fagibe dem people wa do bad ta we. Leh we don
> habe haad tes wen Satan try we. Keep we from ebil.

For many Gullah people, saying grace was akin to the pouring of libations,
a tradition that goes back thousands of years, it is said, to the time when Jacob
erected a pillar of stone in the place where he had spoken to God. He poured
oil on it, made an offering of wine, and made an expression of commitment.
Expressions of grace in Gullah were followed by more elaborate translations,
both from ecclesiastical history and from the Bible. Quite common were ver-
sions of the Lord's Prayer:

> We Fada wa dey een heaben
> Leh ebrybody hona ya nyame
> We pray dat soon ya gwine rule oba de wol.
> Wasoneba ting ya wahn,
> Leh um be so een dis wol
> Same like dey een heaben.
> Gii we de food wa we need
> Dis day yah an ebry day.
> Fagibe we fa we sin
> Same lik we da fagibe dem people
> Wa do bad ta we.
> Leh we dohn hab haad test
> Wen Satan try we
> Keep we fom ebil.

For many years, there was resistance to translating almost any kind of passages into the Gullah/Geechee language, let alone the Bible and other religious
scripture. "It was like breaking the King's English," said one language teacher.
"But you have to realize that Gullah is not 'broken English.' It has a distinct

grammar and vocabulary, and it originated naturally and emphatically with the slaves who were brought to the Sea Islands of America beginning in the 1700s. Slave traders hoped to thwart verbal communication that could lead to plotting and uprisings by mixing slaves who spoke different native tongues. But the slaves, uneducated and downtrodden as they may have been, had a remarkable—almost uncanny—instinct for conversing intelligently with one another. More astonishingly, without much chance or skill at passing the language down through the generations, and across many geographical zones, in any written form, they were able to do so verbally and with an almost scientific accuracy."[18]

Almost a quarter of a century ago came a heroic challenge: to translate portions of the Bible and eventually the entire New Testament into Gullah. It had been found that people who were descendants of slaves and accustomed to many individual words and phrases in native tongues could derive more from a translation of a biblical passage into Gullah than they could from the original English. Hence why not translate lengthy passages from the New Testament and eventually the entire work? As Dr. Emory Campbell, an African American of Gullah decent who served for more than 20 years as the Executive Director of Penn Center and for many years a student of West African tongues, explained, "Even I, who have a graduate degree and have read the Bible in English all my life, can better understand the New Testament in Gullah. It makes a whole lot more sense to me."[19] He should know, for he was at the forefront of the translation that was completed in 2005. But he almost missed his chance.

In the early 1980s, a visiting linguist from the University of Southern California convinced Campbell that Gullah was more than broken English and that its survival was vital to the preservation of the culture of the Sea Islands and the Low Country of Georgia and the Carolinas. "Along with my friends and people my age, I had actually rejected Gullah in my student years," he admitted, "as a kind of stigma that set us apart as outsiders. So everybody I knew in my age bracket wanted to speak standard English."[20]

Shortly thereafter Campbell, who lives on Hilton Head Island, South Carolina, met the late Pat Sharpe and her husband, Claude, who lived on nearby Daufuskie Island, one of the Sea Islands whose inhabitants were, for many years, largely of Gullah origin. As professional translators, they were starting the challenging task of translating the New Testament, and they convinced

Campbell that he should join in this unique venture. Another key person was David Frank, a linguist and translation consultant, whose most challenging assignment was to recruit competent volunteers because he had to warn them that such a venture could take 15 to 20 years. It was decided, however, that the progress would not be so dragged out because they could release advance translations of the Gospel of Luke, which was published in 1994, and the Gospel of John, which was published in 2002. As it turned out, the New Testament (*De Nyew Testament*) was 30 years in the making, actually appearing in November 2005 under the bylines of the Wycliffe Bible Translators and the American Bible Society.

What was most remarkable about the venture—though secondary to the accomplishment itself—was the fact that within a matter of only a few weeks from the date the 900-page edition was released to the public, the entire initial printing—10,000 copies—was all but sold out. Most important, the reviews were excellent and meaningful because they placed great emphasis on the significance of the Gullah language itself and its projected rebirth in society. The success of this venture has led many scholars and authorities in the field of linguistics and languages to take a closer look at the Gullah culture and what it means to society in general, and the Sea Islands and Low Country in particular. Dr. Robert Hodgson, Dean of the NIDA Institute for Biblical Scholarship at the American Bible Society, has said that the translation is one in which everyone can take pride because of its historical and cultural significance, and he points out that this is more than just an unusual translation success story. "The Gullah New Testament raises the Gullah language and culture to a new level by enshrining the Scriptures in a Creole language that was once denigrated as a second-class version of English. African American churches around the country will celebrate this new translation for its lively tone and musical rhythms, reminiscent of today's hip-hop vernacular, but also for its recovery of an almost forgotten chapter in the history of African Americans."[21]

A member of the translation team—a Gullah herself—put it more succinctly and to the point when she remarked, "That's the first time I heard God talk the way I talk!"

Oh yes! I know he will!

On a Sunday morning in a praise house on a Sea Island, the preacher looks out over the small assembled congregation and intones words of hope that the Savior is coming. In a sing-song, deep voice, as though from the tomb, he intones his assurance:

Oh yes! I know he will! All right! Yeah! Amen! Look on the mountain
Beside the hill of Galilee my Lord!
Watch his disciple
Riding on the sea—Yeah. Uh huh!
Tossing by the wind and rain—Yeah. Come up
Going over the sea of temptation—Uh hum
Brother, I don't know
But I begin to think
In this Christian life—Yes
Sometimes you gone be toss—Yes, yeah
By the wind of life—Yes, my Lord!
The wind gonna blow you
From one side to the other—Yes!

Dr. Wilder, a "root doctor" in the Sea Islands in the early 1900s, displaying a snake
TRANSPARENCY NO. 49363. (PHOTO BY JULIAN DIMOCK.)
COURTESY OF THE AMERICAN MUSEUM OF NATURAL HISTORY LIBRARY.

Chapter 6

Healing and Folk Medicine

One of the most bewitching aspects of the Gullah culture is that of medicine and the alleviation of illnesses and injuries of every imaginable kind. This chapter opens with a scene in which a Gullah practitioner is applying strands of spider cobweb to the face of a patient who has acute facial sores, possibly from poison ivy. We then see an update, in the year 2004, in which a noted medical research scientist in Charleston, South Carolina, publishes a dissertation on his laboratory conclusions, in which it has been determined that the secretions from a spider in its web contain elements that have healing properties for treatment of skin infections.

This chapter covers the skills and cures of the Gullah people in medical treatments, particularly in the use of medicinal properties of roots, bark, leaves, herbs, berries, and wild plants. Among the natural sources they employed are teas made from cotton roots applied in hot poultices to aching backs; pellets of softened pine bark to alleviate coughs and sore throat; fermented wild cherry to cure persistent cases of diarrhea; the hot broth from boiled willow root to induce sweating and reduce fevers; pulverized witch hazel leaves soaked in sea-water, and sometimes tidal mud, to apply to aches and pains; a goldenrod lotion to reduce the pain and danger of chigger bites, bee stings, and snake bites; wild cherry tea as a sedative; seaweed and marsh grass to make compresses to treat cramps and bruises; and sweetgrass (so popular in making traditional Gullah baskets) bound in very thin strips to help the healing of broken arms, legs, and feet. Not a few are such that the patient might prefer the illness to the remedy, as in the case of cockroach tea for persistent coughing and earthworms mashed with lard to palliate rashes. Yet, as in the case of the spider webs, many of these centuries-old Gullah folk remedies have been found by botanists and herbalists to contain elements and properties that are used effectively in medications today.

"It has often been said that those hapless occupants of seventeenth- and eighteenth-century slave ships carried nothing with them on their involuntary journeys from their native West Africa to the New World," wrote Roger Pinckney, himself a descendant of slaves, in the introduction to his provocative book, *Blue Roots: African-American Folk Magic of the Gullah People.* But then he makes a meaningful rebuttal:

> This is not true. Though they were stripped of everything but their names, Africans newly impressed into slavery carried fragmented memories of their culture—music, folklore, social structure, and religion—to the mines and plantations of the Americas. Disease and cruel overwork condemned many to their deaths in Central and South America. But on the plantations of the American South, the slaves multiplied and passed their African roots to their descendants in a rich and lasting oral tradition, a tradition that survives to this day.[1]

One of the most vital and enduring elements of their culture that survived even the most devastating of the torments to which these peoples were subjected was the practice of healing and treatment of diseases, accidents, and other assaults on the physical, mental, and emotional structures of individuals and families. This astonishing survival can be traced directly to two factors. The first was the very nature of the individuals forced into slavery: a dominant force in their genes had, through generations, inured them to every kind of danger in the wilderness where they grew up. The second was the geographical locations to which they were sent to serve their masters: the Sea Islands of the Carolinas and Georgia, which provided what Pinckney described as "a fertile environment for the survival of West African culture," where they lived and worked "on moist and verdant ground, not entirely unlike the lands from which they had been taken." As he pointed out, among the slaves were men who had practiced the healing arts in the lands of their births, often referred to by their plantation owners under the erroneous term of *witch doctor*, and sometimes given severe physical punishment when they were found practicing what their white overseers regarded as "allegiance to the devil!"

According to the *Low Country Gullah Culture Special Resource Study*, undertaken over a period of several years by the National Park Service, "Sea Islanders possess vast knowledge about the world around them, particularly as it pertains to maximizing health and wellness. Many folk remedies and beliefs concerning health and medicine suggest the earliest enslaved Africans brought diverse plant knowledge, which has been transplanted throughout the Gullah/ Geechee area.... In a general sense, many Sea Islanders recognize herbal remedies as an option, but a precious few have been able to master this physical world." These specialists were recognized as root doctors, who occupied an esteemed position within their communities, where many of the old-time islanders used ancient tribal remedies as their first line of defense against illness and where many also turned to the root specialists in those areas where the Gullah culture was strong and vibrant.

The extensive research, undertaken by a phalanx of specialists over the years, cited many specific instances of medicinal herbs used by sea islanders. These included "life-everlasting" (*Gnaphalium polycephalum*), which has been used for centuries to relieve cramps, cure colds, combat diseases of the bowels and pulmonary system, and relieve foot pain. Dog fennel (*Anthemis cotula L.*) and mullein (*Verbascum thapsus*) are popular for treating colds, stuffy noses, headaches, and nervous conditions. Bark from a red oak tree (*Quercus falcata*), when boiled and drunk as a tea, was said by many elderly people to alleviate rheumatism, as well as dysentery and other intestinal complaints.

In the early 1970s, a lady named Faith Mitchell began conducting research on traditional folk beliefs and medicine in the Low Country, particularly on St. Helena Island. As a result of her investigations and research, she compiled enough data to author a book that was published in 1978, *Hoodoo Medicine: Gullah Herbal Remedies*. This collection documents the medicinal roots and plants of the Sea Islands of South Carolina. One of its rather unique qualities is that it contains no fewer than 50 detailed drawings of each of the botanical elements that are referred to in the text. "In addition to being an excellent resource concerning plant use," writes one reviewer, "Mitchell sets the historical stage by including a discussion of medicinal plant practices during slavery and the existence of plantation slaves who operated as somewhat official medical personnel. These doctors, or 'doctresses,' were specialists in certain roots and herbs that grew in the Sea Islands, bearers of an oral tradition brought from Africa to America. The similarities of flora and fauna between West Africa and the Carolina coast allowed the plant knowledge to be transferred to their new environment."[2]

According to Mitchell, there were three types of black folk medicine practitioners. First, there were those who practiced healing techniques using barks, berries, herbs, leaves, and roots to combat natural illness, such as common colds, flu, or malaria. Second, there were specialists who dealt with "spiritual illness" by using the laying on of hands or verbal intonations. Third, there were those who really deserved the term *witch doctor* because they were concerned with persons who had occult disturbances that were supposedly caused when they were "hexed" by voodoo (sometimes called "hoodoo") beings who dealt in African mystic beliefs in the supernatural. To this day, many Gullah residents of the Sea Islands wear amulets or necklaces to protect themselves against these unseen beings.

In much the same category is the subject of "rootwork," which has been defined by one fieldwork study as "a system of malign magical beliefs used to explain physical and psychological disturbances and to obtain relief by consulting a specialist or *rootworker* who removes the evil spell and thereby brings about a cure."

During the early 1970s, Daniel E. Moerman, a medical researcher, conducted extensive ethnographic interviews concerning medicinal plant use and indigenous systems of popular medicine and came to the conclusion that folk medical practices and belief systems persisted as an adaptive response to inadequate access to healthcare within the communities he studied. Among those interviewed was the noted Dr. York Bailey, the first black doctor on St. Helena Island, who was long associated with Penn School, founded in 1862 to educate freed slaves, and for whom one of the school's buildings is named. Besides completing extensive research and interviews, Moerman compiled *The St. Helena Popular Pharmacopeia*, a detailed presentation of plants and species with medical applications. He is also given credit for compiling extensive data about the structure of Sea Island households, the relationships of family members, and situations regarding health, medicine, social services, and the availability of medical assistance and pharmaceuticals. Despite these studies and the amount of research and detail involved, a problem facing researchers was one simple frequently asked question: Were the native peoples and communities that were studied on St. Helena Island and Beaufort County, South Carolina, representative of the rich Gullah and Geechee cultural heritage along the entire Gullah Corridor of the Carolinas and Georgia?

One of the most interesting and lucid accounts of these medical and health practices was by Vennie Deas-Moore, a field researcher and writer at the Medical University of South Carolina in Charleston. "During my mother's youth and well into my childhood," she wrote in an article, "Home Remedies, Herb Doctors, and Granny Midwives," in the *World & I Journal*, "during illness, emergencies, and childbirth, my family relied on home remedies, herb doctors, and granny midwives. Home remedies were made mostly from dried plants and other materials that could be gathered from yards and from the woods, such as asafetida, Spanish moss, and milkweed. Many of these remedies have proven to be medically valid. Mama speaks of how her grandmother, Mulsey, doctored her when she was sick or injured. When she was too sick she was taken to the herb doctor of the village. The herb doctor had a cure for anything that ailed you. There were roots, barks, and herbs stored in the mason jars that lined the walls of his house. During those days, there were no doctors for at least twenty or thirty miles, but the old people knew the herbs. Dogwood tea was good for a fever. Sassafras was dug and dried during the winter but could not be drunk during certain summer months. Bitter-bush made another good tea. For bad neck ache, pine-top tea was good. Get a pine the height of you. Get the limb, break off just the top, right at the level of your neck. For a fever, 'When you see a black snake around a root that's a fever root . . . he will eat it.' Another cure for back pain was made from a root that runs across the road. Can't be too much traffic. Cut the root where the wagon hit it. Skin it off and boil it and make a plaster and put that on your back. Draw it up tight, but not too tight." Vennie further explained that, although there was a large variety of herbs and roots, the materia medica of Low Country herbalists were remarkably consistent, falling into three categories: (1) common ingredients that could be purchased at the general store, such as apple cider vinegar, alcohol, table salt, syrup, lard, sulfur, bluestone, and Epsom salts; (2) patent medicines such as witch hazel, saltpeter, ammonia, oil of wintergreen, and pure spirits of gum and turpentine; and (3) common roots and herbs, of which the most common were bloodroot, snakeroot, pokeroot, muckle bush, and life-everlasting. "Gathering, mixing, and prescribing roots and herbs," she emphasized, "required a good knowledge of where to find them at what time of the year, how to prepare them, how much to use, and for which ailments, and so on."[3]

Becoming an herb doctor, therefore, required a long apprenticeship period. Many practicing herbalists acquired their knowledge from their fathers or mothers or from older relatives or friends. . . . My mother doctored her children just as my great-grandmother doctored her. I can remember when I caught a cold, just before I went to bed my mother would boil some "life-everlasting," a tea made from weeds found in the woods and stored in the barn through winter. As I drank the hot tea, I was told not to get out of bed through the night or else I would catch pneumonia. I would awaken the next morning soaking wet. This was a way of sweating the fever out of my body. As a precaution, we would wear little sacks of "asphitti" around our necks in the belief that inhaling the odor would prevent our catching a cold. Mama also laid mullein leaves soaked in alcohol on our heads or chests for headaches and chest colds. Burr ball from the sweet gum tree was rubbed on our burns. Spider webs with burned kerosene taken from lamps was used to stop bleeding. When we had the mumps, hog butt meat was tied with a penny on our chin. In cases of high blood pressure, the head of the patient would be tapped to facilitate bleeding, a form of bloodletting. High blood pressure was controlled by wearing Spanish moss in the shoes. Penn School, located in Frogmore, South Carolina, below Beaufort, retrained many of the grannies and gave them certification. One of the school's main purposes was to introduce sanitary techniques. A vicious practice that gave much concern was the use of cobwebs on the stump of the umbilical cord just after it had been cut. The cobweb was used as a means of stopping the flow of blood from the cut area. Since some of the cobwebs were gathered from stable walls, it was not unusual to have infants die of "nine-day fit," so called because convulsions would occur usually about nine days after the tetanus germ had been introduced into the navel with the cobwebs.

Attempts at Modernization

It was obvious that, through the years, medical and health organizations would increase their efforts to introduce 20th-century science to the regions where the old Gullah methods of healing still held sway. At Penn School on St. Helena Island, for example, a program was instituted in the 1930s that, even though it recognized the value, practical knowledge, and traditional community status of the granny midwives, was aimed at retraining and certifying them. "The program's goal," explained a release from Penn, "was to discourage traditional midwifery practices that were harmful and to introduce sanitary techniques to the grannies without alienating or discrediting them."[4] The use of cobwebs in the navel, for example, was cited as one of the practices that should be abandoned. At this time, in conjunction with the State Board of Health, licensed nurses began regular courses of training for the native practitioners at Penn School (later renamed Penn Center). The students received supplies and instruments, such as sterile dressings, medical scissors, and needles, and were taught new procedures. They were also given instructions about the need to supplement their basic skills by seeking professional assistance from licensed physicians, technologists, and nurses. Every attempt was made at this time to show deep and abiding respect for the grannies by inviting them to periodic health and medical meetings, which invariably opened with prayers and the singing of spirituals. This respect earned the grannies' trust and ensured their cooperation in spreading knowledge about hygiene and sanitation practices.

From the 1920s on, public health nurses, largely African Americans, traveled the South Carolina Sea Islands and Low Country providing a compassionate link between modern clinical medicine and the old-time health practices. County health nurses instructed the rural population about sanitary procedures and alerted families about signs of communicable diseases or other threats to their health and well-being. In the meantime, however, those few licensed physicians (predominantly black) who practiced in the region faced formidable challenges, not the least of which were suspicion and lack of trust from local families because their procedures were unfamiliar and the medications they prescribed differed completely from the traditional folk medicine that the people were accustomed to when sick or ailing. In some cases, these new-style doctors were accused of trying to usurp the authority of the root doctors or herb doctors who had been treating the local populations for generations. If they tried to oppose any of the methods or medications prescribed by the old-time practitioners, they risked losing much of their practice in the community. In some cases, they also risked losing their fees for services because patients who were cured of an illness ascribed the results to the herb doctor who was also treating them and not to the modern-age physician.

Doctors who succeeded best were likely to be those who had the sense to acknowledge some of the ancient practices by working through a granny or midwife, thus achieving a kind of "seal of approval." It was essential, too, that doctors make house calls for the most part, seldom requiring patients to visit their offices.

Gullah Medical and Health Traditions

When Laura Towne, founder of Penn School, first arrived on the scene in 1862, she was in a good position to be helpful to the native peoples in matters of medicine and health because she herself had been trained not only as an educator and missionary but also as a homeopathic practitioner at Penn Medical University in Philadelphia. Homeopathic medicine had been developed in the mid-1880s as a system for treating disease based on the administration of doses of drugs that produced symptoms in healthy individuals similar to those of the disease itself, and later protected them from such diseases during epidemics. Homeopathy had enjoyed some success in treating, for example, typhoid, cholera, measles, mumps, tuberculosis, and smallpox.

Although she was at a great disadvantage because of a lack of homeopathic drugs, limited supplies of even the most basic medicines and equipment, and little experience with the most prevalent health problems of the South, Laura nevertheless had an uncanny sense of treating the sick. She quickly acquainted herself, too, with the Gullah folk medicine that had been brought to the Sea Islands from West Africa and the uses of plants, roots, and herbs to cure or alleviate maladies. She discovered, for example, that combinations of certain herbs and seaweeds, when boiled together, could relieve cramps, diseases of the bowels, and pulmonary complaints and that a plant described by the natives as "life-everlasting" could be dried and smoked to assuage asthma, or chewed to ease toothache.

There were said to be almost 100 plants known to the Gullah peoples of Africa for healing aches and pains, and many of them were also available in the coastal corridors of America. Among those mentioned in Laura Towne's diaries and letters, and those of her compatriots, were sweet gum, myrtle, and blackberry for diarrhea and dysentery; swamp grass for poultices; sassafras tea as a tonic for colds; galax (an evergreen) for high blood pressure; kidney weed as a diuretic; sassafras roots for colic; ironweed combined with mare's milk as an eye wash to improve sexual potency; acid from willow leaves to treat rheumatism; the juice of wild figs for skin lesions; okra for snake bites; nightshade to reduce fevers; jimson weed as a salve; chinaberry to purge intestinal worms; and basil for sore throats. Common, too, was the practice of applying a mash of stems, flowers, and leaves to rashes or applying a scrap of brown paper, licked lightly and placed at the center of a baby's forehead, to eliminate hiccups.

One form of medication that was of special interest, in part because of its unusual nature and substance, was the application of spider webs to the skin—most often to the face and neck—to alleviate sores and painful insect bites. Strange though this practice may have seemed, it apparently was effective. Was this a practice that was more effective mentally than medically? An article in the Associated Press on October 31, 2004, provides some credible insight. Headlined "Healing Power of Spider Silk Examined," it covered the work of

Michael Ellison, a Clemson University materials science professor whose laboratory research indicated that spider's silk was proving to be effective in helping wounds heal more quickly.

Among the Gullah peoples, root doctors, generally elders, were also prevalent, and not all of them were appreciated by Towne and her fellow teachers. She wrote in her diaries, for example, about a certain "Doctor Jacobs" as being "a man who has poisoned enough people with his herbs and roots and magic, for his chief remedy with drugs is spells and incantations." She wanted no part of a voodoo man whose "pharmacopeia" included rat tea, dried frogs, nail clippings, graveyard dirt, and lizard legs. But she eventually discovered that many of the beneficial native medications in common use by families actually contained elements that were medically viable. So, by combining her knowledge of homeopathic medicine with what she garnered from the old-time residents of St. Helena Island, and using what few medical supplies arrived from time to time from Philadelphia, she was able to administer to medical and health demands at Penn Center, and at times of crisis, even in the surrounding communities.

"Sea Islanders possess vast knowledge about the world around them, particularly as it pertains to maximizing health and wellness," reported the NPS study. "Many folk remedies and beliefs concerning health and medicine suggest the earliest enslaved Africans brought diverse plant knowledge, which has been transplanted throughout the Gullah/Geechee area. . . . Several studies have been conducted which have added bits and pieces to our knowledge of Gullah folk medicine and perspectives on faith and healing. . . . In a general sense, many Sea Islanders recognize herbal remedies as an option, but a precious few have been able to master this physical world. These knowledgeable few are recognized as 'root doctors' and/or 'herbalists,' who occupy an esteemed position within their communities. Many Sea Islanders readily turn to home remedies as their first line of defense against illness and overall physical and mental maintenance; but some turn to the root specialists who dot the Gullah/Geechee landscape." As can be seen by visitors to the Penn Center area and, in fact, throughout the Sea Islands of the Carolinas and Georgia, wherever there are people of Gullah descent, it is likely that there are stories about native medications that have been handed down through the generations.

Healing Herbs and Other Medications

One of the most popular herbs was an annual known as "life-everlasting," whose leaves, stems, and yellow flowers were boiled and taken by patients to ease a cold, cough, or congestion and fever. Often it was combined with mullein or sea myrtle to relieve cramps, pulmonary distress, and loose bowels. When dried and smoked, this plant was said to relieve asthma, and it could also be applied to sore feet and when chewed could ease the pain of a toothache. But this was only one of more than 100 plants that were in common use in the Sea Islands going back to the 17th century, and all were similar to plants that had served the same purposes back in the most isolated villages of West Africa. It is incredible to realize that, although the slaves brought *memories* of the native plants that they and their forebears used in the Old World, there are almost no records of plants being imported along with the human cargo on the slave ships.

"Several different herbs were employed to combat one illness," reported the *Low Country Gullah Culture Special Resource Study*, "and many different complaints were treated with the same plant. Tannin-rich astringents, like the leaves of sweet gum, myrtle, and blackberry, were invaluable in treating the all-too-common profuse diarrhea and dysentery; bitterness was prized in searching for a cure for ever-present malaria. More than a dozen plants were used to treat colds, a dozen more for fever; a half dozen were applied to sores, and as many again were taken as tonics, considered especially beneficial when whiskey was added."[5]

Further examples are found, such as the use of the leaves of aloe and the bark of the angelica tree, known to natives as "rattlesnake master" because of their use as an antidote to the bites of deadly snakes. An example of a lesser concoction is sassafras roots for brewing tea as a health tonic. Sassafras also earned a reputation as a cure for colic, venereal disease, and even blindness, when combined with milk from a mare and applied as an eye wash. Another form of eye wash was one made from roots of the heartleaf plant, which was said to treat bloodshot eyes effectively and clear the vision.

In one of his articles on the subject, Roger Pinckney lists any number of home remedies that were not just hearsay but passed down in his own family. These included green cockleburs folded into a poultice for various skin afflictions; alligator root as a sedative; ginger root tea for females with irregular menses; bitterweed to cure chills; a variety of teas concocted from cherry roots, oak bark, and dogwood to alleviate muscular aches and swellings; and several palliatives most people would shudder at taking—such as "cockroach tea" for persistent coughing and "earthworm tea, mixed with lard," as an effective salve for rashes and burns. He also recommended bloodroot tea for the skin, peppermint oil to ease stomach pains, wild grapevine sap for patients having difficulties urinating, and basil leaves in the bath to serve as a natural deodorant. As he further explained, the Gullah peoples "widely used turpentine as an emergency balm, antibiotic, and sealant for cuts, abrasions, and lacerations while working in the pinewoods. Gunpowder mixed with whiskey will calm the heart and give power. Benefits from turpentine and whiskey may be enthusiastically debated with less than certain conclusions, but smokeless gunpowder contains nitroglycerine, a common heart stimulant." Also, he added, "if you happen to have a buzzard's carcass handy, you can extract a lard from its innards to rub on your legs if they suffer from stiffness." This was especially effective, it was said, if the stiffness problem had come about because the patient had walked over an "evil root buried beneath the doorstep."[6] Although it was admitted that the odor of a dead buzzard was pretty hard to take, it was definitely effective—so much so that if a person overdid the application on his legs, he could get "so limber that he could no longer walk!"

The National Park Service research revealed the truth behind many of the remedies and nostrums that were mentioned in Gullah lore or were often cited by non-Gullah practitioners as being questionable. "A surprising number of food plants, especially fruits, also yielded products used to treat disease," it reported. "Fig, peach, pomegranate, persimmon, along with basil, okra, and pumpkin, found their way into the pharmacological lore of the Sea Islands. No line can be drawn between folk medicine and the scientific medicine of the time." Comparative studies revealed that many of the species of plants common to Gullah application were actually mentioned independently in the *U.S. Pharmacopeia*, the *National Formulary*, or both, from as far back as 1820 to the present century. Research also was done to compare the plants and natural substances that were traditionally used in Africa with similar species in the Americas. In one case, at least 14 plants that were said to have healing properties were found in the Low Country and Sea Islands as well as in West Africa. "Although most of the items are employed to treat more than one condition," said the report, "the same plant is often used in the same way on both sides of the Atlantic. Thus wormseed and the chinaberry tree are taken as a vermifuge, especially against hookworm. The crushed flowers of okra are applied to snake bites, and cotton is used for abortion or uterine contraction in the Old World and the New. Nightshade, taken for fever in the Low Country and in Africa, has known antibacterial action. Jimson weed, used as a vermifuge, cold medicine, and salve in Carolina, is taken as a narcotic in West Africa. . . . Basil, taken for colds and other ailments, and pomegranate, used to stop diarrhea in South Carolina, are best known as antihelmintics in West Africa; pumpkin, taken for dropsy as a diuretic, is also used to treat worms there." The conclusion was that there was evidence of a very strong link, medicinally, between where the slaves came from and where they ended up, but even more conclusive was the fact that the art of healing, the natural substances, and the beliefs surrounding them were so strikingly similar.

There is no doubt also that all along the Gullah Corridor, whether on the islands or within 30 or 40 miles inland, there was, is, and always has been a surprising abundance of natural sources for healing the body, and even the mind and the spirit. Applications of these innumerable plants, herbs, roots, and other gatherings from forests, fields, marshes, and streams was largely in the hands of the root doctors, who knew the sources, the seasons, and the methods of preparation—not to mention, very often, some of the occult incantations that were necessary during the applications of the remedies. These specialists were not only herbalists but very often also preachers or conjurers whose physical actions and verbal communications played a vital part in the treatment.

Something of a turning point occurred in the 1920s, when public health nurses began to play a more important role in the Carolinas and Georgia, trained in clinical medical practices but also knowledgeable of the traditional beliefs about sickness and cures. They helped to fill a need in those villages and remote areas where there were few doctors and almost no medical facilities or pharmacies. Equally important, they kept a lookout for communicable diseases and were at the forefront when it came to improving the sanitary conditions in homes that had no indoor toilets, running water, or insecticides. Many of these practitioners were well-educated nurse-midwives with a working knowledge of obstetrics. One outstanding example was Maude Cullen, who was born in Quincy, Florida, in 1898, educated at Florida A&M, and a graduate of a nursing course before moving to South Carolina. She was so successful in her calling as nurse, dietician, midwife, and psychologist that *Life* magazine published an award-winning 12-page photographic profile of her work in 1951, which generated great interest and some $27,000 in contributions that were used to construct a modern clinic in Pineville, South Carolina. But even as recently as mid-century, old-time residents in the more remote areas of the Low Country still held doggedly to the healing practices of their forebears and looked sometimes with suspicion on modern medical technology.

The Infamous Dr. Buzzard

Root doctors traditionally had trade names or nicknames that set them apart from other kinds of practitioners. Most of these names related, in one way or another, to beings from the animal kingdom. Thus we find numerous stories about Dr. Lizard, Dr. Crow, Dr. Snake, Dr. Wasp, and the like. But the one who stood out above all for many years was Dr. Buzzard. According to Roger Pinckney, his real name was Robinson and he lived in the tiny village of Frogmore (famous for the Gullah stew that bears its name) in the central region of St. Helena Island, South Carolina. "Dr. Buzzard not only sold roots to a nationwide clientele that numbered in the thousands and predicted winning numbers in clandestine lotteries," wrote Pinckney, "he was reputed to have spirits at his command—various haunts and hags that flirted around the edges of island reality. If Dr. Buzzard put an evil root on a man, locals said, that man was as good as dead."[7] On the other hand, he was said to have been highly successful in banishing mental illness, bringing success to people in love, and protecting people from evil spirits who tried to do them bodily harm or destroy their businesses.

In her charming book, *God, Dr. Buzzard, and the Bolito Man*, author Cornelia Walker Bailey, herself a "saltwater Geechee from Sapelo Island," a barrier island off the Georgia coast, has much to say about the famed doctor. In her rhythmic, conversational prose, she writes:

> The church was a huge part of our lives. We went there to worship and to settle disputes. People were called before the elders for adultery disputes, stealing disputes, fistfights, name calling, and to try to prove who was the rightful father of a child if a man denied he was or if any woman other than Grandma had the nerve not to tell.
>
> But we had Dr. Buzzard too. Let's say I tried the church and that didn't work. I'm still angry so I need to do something a little more drastic. I'll try Dr. Buzzard. And *in come* Dr. Buzzard. Dr. Buzzard was the root doctor. The conjurer. The worker of *black magic*. He could put a spell on you and do you bodily harm. He could lift a spell off you. He could even turn a spell around and throw it back on the one that put it on you to begin with. Some places people call that voodoo or hoodoo, but over here we mostly said "root" or "mojo" to refer to the mysterious roots and herbs Dr. Buzzard used. No one was safe from root, absolutely no one, and the old people had a hard time believing in natural illness. It was hard for them to take the word of a doctor about anything. Even if someone persuaded them and said, "Take them to the doctor, take them to the doctor," if the doctor didn't find an instant cure, then the illness was blamed on something different. *Entirely different.* Root. Somebody "fixed" somebody.
>
> When my aunt Della got breast cancer, Grandma refused to believe it was cancer. She said those doctors removed Della's breasts for nothing, that somebody worked root on her daughter. She went to Brunswick [Georgia] and got Aunt Della out of that hospital and brought her back over here. Aunt Della died at home, and after that Grandma didn't believe in hospitals any more.[8]

Cornelia Walker Bailey was also a great believer in the previously mentioned life-everlasting tea. As she wrote, "Grandma and Grandpa raised Mama on life everlasting tea, and Grandpa never gave it up, even when he could afford coffee. Papa drank life everlasting tea, and he drank it more than Mama did. That's probably because Papa was practically raised by Uncle Nero. His uncle was the only relative left still around after Grandma Gibb left Sapelo and went off to Florida. Papa would come across life everlasting growing in the woods while he was driving his tractor, and he would bring home these huge bunches of it tied to his knapsack and hang them up outside in the corn house to dry. Life everlasting's got tiny little leaves that turn kinda silver-gray in the fall, when it's ready for you to pick it, and little white blossoms on top. So when he wanted some tea, he'd go out back, break a piece off, and boil it up."[9]

In the 19th century, root doctors thrived because "ordinary" doctors had limited skills and medications. On the plantations, there was a constant call for medical doctors who were able to take care of simple illnesses as well as accidents, such as broken arms and legs, cuts and bruises, common skin ailments, simple hernias, and a few other aches and pains. But when it came to ulcers, yellow fever, pneumonia, cholera, malaria (then referred to as "swamp fever"), and various degenerative diseases, the only hope for most victims was to turn to root doctors. Even in the case of illnesses that could be cured or alleviated by medical doctors, the patients preferred to rely on root doctors rather than suffer "cures" that were almost worse than the disease—blood-letting, bone-setting, and drastic purges, to name a few of the more traumatic alternatives. Yet an ailing patient could endure some procedures of root doctors that would repulse us today, such as the evil eye, mournful incantations at midnight, or being isolated in the wilderness and "visited" by unknown spirits.

A Land of Shades and Shadows

A common phrase used to describe the old Gullah healing practice is that it was "a land of shades and shadows, where one can see his way through life, yet more in the dark than the light."[10] In the early days, the nurses had to deal with conjuring as well as root doctors in handling patients. Many examples of this appeared in interviews with native peoples, as described in *Drums and Shadows*, the book published by the Georgia Writers' Project, under the WPA, during the 1930s. The following is a typical example of a quote gleaned from an interview:

> Well, dey's some belieb in cunjuh an some wut dohn. Dey's lots wut say
> sickness ain natchul an somebody put sumpm down fuh yuh. I ain belieb in it

much muhsef but dey's curious tings happen. Now, wen I wuz a boy, deah's a
root makuh wut lib yuh name Alexanduh. He wuz African an he say he kin
do any kine uh cunjuh wut kin be done an he kin cuo any kine uh disease.
He wuz a small man, slim an bery black. Alexanduh say he could fly. He
say all his fambly in Africa could fly. I ain seen em fly muhsef but he say he
could do it all right. We's sked ub im wen we's boys an use tuh run wen we
see im come. [11]

In a section of their lengthy report on the Gullah culture, the National
Park Service researchers had the following pertinent comments about root
doctors and their practices:

> While anything may be used to fix a person, from roots and pow-
> der to hair and nail-clippings, most effective is graveyard dirt, prefer-
> ably from the grave of one who has been murdered. Serpents, feared in
> Dahomey and among the Ibibio and other people of southern Nigeria,
> frequently play a prominent role in conjuring. One Gullah woman said
> of another, "*She wok a root on me so strong dat she put a big snake in muh*
> *bed, and uh could feel tings moobin all tru muh body. I could feel duh snake*
> *runnin all tru me.*"
>
> Root doctors take their name from the various roots and herbs used
> in healing, for their magic is not all harmful. George Little, who said he
> had been born with a special knowledge of healing, listed a dozen roots
> in his pharmacopeia. A self-professed root doctor and fortune teller,
> James Washington, explained that he could tell the future because he
> was born with a double caul. He said that some magic can guard you
> from harm, but evil magic can put you down sick; hair is the most pow-
> erful thing an enemy can get hold of because it is so close to the brain. The
> root doctor thus revealed several beliefs with well-known African anteced-
> ents. The special power of those born with a caul is recognized in Dahomey;
> the importance of the diviner or fortune teller is known to the Ashanti;
> the place of hair in magic is widespread among many Africans from the
> Ewe to the Mpongwe; and the role of conjure and charms is universal. [12]

One of the authoritative works on this subject is *Hoodoo Medicine: Gullah
Herbal Remedies* by Faith Mitchell. Having grown up in Michigan, she was both
shocked and moved by the conditions of some of the villages. "I was stunned by
some of the more remote backwoods settlements, where very little has changed

since slavery. But I was most deeply affected by the rich, fertile beauty of the islands, and by the strength and integrity of the families I met." She had this to say, in a nutshell, about the treatment of illnesses:

> Hoodoo medicine is a unique record of nearly lost African American folk culture. It documents herbal medicines used for centuries, from the 1600s until recent decades, by the slaves and later their freed descendants, in the South Carolina Sea Islands. The Sea Island people, also called the Gullah, were unusually isolated from other slave groups by the creeks and marshes of the Low Country. They maintained strong African influences on their speech, social customs, and beliefs, long after other American blacks had lost this connection. Likewise, their folk medicine mixed medicines that originated in Africa with cures learned from the American Indians and European settlers. Hoodoo medicine is a window into Gullah traditions, which in recent years have been threatened by the migration of families, the invasion of the Sea Islands by suburban developers, and the gradual death of the elder generation. More than that, it captures folk practices that lasted longer in the Sea Islands than elsewhere, but were once widespread throughout African American communities of the South.[13]

The Case for Conjuring

Some 10 miles south of Savannah, Georgia, lies what is left of a small Gullah village called Sandfly, once described as a "scattered community spreading through the hot pine barrens to the nearby Isle of Hope," with a population of about 300 inhabitants "who appeared to lead a placid, uneventful existence."[14] In what is considered one of the oldest African American settlements in America, some of the modest homes are still brightened by flower gardens in the front yards, and some have small truck gardens on the sides or in the rear for vegetables and herbs. A few homes are set in deeply wooded sections of giant moss-hung live oaks, reached by narrow, winding paths. Some of the men who live there are fishermen along the Atlantic coast, whereas the women keep house or have day jobs at homes in the upscale vacationland of the Isle of Hope.

Sandfly had its origins as a small, marshy African American community right after the Civil War when freed slaves from Wormsloe Plantation settled there. What marked this little, buggy strip of coastal Georgia as outstanding in a different way was the reliance of many of its people on the beliefs of their families and forebears in the ancient Gullah traditions of conjuring. Even recently, when interviewed by a reporter, they readily described many of their experiences and the reasons why this was a distinct part of their spiritual, supernatural, and metaphysical lives. As the interviewer quoted one of the residents, "*A woman jis couldn't seem to have nuthin but bad luck. She thought maybe an enemy had conjuhed uh, so she looked in the yahd an sho nough theah was a conjuh bag . . . .a queah lookin bundle with a lot of brown clay in it. She destroyed the bag an the bad luck stopped an the evil spirits didn't bothuh us none.*" As was explained, graveyard dirt was used in the making of "conjure bags" and was most effective if the dirt had been taken from the grave of a murder victim and if at the same time a few coins had been left at the gravesite in payment to the deceased to use in the other world. There were other examples, too, where people believed that powerful charms (usually malicious rather than favorable) could be made from the dust of a person's foot tracks on a dirt path. One woman was so scared that such dust would be used against her that she carried a small rake, and "*down du road she would go, rakin' up uh footsteps in back of uh, so dat nobody could git dat dus an fix uh.*"

In another typical case, a small boy in the village evidenced great emotional upset, and when his parents tried to determine the cause, he kept repeating that he had "snakes sliding about in my head." When they called in a local doctor, he diagnosed the illness as ringworm, which was prevalent in children and often affected the scalp, causing patches on the skin and in some cases extreme itchiness, which could give a child the sensation of something moving around on or in his head. He gave the mother some fungus-killing cream to apply to the head with the assurance that the problem would soon be solved. But such was not the case. The boy called out from his bed shortly after dark, screaming in terror that there were snakes in his hair. The mother applied more ointment, to no avail. But early the next morning, she looked out the window and saw a snake—an omen. She grabbed a stove shovel and killed it. And lo, within a few hours, her young son said the snakes had "gone away" from his head. He was cured.

The book *Drums and Shadows* contains many graphic accounts of the part played by root doctors, along with examples of "cunjah" and the presence and riddance of evil spirits.

Witness the following typical example:

> Professional witch doctors and root doctors ply an active trade and are employed in the more extreme cases, but often the people take matters in their own hands and by means of conjure bags and charms seek to alter their own destinies and those of their neighbors. . . .
>
> In a section of Sandfly known as Baker's Crossing lives Ophelia Baker—better known as Madam Truth, professed fortune teller and clairvoyant. The woman's sober attire and her modern, attractive house give little evidence of her profession. When holding a séance, she undergoes a change. Her body becomes tense and jerks spasmodically; her dark eyes roll wildly. Of her ability in her chosen field, the medium says, *"I advise on business an love affeahs. I tell good an bad nooz comin tuh yuh. Deah's a remedy fuh ebry trouble and I hab dat remedy, fuh a spirit hab brung it tuh me."*
>
> Madam Truth, a member of the Holy Sanctified Church of Sandfly, said that all members must undergo a sanctifying process in order to be saved. After this has been accomplished members claim to be able to hear, from a great distance, singing, talking, and the sounding of drums. We were told that the beating of the drums has a special significance, but that was all we could learn on the subject; we were told that this was a secret, divulged only to members.
>
> Members of the church are forbidden to eat certain kinds of fish and also cabbage, lettuce, and other green vegetables. The reason they give is that they have received a warning from the spirits that it is unwise to eat these foods.
>
> The plump, dark-skinned fortune teller said that she had spent her childhood on Skidaway Island. She remembered hearing the drums beaten to tell the people in the nearby settlements of an approaching dance or festival. Her father had been one of those who beat the drum and thumped out a regular message on it, a message that could be heard for miles and was clearly understood by all those who had heard it.
>
> Another method of avoiding the evil spirits was the wearing of a silver coin on the ankle, or on other parts of the body if desired. The practice initially was the wearing of, or attachment of, a *gold* coin. However,

as one woman who was married to a man *"wid duh powuh to see tings"* explained, *"duh folks roun yuh use tuh weah five-dolluh gole pieces on deah ankle, but hahd times jis nachly make dem gole pieces jump off."*[15]

Native American Herbal Remedies

Hand in hand with accounts of the Gullah viewpoints on sickness and treatment and the use of natural materials are those of the American Indians and their ways of curing the sick and the disabled. These included beliefs, magical practices, spirits, talismans, omens, the use of drums, dancing, rituals, taboos, and other aspects of ethnology and folklore. Here, as examples, are representative Native American herbal remedies that closely simulate some that are prevalent in the Gullah culture.

Snakeweed: chewed up and applied to insect bites and stings, also as a tea for help with labor pains

Skunk cabbage roots: to ease spells of asthma

Wormwood leaves: boiled as a tea to cure bronchitis

Horsemint leaves: crushed in cold water and imbibed to alleviate back pain

Thistle blossoms: boiled into a thick liquid to apply to burns and skin lesions

Chokeberry juice: swallowed to stop internal bleeding

Cotton roots: boiled as a tea to relieve labor pains

Catnip leaf tea: to ease infants with colic

Wild cherry bark: ground, steeped in hot water, and gargled for coughs

Sarsaparilla: dried roots in warm water, used as a cough remedy

Dandelions: simmered into a broth to help heartburn and act as a tonic

Witch hazel leaves: boiled into a liquid and applied to aching backs and bones

Pokeweed berries: pulverized and applied to ease pains of rheumatism and gout

Dogwood bark: in hot water, for rectal distress, applied with a syringe made from a rabbit's bladder or injected through a syringe made from the hollow bone of a bird

Wild lettuce: chewed slowly for sedative purposes and nervousness

Persimmon bark: boiled in water to form a dark liquid used as a mouth rinse, especially for infants with thrush

It is important to remember that the region we now have come to know as the Gullah/Geechee Corridor, stretching through the coastal areas of the Carolinas and Georgia, was Indian territory for thousands of years, long before the slaves from West Africa began arriving on these shores. For the most part, the early relationships between the white settlers and the Indians were not only peaceful but also productive, as indicated in a statement made by Governor James Glen of the Province of South Carolina in 1763: "The concerns of this country are so closely connected and interwoven with Indian affairs, and not only a great branch of our trade, but even the safety of this Province, do so much depend upon our continuing friendship with the Indians, that I thought it highly necessary to gain all the knowledge I could of them."[16]

At least 29 distinct tribes of Indians lived within the area that is now South Carolina, and many left behind names that are to this day still being used in the state, albeit converted to more Anglicized terminology. Although many of the tribes in the region are now extinct, there are a number that still do exist and whose descendants are active in retaining some of the activities and outlooks of the past. These include the Awendaw, Catawba, Cherokee, Chicora, Edisto, Santee, Waccamaw, and Yemassee tribes.

Old-Time Treatments Live On

Root doctors are by no means extinct along the Gullah Corridor and in the Sea Island and Low Country villages, where generations of families have relied on them for treatment. Here, at random, are some of the old-time prescriptions and treatments that are still being used for specific diseases, accidents, and other physiological, psychological, and even spiritual ailments.

Bladder distress: Mix two tablespoons of flax seed with two tablespoons of cream of tartar in a glass of water and drink half in the morning and half at night.

Rheumatism: Steep six leaves of wild Aaron's rod (mullein) in a quart of water and drink half a glass of the liquid four times a day.

Temporary blindness: Mix slate dust with pulverized sugar and have someone blow it in the eyes of the patient. Another remedy is the juice from the gall bladder of a catfish, placed in the affected eyes with an eye dropper.

Swelling of the skin or joints: Mix the oil from blending white roses, lavender, and honeysuckle; apply this to the affected part and rub well into the skin.

Stomachache: Make a gravy of bay leaves and parched rice, well blended, and drink a cup of it very slowly.

Wounds: Especially for injuries from rusty nails or other metal objects piercing the skin and likely to cause lock-jaw, mix a compound of bacon fat and tobacco leaves and squeeze it into the wound. The treatment is most effective if a copper penny is then taped against the sore.

Loss of memory: Mix bay leaves, sarsaparilla root, and sheep weed bark, ground well to a powder. Boil mixture in water as a tea and drink during the day until the memory improves.

Chapter 7

The Mellifluous
Gullah Tongue

"Ef oona ent kno weh oona da gwuine, oona should kno weh oona kum from."
"If you don't know where you are going, you should know where you come from." It is as simple as that. This chapter provides a mini-lesson in Gullah, with examples of words and phrases, proverbs, jokes, and conundrums. It also contains traditional short stories and tales, with English and Gullah side by side. Many of the favorite stories are from Uncle Remus and Br'er Rabbit, Aesop's Fables, and Grimm's Fairy Tales. We also are introduced to Geechee, that genre of Gullah common to some locations in Georgia. Samples of the language will bring the reader into close contact with not only the dialect but also the subject and philosophy of native communication. Some examples follow:

Milk ain't dry off e mout yet. Said of a person who is very young.

Evry frog praise e ownt pond. Everybody favors his own home.

Fox da watch de henhouse. It is a mistake to put a crook in charge of an establishment.

Young slaves with a donkey cart on Hopkinson's Plantation, Edisto Island, South Carolina
COURTESY OF THE LIBRARY OF CONGRESS

Throughout the history of the culture, place has always been important, whether it was a huge live oak in the forest where people went to meditate, the landing where local fishermen kept their boats, or a tiny praise house for religious services. However, the language, more than any other cultural asset, has allowed individuals to remain part of one big family despite the devastation of wars, famines, slavery, and epidemics. The spirituality of the communities and the forms of communication—whether hymns, art forms, or prayers—have resulted in an abiding faith that has transcended religions and denominations. As Du Bois and other prominent African American writers have pointed out, Gullah is a language of cadence and accents, words and intonations, as exemplified in the religious "shout," the lyrics of songs in everyday life, and even in the world of the marketplace.

A favorite saying in Gullah lands throughout the Sea Islands and Low Country is sometimes startling to visitors who are not quite prepared for it: *"Ef oona ent kno weh oona da gwuine, oona should kno weh oona kum from."* Translated it makes a great deal of sense: "If you don't know where you are going, you should know where you come from."

Although places such as Charleston, Beaufort, and Savannah and islands such as St. Helena, Hilton Head, and St. Simons do not seem like foreign countries for the many tourists who visit them at all seasons of the year, the Gullah ancestry, heritage, and customs have all been a distinctive part of the locales from early times. Most important, although Gullah was a culture that was in imminent danger of dying away, its roots were strong enough to grow again, and its language was ingrained enough to be influential and of increasing importance in the annals of America. Fortunately an increasing number of associations, studies, and groups of people have become interested in the culture and are actively researching it and spreading the interest to others.

"The Gullah people of the Georgia and South Carolina coast are among the most studied populations in the United States," according to David Moltke-Hanson, an authority and historian on the Sea Islands, "and for several different reasons: they are generally of a purer strain than any other African American group, show more resistance to changes affecting the historical traditions and customs of their race, and are rich in music, dance, arts, and skills whose origins generations ago have been described as 'powerful, beautiful, and evocative.'"[1]

The Gullah language, a Creole blend of Elizabethan English and African languages, was born on Africa's slave coast and then developed in the slave communities of isolated plantations in the coastal South. Not only did the language cross the Atlantic on the slave ships, but the dress, food preparation, art forms, religion and spirituality, and medicinal practices did as well. Even after the Sea Islands were finally freed in the early 1860s and people were at liberty to travel, the Gullah speech and customs flourished because access to the islands was by water only until the middle of the next century. In effect, most of the Gullah peoples along the coast were as isolated as if they lived in another country. Interestingly, during the 1930s and 1940s, when island communities

A Sampling of Gullah Proverbs

Dog got four feet but can't walk but one road.
No matter how many things you'd like to do, you can do only one at a time.

E teet da dig e grave.
He (or she) is overeating.

New broom sweeps clean but old broom gets corners.
To get the job done, use someone familiar with it.

Li'l pitcher got big ears.
Be careful what you say around children.

Evry sick ain't fa tell de doctor.
Don't tell the doctor all your ailments.

Mus tek cyear a de root fa heal de tree.
Take care of the roots in order to heal the tree.

began building bridges in order to have better access to medical facilities, shopping centers, and other desirable facilities, their residents, reminiscing about the past, often came to use the phrase "before the bridge" or "after the bridge."

Thousands of enslaved Africans survived to reach the Sea Island shores, the majority of them from a section of Africa known as Angola. Their ancestral traditions and ways of life survived, and the words *Gullah* and *Geechee* have come to describe that legacy. West Africans not only survived, they thrived—spiritually, intellectually, and physically—mainly because family members and families bonded with one another. After slavery, a close-knit community evolved with these basic qualities already in place, drawing on each other individually and collectively.

The Gullah language itself, perhaps more than any other cultural asset, allowed the people to remain one expansive family, helping to keep them intellectually, collectively, and ethnically protected. Their spirituality had always

Body Language

The Gullah tongue, like almost every other language, is often accompanied by motions and gestures to emphasize what is being said verbally, whether with or without grunts, groans, or other variations of emphasis. The following examples are typical.

If a conversation between two men becomes heated, one of them is likely to cross his arms over his chest to signal the end of the conversation. Among the Congo people, this was called *tuluwa lwa luumba* and was considered to be more emphatic than the spoken word.

A simple left or right movement of the head by a person listening to a conversation can signal yes or no, but is so subtle that only people who are familiar with each other can interpret which is which.

Children who are being rebuked by a parent and who feel that the reprimand is not justified will often turn their heads and purse their lips to avert a direct gaze. Known as a gesture of *nunsa*, this is sometimes captured in sculpture to add emotion to the piece of art.

When people stand with their arms akimbo, the pose is referred to as *pakalala*, and proclaims that they are ready to accept a challenge.

been—and to some extent still is—secured by an abiding faith in varied historic beliefs that transcended traditional religions and denominations. In addition, art forms have always been critical to the Gullah people, enabling them to use natural assets for both artistic and practical purposes. Sweetgrass baskets, household wood carvings, and beautiful fabrics, for example, have traditionally combined art and utility in one. As in several other native cultures, obtaining and blending foods—whether from field, forest, stream, or ocean—has played an immeasurable part for ages past in more than simply the preparation of nourishment for the body. The fact that West Africans had been growing and preparing succulent rice dishes for 5,000 years before the slave trade even began has left its mark firmly on the customs of the Gullah peoples today, influencing not just the food ways but the beliefs, spirituality, customs, language, and even art forms.

Origins of Gullah Influence at Penn Center

Historically the Gullah language was part of the everyday life at Penn School from its very beginnings, though in the 1860s it had not yet been realized or identified by outsiders from the North. Shortly after she arrived on St. Helena Island and began establishing Penn School, Laura Towne recognized the melodic speech patterns of the freed slaves and the young children under her care and wrote about them in her diaries and letters home. But of course she had no idea of the origins of their speech or its name. What she did not know, and what has since been documented by scholars, was that as many as 20 percent of the words were (and are) West African, and even words of local origin tended to be influenced by the basic tongue and traditional manners of speech.

In his book *Souls of Black Folk*, the noted African American writer and statesman W. E. B. Du Bois describes the first time the Yankees—whether soldiers or civilians—arrived in the Sea Islands early in the Civil War and encountered Africans. These outsiders had not even an inkling of what they were hearing in speech, songs, and spiritual chants. And yet these unique peoples were the cause for fighting the war—to release human beings from bondage.

As Du Bois and other African American writers have pointed out, Gullah is a language of cadence and accents, words and intonations. The Gullah shout, for example, so strongly associated with the spiritual lives of the Gullah/Geechee peoples, is "a sacred voice," a rhythmic translation of forbidden drums and the oldest of plantation melodies.[2] Old spirituals and songs spoke of storms and other events in the lives of the slaves and were often times used as codes for

Spiritual of Unknown Origin

This spiritual was said to have been composed shortly after Lincoln's Emancipation Proclamation of January 1, 1863.

Slavery chain done broke at last, broke at last, broke at last,
Slavery chain done broke at last,
Going to praise God till I die.
Way down in-a dat valley
Praying on my knees
Told God about my troubles,
And to help me ef-a He please.
I did tell him how I suffer,
In de dungeon and de chain,
And de days were with head bowed down,
And my broken flesh and pain.
I did know my Jesus heard me,
'Cause de spirit spoke to me
And said, "Rise my child, your chillun
And you shall be free.
I done 'p'int one mighty captain
For to marshal all my hosts
And to bring my bleeding ones to me
And not one shall be lost."
Slavery chain done broke at last, broke at last, broke at last,
Slavery chain done broke at last,
Going to praise God till I die.

transmitting meeting times and places and as messages for freedom. However, it is not easy to define the mysticism that is part of the culture. As a former director of Penn Center whose family has lived in the Low Country for many generations and who himself spoke Gullah as a first language explained, "I was nearly half a century old when I comprehended that the culture in which I was born, Gullah, contains uniquely rich folklore and a fascinating, distinguished idiom. I realized that the waterways and the Atlantic Ocean that encircled our islands kept our peoples from mainstream America for more than 200 years, and also kept our culture relatively pure and free from outside influences. But even more revealing was the fact, as I later learned, that nearly half a million African Americans who live among the Sea Islands were equally distinguished."[3]

As he further pointed out, he, his family, and their friends and associates took it for granted that the food they ate, the songs they sang, the spirits they embraced, the daily rituals they followed, and of course the language they spoke were all as "American" as lifestyles anywhere else in the United States. For many years the differences became apparent mostly to those islanders who moved away—to New York, Boston, Philadelphia, and other regions north of the Mason-Dixon line. Strong though the convictions of Gullah peoples are, and in spite of their determination to endure, the sites and artifacts of the early Gullah/Geechee culture have unfortunately been slowly slipping away along the Sea Islands. Stories and traditions of this fusion of African and European cultures brought long ago to these shores have been lost because of the encroachment of developments and the pressures to assimilate into the "modern" world. Small enclaves of Gullah on St. Helena Island remain, in the form of houses trimmed in indigo, believed to ward off evil spirits. There you hear talk of life before the *cumyas*, those who are recent arrivals to the area, and the problems brought by the *benyas*, those whose domiciles can be traced back to plantation life. In the Sea Islands, during celebrations of Gullah culture, you can still listen to traditional spirituals such as *"Kumbaya"* ("Come By Here"), and you can watch nimble hands weave gorgeous sweetgrass baskets with a skill that has been handed down for generations. You can enjoy the aroma and tastes of hoppin' john, sweet potato pie, and benne wafers—a few of the Gullah specialties that have found their way into our modern culture.

The television program, *NOW with Bill Moyers* reported: "Recently historians, anthropologists, and preservationists have come together to realize that preserving a culture is akin to preserving an ecosystem. There are many interlocking parts to the whole. The Gullah culture of the Low Country is such a system. It has a language, history, economic system, and artistic vision found nowhere else. It is, indeed, a heritage so rich no price tag can measure its value."[4]

Lorenzo Dow Turner

If there is any single person who deserves credit for rescuing the Gullah language from possible oblivion it is Lorenzo Dow Turner, an African American linguist whose skin color and family background made it possible for him to mingle with ease among even the remotest and most lowly Gullah peoples in the Sea Islands. This was a remarkable feat, given the fact that Turner made many of his unique studies at a time when he was a high-ranking scholar with a PhD in English literature from the University of Chicago, head of the English Department at Howard University, and editor and publisher of the *Washington Sun* newspaper.

Turner, a graduate of Howard University in 1910 who had worked his way through college as a Pullman car porter and waiter with the Commonwealth Steamboat Line, was unique: a person who could hold his own in the highest level of the halls of ivy, yet was perfectly at home and at ease with a farmhand in the cotton fields, a shrimp boat crew in Port Royal Sound, or a midwife in a Sea Island shack. Most importantly he could speak Gullah and distinguish its nuances so well that he could tell you whether the speaker was from an inland produce farm in the Low Country of South Carolina, Daufuskie Island off Savannah, or the waterfront of Sapelo Island, Georgia. In the field of languages he was astonishingly gifted. During his early academic career he became eminently well qualified in documenting, analyzing, and comparing the Gullah dialect with African, Louisiana Creole, Afro-Brazilian Creole, Native American, and Arabic languages. He studied Portuguese, Arabic, German, French, Italian, Kino, Igbo, Yoruba, Krio, Mende, and two Native American dialects, and had a reading knowledge of Latin and Greek. During his studies he identified many unusual findings to prove that Gullah was strongly influenced by African languages, not only in the variety of sounds but also in vocabulary, grammar, sentence structure, and semantics. He identified, for example, more than 300 "loan words" from African sources that are common in Gullah speech and some 4,000 African personal names that are also used by the Gullah peoples in America. Even in the remotest villages in the Sea Islands of the Carolinas and Georgia, he met people who readily recited tales and sang songs of African origin, although it was obvious that they had never set foot outside their own tiny communities. Some could even do simple arithmetic in the Mende, Vai, or Fulani vernacular of West Africa.

For Turner there was a seemingly endless source of information that had to be accumulated in what at first had seemed like a fairly simple study of an African-based language. It was said that he explored more than 20 African languages, including Wolof, spoken in Senegal; Malinke and Bambara, spoken in Guinea; Mandinka, spoken in Senegal and Guinea; Fula, spoken in Senegal, Gambia, and Guinea; Mende, spoken in Sierra Leone; Vai, spoken in Liberia; Twi and Fante, spoken in Ghana; Ga and Ewe, spoken in Togo; Fon, spoken in Benin; Yoruba, Bini, Hausa, Ibo, Ibibio, and Efik, spoken in Nigeria; and Kongo, Umbundu, and Kimbundu, spoken in Angola.

Despite the drawback of being an African American at a time when a majority of those he associated with in the higher levels of academia were white upper crust, he not only held his own but dared to take issue with some of the top practitioners in the field of linguistics. He particularly took issue with three of the most noted men in his field: Henry Mencken, George Krapp, and Ambrose Gonzalez, who looked down on his studies of Gullah, whose grammar and pronunciation they termed as "incorrect English grammar" and of little value as a language. He described all three as "shocking" in their lack of knowledge about, or interest in, the Gullah tongue as a language in its own right.

Beginning in 1932 Turner was a virtual resident in the lands of the Gullah, living among them in many places, listening, conversing, writing, and recording. Over a period of some 15 years, he created a phonetic alphabet, comparing it bit by bit with the alphabets he had compiled in West Africa. Attesting to his thoroughness, those who knew him said that he did not rely on his own judgment alone but enlisted the help of 27 researchers who between them had an accumulated knowledge of more than 15 African languages. He also was in touch with more than 50 informants in a number of key Gullah communities in Georgia and South Carolina. He focused his investigations in four categories: distinctive figures of speech, the dynamics of language usage, the role of the language within the Gullah culture, and the origins and composition as a Creole language system. In regard to the origins, he suggested that the Gullah language resulted from a merging of English and West African languages, particularly Yoruba, Igbo, Efik, and Twi.

One of the results of his studies was a book, *Africanisms in the Gullah Dialect*, published in 1949 by Arno Press and the *New York Times* through the University of Chicago Press. This unparalleled work included a history of the importation of slaves to Georgia and South Carolina direct from Africa; a phonetic alphabet; West African words used in Gullah originating from African tribes, along with expressions heard only in stories, songs, and prayers; syntactical features; and morphological features—the forms, structures, and derivations of words.

In his Preface, Turner wrote:

> Gullah is a Creolized form of English revealing survivals from many of the African languages spoken by the slaves who were brought to South Carolina and Georgia during the eighteenth century and the first half of the nineteenth. These survivals are most numerous in the vocabulary of the dialect but can be observed also in its sounds, syntax, morphology, and intonation; and there are many striking similarities between Gullah and the African languages in the methods used to form words. The purpose of this study is to record the most important of these Africanisms and to list their equivalents in the West African languages. One chapter in the volume is devoted to Gullah texts, in phonetic notation, that show varying degrees of indebtedness to African sources.
>
> The present study is the result of an investigation of the dialect that has extended over a period of fifteen years. The communities in coastal South Carolina that furnished the most distinctive specimens of the dialect were Waccamaw (a peninsula near Georgetown) and James, John's, Wadmalaw, Edisto, St. Helena, and Hilton Head Islands. Those in Georgia were Darien, Harris Neck (a peninsula near Darien), Sapeloe Island, St. Simon Island, and St. Mary's. On the mainland of both South Carolina and Georgia many of the communities in which specimens of

the dialect were recorded are situated twenty miles or further from the coast.

Equally important, Turner devoted a large segment of his research time to listening to and recording not only spirituals but also the local songs that had been passed down from generation to generation in America that had their origins in West Africa. These are available today in the *Lorenzo Dow Turner Collection of Audio Recordings*, available in some public libraries, most notably the Hog Hammock Public Library, Sapelo Island, Georgia. An example is "What Am I Going to Do with the Old Cow?" in Gullah, originally recorded by Turner on August 12, 1933:

> *What am I going to do with the old cow hoof, sir?*
> *Make a good water cup you ever did see, sir.*
> *Water cup, drinking cup, tea cup*
> *Any kind of cup, sir.*

[Chorus]

> *What am I going to do with the old cow tail, sir?*
> *Make a good buggy whip you ever did see, sir.*
> *Buggy whip, chariot whip, licking whip*
> *Any kind of whip, sir.*

[Chorus]

Another favorite was Katie Brown's "Getting Religion":

> *An' I first got religion, that is,*
> *By goin' to church with my mother.*
> *Every night, I would beg her to let me go to church*
> *An' she carry me to church.*
> *An' then I heard the old people singing.*
> *It make me feel like I ought to been a Christian.*
> *An' I went to pray.*
> *An' I prayed an' I prayed*
> *Until I got my religion.*

Turner also composed many of the Br'er Rabbit and Br'er Wolf tales, which were popular with adults as well as with children and are much quoted even today. He pointed out many common words in English that are almost directly related to their African counterparts. These include, for example, the following:

Animal names: Bambi, gorilla, zebra

Plant names and foods: banana, goober, okra, yam

Action words: bogus, booboo, boogie, dig, hippie, honkie, jamboree, juke, sock, tote

Religious and "otherworld" terms: bad eye, booger, boogie, mojo, voodoo, zombie

Musical and dance terms: bamboula, banjo, bongo, jive, mambo, samba

According to Dr. John E. Holloway, a linguist at California State University:

Most Americans are not aware that many of the words they speak and write every day are derived from African words. Who would have thought that the word *doggies* in the cowboy lyric "get along little doggies, for Wyoming shall be your new home," stems from the African word *kidogo*, which means "a little something," or "something small." How did this African word become part of the American language? Part of the explanation is that one in every five American cowboys was black in the 1880s, and much of what we think of as "cowboy culture" is rooted in African cattle herding. For example, some historians believe that the trail-driving practices of American cowboys (such as the open grazing of cattle) were based on the ways Fulani cattle herders in Western Africa had tended their animals for centuries. So, we should not be surprised to find African words as part of our cowboy culture. The word *bronco* (probably of Efik/Ibibio and Spanish origins) was used by the Spanish and by enslaved Africans to indicate the horses they rode in herding cattle. *Buckra* comes from *mbakara*, the Efik/Ibibio word for "white man," and *buckaroo* also comes from *mbakara*. These words described a class of whites who worked as "broncobusters." Although such African-derived words came from all of the five or six major cultural groups of West Africans enslaved in North America, many of the earliest words were introduced by the Wolof people. The African Wolofs were brought to the North American colonies as enslaved people between 1670 and 1700. Working principally as house slaves, they may have been the first Africans whose cultural elements and language were assimilated into the developing culture of America.

The Gullah People and Their African Heritage

Another noted linguist whose research uncovered many captivating facts and examples was the late Dr. William S. Pollitzer (1923–2002), a professor of anatomy and anthropology at the University of North Carolina–Chapel Hill. In addition to his most noted book, *The Gullah People and Their African Heritage*, he published almost 100 articles on the subject of African American culture and related subjects. According to Pollitzer, the first known appearance in print of a word resembling *Gullah* was on May 12, 1739, in which an ad had been placed seeking a runaway slave named "Golla Harry," which apparently referred to a person from the Gola tribe in Liberia, many of whose people had been captured and sold into slavery. Much later, in 1822, the name again surfaced in a reference to "Gullah Jack," who had been involved in a rebellion, and who had originally been purchased as a prisoner of war in Zinguebar.

Pollitzer's research indicated that the first known effort to reproduce the Gullah dialect appeared in the *South Carolina Gazette* on September 25, 1794. Edgar Allan Poe tried to reproduce Gullah in his curious tale "The Gold Bug," published in 1843, whose setting was Sullivan's Island, just off the port of Charleston, South Carolina. The name became much more prevalent when the late Ambrose Gonzales, a wealthy newspaper publisher and son of a Cuban revolutionary leader, wrote a series of books starting with *The Black Border: Gullah Stories of the Carolina Coast*, published first in 1922. Although Gonzales based his dialogues on his many conversations with former slaves on his family's rice plantations, he tended to take almost a condescending view of the Gullahs, referring to their speech as clumsy and the manner of presentation

Buh Lion and Buh Goat

This little tale, entitled *"Buh Lion and Buh Goat,"* was first published in 1888 by Charles Colcock Jones, who was an avid collector of Gullah stories.

> Buh lion bin a hunt, an eh spy Buh Goat duh leddown topper er big rock duh wuk eh mout an der chaw. Eh creep up fuh ketch um. Wen eh git close ter um eh notus um good. Buh Goat keep on chaw. Buh Lion try fuh fine out wuh Buh Goat duh eat. Eh yent see nuttne nigh um ceptin de nekked rock wuh eh duh leddown on. Buh Lion stonish. Eh wait topper Buh Goat. Buh Goat keep on chaw, an chaw, an chaw. Buh Lion cant mek de ting out, an eh come close, an eh say: "Hay! Buh Goat, wuh you duh eat?" Buh Goat skade wen Buh Lion rise up befo um, but eh keep er bole harte, an eh mek ansur: "Me duh chaw dis rock, an ef you dont leff, wen me done long um me guine eat you." Dis big wud sabe Buh Goat. Bole man git outer diffikelty way coward man lose eh life.

Translation

Brother Lion was out hunting when he spotted Brother Goat lying down on top of a big rock working his mouth and chewing. He crept up to catch him. When he got close to him, he watched him good. Brother Goat kept on chewing. Brother Lion tried to find out what the goat was eating. He didn't see anything near him except the naked rock, which he was lying down on. The lion was astonished. He waited for Brother Goat. But Brother Goat just kept on chewing, and chewing, and chewing. When the lion couldn't make the thing out, he came close, and he said: "Hey! Brother Goat, what are you eating?" The goat was scared when the lion rose up before him, but he kept a bold heart, and he answered: "I am chewing this rock, and if you don't leave me in peace, when I am done with my eating, I will eat you." This big word saved Brother Goat. The message: A bold man gets out of difficulty where a cowardly man loses his life.

as somewhat lazy or careless. He has been cited as having stimulated a great deal of public interest in the Gullah culture, but he seldom used the kinds of true Africanisms that scholars such as Turner were later to pinpoint in their writings.

Pollitzer's linguistic and cultural research was of a much higher order, and in his book he presented many findings that had previously been little known. One interesting highlight was the fact that most Gullah-speaking people in the United States had two kinds of given names: one used in school and with strangers, which was English, and the other a nickname, or "basket name," which was nearly always of African origin. "To the African," he wrote, "the power to name is the power to control. Even when the Gullah name is English, it follows African naming practices, like those of the Twi, Dahomeans, Mandingo, Yoruba, and Ibo tribes of northern Nigeria, and the Ovimbundu of Angola. Almost universally in Africa a child has at least two given names, bestowed by an intriguing array of circumstances. Widespread is the practice of naming the baby for the day of the week. . . . Also common is the month or season of its birth [or] birth order. . . . Conditions at birth, such as feet foremost, head presentation, born of a prolonged pregnancy, or with the cord or caul about the neck, are well-known sources of names among the Dahomeans. . . . In addition to individual names, the Mandingo, among others, stress clan names, the descendants of a real or mythical ancestor, such as a crocodile. Animals, plants, or places inspire a cognomen, especially among the Twi and tribes of northern Nigeria." In some instances, the first name is considered a secret, and thus is not spoken aloud but whispered into the ear of the infant, "lest some supernatural power, knowing it, could harm the child."

"The list of reasons for naming a newborn child are endless: time and dates; appearance of the infant, such as skin color, small size, fat, or wide-lipped; parts of the body; animals and birds; feelings and emotions seemingly expressed at the start of life; regions of the country; kings, queens, and other rulers; and occupations. *Do-um*, suggesting 'Do it,'" says Pollitzer, "was earned for assiduous application to an endeavor and audacity in sexual adventure. *Cunjie*, with very broad cheekbones, may have come from the Hausa word for cheek. *Yaa* for a girl and *Yao* for a boy, meaning Thursday, keeps alive the Ewe practice for naming a baby for the day of the week on which it was born. Even an

Spoken Gullah

These sample sentences show how Gullah was spoken in the Sea Islands in the 19th century.

Uh gwine gone dey tomorruh.
I will go there tomorrow.

We blan ketch 'nuf cootuh dey.
We always catch a lot of turtles there.

Dem yent yeddy wuh oonuh say.
They did not hear what you said.

Dem chillun binnuh nyam all we rice.
Those children were eating all our rice.

E tell um say e haffuh do um.
He told him that he had to do it.

Duh him tell we say dem duh faa'muh.
He's the one who told us that they are farmers.

De buckruh dey duh 'ood duh hunt tuckrey.
The white man is in the woods hunting turkeys.

Alltwo dem 'ooman done fuh smaa't.
Both those women are really smart.

Enty duh dem shum dey?
Aren't they the ones who saw him there?

Dem dey duh wait fuh we.
They are there waiting for us.

English-appearing name like *Joe* may be an abbreviation for *Cudjo*, a male born on Monday. Similarly, *Phoebe* may really be *Fibu*, a girl born on Friday. *Gussie* may not be from Augustus, but from the Bambari *gasi*, meaning misfortune; and *Pompey* is not necessarily the famed Roman general but the Mende name *Kpambi*, meaning a line, course, or red handkerchief." He also points out that derogatory terms, such as *Boogah*, which means something frightful, or *Nuttin*, for what it sounds like in slang—"nothing"—are often given to African children at birth so that their ancestors might not become jealous and try to take the child back. In general, however, the names are given with the idea of being appealing because kinship is highly cherished, and thus there are numerous examples of double names in which one is the child and the other the grandparent—such as *Minna Bill* as a nickname for Bill, the grandson of a lady named Minna.

Turner also discovered that some of the names that were considered most impressive for an individual related to the place of birth or other location meaningful to the person so named. Thus he gave as examples *Asante*, referring to the Gold Coast, *Loanda* in Angola, and *Wida* in Dahomey. *Nago* refers to southern Nigeria, and *Uzebu* relates to the home of a chief at Benin City. He mentions also that the Islamic influence is evident in a number of names, including *Aluwa* in Wolof, which is a wooden tablet containing verses of the Koran, and *Hadijata*, the name of Mohammed's first wife; legends and folklore also play a part, with names like *Akiti*, a famous hunter, and other characters who were well known in the tales told by parents and storytellers.

Gullah pronouns make no distinction between men and women. "In this behavior," says one of the most recognized scholars in the Gullah language, Charles Joyner, in *Down by the Riverside*, his personalized book about a South Carolina slave community, "Gullah retained a structure common to a number of African languages, such as Ibo, Ga, and Yoruba."

> The initial all-purpose Gullah pronoun was *e*, as in *"After de war e come back and took into big drinking and was' em till e fall tru"* ("After the war he came back and took to big drinking and wasted it [his money] until it fell through [he lost it]"). *E* served as the masculine, feminine, and neuter pronoun. Later, under the influence of English, *he* became the all-purpose Gullah pronoun, although *e* was not completely replaced

during slavery, when the last generation of slaves was learning to speak the language. The Gullah pronoun *he* was not the same, however, as the English pronoun *he* but served for masculine, feminine, and neuter gender. Interchangeable with *e*, *he* could serve as a subject or to indicate possession, as in "*He broke he whiskey jug*" ("He broke his whiskey jug") or "*Sam he husband name*" ("Sam was her husband's name"). The Gullah pronoun for objects in All Saints Parish was *em*, which served for masculine, feminine, and neuter gender, whether singular or plural, as in "*See em the one time*" ("I saw him once"); "*Grandfather took old Miss Sally on he back to hid em in the wood where Maussa*" ("Grandfather took old Miss Sally on his back to hide her in the woods where the master [was hiding]"); "*He couldn't believe em*" ("He couldn't believe it"); and "*Flat em all up to Marlboro*"("They took them all on flatboats up to Marlboro District").[5]

Joyner, who with Mary Arnold Twining has done extensive research in such Gullah strongholds as Waccamaw Neck and the islands of Wadmalaw, Yonges, Edisto, and St. Simons, explained further that two other features of the Gullah system distinguished it from English. First, Gullah speakers marked possession by *juxtaposition* rather than by word forms, as in "*He people wuz always free*" ("His people were always free") or "*Joshuway been Cindy pa*"("Joshua was Cindy's father"). The other distinctive feature was the practice of non-redundant plurals. If pluralization were otherwise indicated in a Gullah sentence, it was not also indicated by the noun, as in "*Dan'l and Summer two both my uncle*" ("Both Daniel and Summer were my uncles"). As Joyner concluded, "This practice was in sharp contrast to English, which required agreement in number between determiners and the nouns they modified."

When Roots Die

"She was beautiful. That was the first thing most people noticed about Patricia Jones-Jackson. Those who knew her found her inner beauty—her charm and kindness and intelligence—even more striking than her appearance. Hers was a very special grace." That was the beginning of the "In Memoriam" to this fine Gullah lady in her last and probably most important work, *When Roots*

Die: Endangered Traditions on the Sea Islands, before she died tragically in an accident while on an assignment for the National Geographic Society. Her book is about the lives and literature and language of the Gullah peoples of the Sea Islands, the free descendants of slaves. Dr. Jones-Jackson, an associate professor of English at Howard University, spent five years living among and studying the people she wrote about—their habits of work, their family lives, their methods of communication, and the stories they had to tell. And she had much to say about their language, or, as she said in Gullah, "*The old-time talk we still de talkem here.*"

After extensive years of research, she made the basic prediction, as a result of her studies, that the Gullah language can live and remain intact, but only as long as the families and the communities themselves remain intact. It was vital, too, that those who spoke Gullah be educated in the origins and roots of their language because when the roots die, the language dies. She expressed it in the beginning of a key chapter of her book:

> The factors which nurtured the Sea Island culture also nurtured the development and perpetuation of the unusual Sea Island language called Gullah or Geechee. The geographical isolation, the marginal contact with speakers outside the Sea Island communities, and the social and economic independence contributed to creating an environment where a mixed language could thrive. Gullah is defined as a Creole, the language that results when a pidgin, which has no native speakers but comes into existence as the product of communication among speakers of different linguistic backgrounds, takes over as the only language of the community.
>
> The Sea Island language, like the culture, is undergoing transformations. Several varieties of contemporary Gullah can be heard in day-to-day conversation on topics ranging from who is running for president to the best bogging place in the creek. With the exception of the unusual accent, some speakers show little deviation from standard English at all. The degree of standard English acquisition is a reflection of such factors as the level of education, the accessibility or inaccessibility of a given island to outside forces, and the extent of inside social mobility. Just as one hears a form of standard English, one also hears the "real Gullah" spoken by children and adults in all aspects of community life.[6]

As she explained, the history of Gullah is complicated. It is called a Creole language because it was determined to have resulted along the West African coast from the merger of English and the many languages in that region, including Ewe, Fante, Efik, Ibebio, Igbo, Yoruba, Twi, Kono, and Mandinka. Some researchers, she reported, suggested that Angola was a possible source for the word *Gullah*, and that *Geechee* may have been derived from the Gidzi, a language and people in the Kissy country of Liberia.

Dr. Jones-Jackson concluded that the very isolation of so many communities and tiny pockets of isolated neighborhoods in the Sea Islands of the Carolinas and Georgia was fortunate as far as the Gullah language was concerned because there were so few mixtures with people speaking standard English or other vernaculars. She said, "It can be credited with achieving even more than that. Growing up as a black majority almost free from outside social influences, such as racial prejudice . . . undoubtedly affected the attitudes and perceptions of the islanders, to the extent that few of them wish to leave the islands today."

This was particularly true until the middle of the 20th century in many of the islands where there were no bridges and where some of the inhabitants had never even been to the mainland. Even when she was completing her research in the 1980s, she reported that "several of the elderly informants for this study reported that they had not left their island in at least forty years." And she added, "The islanders are very private people and will often guard the secrets of their culture just as they make attempts to guard their language."

Dr. Jones-Jackson reported another interesting observation that had been overlooked even by some of the most accomplished researchers. Very minor details of speech, such as a consistent use of certain letters or a distinctive "frizzing" sound on words beginning with *w*, subtle though they may be, permit Gullahs to determine which island the speaker is from. "During my first few years on the islands," she wrote, as an African American who could perfectly well pass muster in looks and bearing, "I learned that I should not try to pass myself off as an islander by an attempt to imitate the local language. While I may have had the syntax right, I was never able to perfect the accent, and it is the stress and intonation that give one away. When I asked the islanders how they were able to detect such small differences, I was often told, '*I ain't know how I de know, but I de know*.'

As was pointed out in her sampling of characteristic "interpretations" of Gullah talk, a number of idioms were found to be common in the speech of elderly islanders. She gives the following examples:

dark the light: the sun was set

out the light: turn the light out

hot the water: bring the water to a boil

ugly too much: very ugly

the old man bury: the old man is dead

this side: this island

do the feet to you: cause harm to come to you

can't bring the word right now: I can't remember at the moment, or I
    will not speak of it at this time

pull off my hat: I had to run

de fix for you: lie in wait for you

watchitsir!: watch your step!

dayclean: daybreak

clean skin: a person with light skin color

one day mong all!: finally!

nothing for dead: nothing dying

the sun de red for down: sunset

knock em: hit

sweetmouth: flatter

rest you mouth!: shut up!

long eye: envy

Jones-Jackson explained, too, that many characteristic features of grammar and syntax differ from those of other African American forms of speech and writing. "Unlike standard English," she says, "which relies heavily on subordination to convey relationships between ideas, contemporary Gullah relies on coordination, or the combination of sentences that are short, abrupt, and loosely strung together." In Gullah we see few of the parts of speech—verbs, adjectives, adverbs, conjunctions, and participles—that tie together complex English sentences. What results is a language that emphasizes the more vivid words and dispenses with the "joining" words. When Gullahs speak, they tend to use a single verb stem whether to refer to a present, past, or future action that is taking place, was taking place, or might take place. The time is not as important as the mood or tone of the action, and there is little or no passive construction. Neither are there plurals on nouns in the same sense that they are used in other languages. For example, *tu baskit* is "two baskets" and *dem boi* is "those boys." To say in English "I heard he knows some old stories" would translate into "*I hear tell e know sum old story.*"

The Language You Cry In

"While millions of black Americans must wonder where in the vast continent of Africa their ancestors might have come from, one family from the U.S. need not ask that question. Mary Moran, a seventy-five-year-old grandmother from Harris Neck, Georgia, could sing an ancient song in the Mende language of Sierra Leone, a song passed down in the family from mother to daughter for generations. And, due to the efforts of a number of scholars, Moran and her family were finally reunited with their long-lost kinfolk in Sierra Leone."[7]

This opening paragraph of an article in *West Africa* magazine leads to a remarkable story of how words and music combined to change the lives of an entire family of Gullah people at a time when so little was known about this remarkable culture, its history, and its language. It all began in 1932, when Mary's mother, Amelia Dawley, sang an old family song for Lorenzo Dow Turner when he was recording it on one of the primitive wire recorders of those days. Turner was sure that the song, so familiar to the family, was a key to the past, and that the lyrics, which on the surface of the young girl's own recollection were "just a silly little old thing," were indeed meaningful. Once he had made the recording, Turner played it on one occasion after another as he traveled extensively throughout the South and across the seas to West Africa, hoping that someone would recognize its origin and that he thus would be able to trace the family roots back to a specific location. Success came one day when he was

ion of the Lord's Prayer in Gullah

We Fada wa dey een heaben
Leb ebrybody hona ya nyame
Cause ya holy.
We pray dat soonya
Gwine rule oba de wol.
Wasoneba ting ya wahn
Let urn be so een dis wol
Same like e da dey een heaben.
Gii we de food wa we need
Dis day yah, an ebry day.
Fagibe we de bad ting we da do,
Same like we fagibe dem people
Wa do bad ta we.
Leh we down habe haad test
Wen Satan try we.
Keep we fom ebil.

interviewing Solomon Caulker, then a young student but later a vice principal at Fourah Bay College in Sierra Leone, one of the countries from whence hundreds of slaves had come to America. When he played the music, Caulker identified it right away as a funeral song, and thus Turner was able to deduce that the roots of the Moran family went back to that particular region. Turner published the song and its English translation in his remarkable book, *Africanisms in the Gullah Dialect*, in 1949. But it was not until 1989 that a group of African Americans, under the leadership of Dr. Emory Campbell, a Gullah himself, and Dr. Joseph Opala, an American anthropologist who is among the topmost scholars in the field of Gullah history, initiated the first of several trips by Gullah groups to West Africa. And not until 1997 did Mary Moran make her own pilgrimage, based so unbelievably on the "silly little old thing" of a song from her childhood.

The ultimate outcome of this experience, as far as the American public was concerned, turned out to be a very moving documentary film that received many reviews as one of the finest of its kind, entitled appropriately, *The Language You Cry In*. When Dr. Opala had asked one of the elders of a tribe in Senehun Ngola, West Africa, why a Mende woman, stolen away from Sierra Leone 200 years earlier, would have carried that song in her memory instead of some other, the old man explained that it was an ancient funeral song and thus far more important than any other she was likely to have known in her lifetime. "All her people were buried with it," he explained, "and by singing it, she would always be connected to her ancestors in Africa."

He then quoted an ancient Mende proverb: "You know who a person is by the language he cries in."

Gullah and the Poetic Tradition

Gullah by its very nature is an ebullient and exuberant language, and so it is only natural that many well-recognized poets—and quite a few lost in obscurity—have found a place in the creative history of the culture. Many compositions express the emotions of the black and enslaved populations of Africa and America, with themes relating to oppression, family life, hard work, and lifestyles. One of the most noted poets was Phillis Wheatley, who had been captured and sold as a slave at the age of seven. It was almost unbelievable that she was talented enough not only to have mastered the English language but also to have published a volume entitled *Poems on Various Subjects* in 1793 and to have won praises from several of the greatest people in America, including George Washington. An early sample of her talent was "On Being Brought from Africa to America":

> 'Twas mercy brought me from my Pagan land,
> Taught my benighted soul to understand
> That there's a God, that there's a Saviour too:
> Once I redemption neither sought nor knew.
> Some view our sable race with scornful eye,
> "Their colour is a diabolic die."

Remember, Christians, Negros, black as Cain,
May be refin'd and join th' angelic train.[8]

There is little doubt that the most talented African American poet, and indeed one of the most talented poets of his time regardless of race, was Paul Laurence Dunbar, who died in 1906 at the age of 34. Unfortunately he suffered not only from the general bias against blacks but also from the prejudices of the literary establishment, which refused to believe that uneducated people of color could possibly forge the English language into readable text, let alone poetic expression. One of his most memorable poems was "Sympathy," which in its extraordinarily beautiful expressiveness and sense of melancholy captured the centuries-old plight of African Americans in the New World:

I know what the caged bird feels, alas!
When the sun is bright on the upland slopes;
When the wind stirs soft through the springing grass,
And the river flows like a stream of glass;
When the first bird sings and the first bud opes,
And the faint perfume from its chalice steals—
I know what the caged bird feels!

I know why the caged bird beats his wing
Till its blood is red on the cruel bars;
For he must fly back to his perch and cling
When he fain would be on the bough a-swing;
And a pain still throbs in the old, old scars
And they pulse again with a keener sting—
I know why he beats his wing!

I know why the caged bird sings, ah me,
When his wing is bruised and his bosom sore,—
When he beats his bars and he would be free;
It is not a carol of joy or glee,
But a prayer that he sends from his heart's deep core,
But a plea, that upward to Heaven he flings—
I know why the caged bird sings![9]

A Sample of a Typical Gullah Folk Tale with Animal Characters

Why Bro Cat na da wash e face fo e eat e brekwas

Once upon a tim fo day was clean, one monin Bro Rat bina wanda roun de rim ob barril wuh bin half ful wid watuh an bin slip an fal een.

E binah tri fa gjt out, but ebry tim e fa grab de wal e slip and fal bac in da watuh. Wen e bin dun bout gib up e yeddy a nise.

Da nise binab Bro Cat who bim saach fa brekwas. Bro Cat cock e yez and yeddy de watuh da splas. E clim up de side de barril and lok een and bi see Bro Cat. E sae, "How yu git down en da, Bro Rat?" Bro Rat sae, "Maan, a bina wak roun de edge ob de barril fa lok een an a slip an a fall een. Eef you hep me fa git outa ya, I let you eat me fa brekwas." Bro Cat say, "Fa tru?" Bro Rat say, "Yeah fa true."

Bro Cat gon an clim up tuh de top ob de barril an bi rech down an grab Bro Rat by e tail.

E bi lay Bro Rat on de broad sid de barril an bi staat fa eat Bro Rat. Bro Rat holluh, "Oh no Bro Cat. Yu baffa leh me dri fus fo you choke yourself tu det. Go wush you face wile a dry."

Bro Cat gon fa wush e face an wen e bi git bac e brekwas bin gon. Bro Cat nebuh wush e face fo brekwas from dat dae tuh dis.

The English Translation
Why Bro Cat Does Not Wash His Face before Breakfast

Once upon a time, Bro Rat was wandering around the rim of a barrel half filled with water and slipped and fell in. He was futilely trying to climb up the slippery side of the barrel when Bro Cat, looking for breakfast, heard Bro Rat splashing in the barrel.

Bro Cat climbed up the side of the barrel to see who was in there and saw Bro Rat.

"How did you get yourself in such a fix?" asked Bro Cat.

Bro Rat answered, "Man, I was curious about what was inside the barrel and slipped and fell in. If you help me get out, I'll let you eat me."

"Would you really?" asked Bro Cat.

"Sure, I'll let you eat me," answered Bro Rat.

"That's a deal," said Bro Cat. Then he reached down with his two front paws and grabbed Bro Rat by the tail and laid him on a nearby board.

As Bro Rat lay there soggy, Bro Cat approached to begin his meal.

"Oh, no!" screamed Bro Rat. "You don't want to eat me like this. Man, my wet hair will choke you to death. You'd better let me dry so you can take my hair off. Why don't you go and wash your face while I dry here in this sun."

Bro Cat went and washed his face, but when he returned, Bro Rat had disappeared. From that day to this, Bro Cat has never washed his face before he eats breakfast.

CHAPTER 8

Geography

The map at the front of this book shows the Gullah Corridor from North Carolina through South Carolina and Georgia and on to northern Florida. Some key locations, which will be described and seen through the eyes of residents, include the following: Tibwin Plantation, one of the oldest agricultural sites on the South Carolina coast, and the adjacent African American community with close ties to the Tibwin land and a long Gullah history; Hampton, on the South Santee River, site of a major rice plantation; major portions of St. Helena Island, South Carolina, especially the Penn Historic District; communities in McIntosh County, Georgia, located along the southern coast; the Hog Hammock community on Sapelo Island, Georgia; Seabrook Village in Midway, Georgia; St. Simons Island and Cumberland Island; Hofwyl-Broadfield Plantation and nearby communities in Glynn County, Georgia; Butler Island, Georgia; Harris Neck, Georgia; areas and islands adjacent to Beaufort, South Carolina; 10 sites on Hilton Head Island, South Carolina, and along

*Before its destruction in the 1860s, Haig Point Plantation had the largest tabby
domestic buildings in coastal South Carolina. Today, these ruins at
Daufuskie Landing are the best-preserved tabby slave dwellings in the country.*
COURTESY OF THE LIBRARY OF CONGRESS

the May River in Bluffton; and many sites in the vicinity of Charleston and Edisto Island, South Carolina. There are also numerous Gullah clusters along the coast near Savannah, Georgia, and the Savannah River.

※※※

In October 2006, the president of the United States signed a bill that had been long pending in Congress, and before that in preliminary stages in various legislative bodies in the American Southeast, to preserve and interpret the Gullah/Geechee culture. One of the basic features was geographical in nature, establishing the territory to be covered as "a coastal area running from southern North Carolina to northern Florida, which is home to the culture that is a unique blend of African and European influences brought to America in Colonial days." Although the news was a matter of jubilation and success for many of the 500,000 people of Gullah descent who live in this region, it was an enigma to most Americans even in the Southeast, who were unfamiliar with the native cultures in this area described as a cultural "Corridor." Among the initial projects aimed at recognizing and describing this native culture was a program of the National Park Service (NPS) to open up to the public Tibwin Plantation, Hampton Plantation State Historic Site, and Snee Farm at the Charles Pinckney National Historic Site, all of which are located near U.S. Highway 17 in upper Charleston County. The NPS reported the following:

> Tibwin, Hampton, and Snee Farm (Charles Pinckney National Historic Site) each have an important story to tell. Each of the sites was owned by founding families of South Carolina. Each had numerous enslaved Africans who cleared the land, constructed the homes, planted the crops, and made other significant contributions to the infrastructure and wealth of the state and nation. Together, these sites have a synergistic relationship that enhances interpretation of South Carolina from the earliest colonial beginnings to the signing of the Declaration of Independence, the Revolutionary War, the framing and signing of the Constitution, the growth of the new nation, the Civil War, and beyond. The three sites represent a 300-year continuum of coastal history intertwined with the story of the Gullah/Geechee people, their language, their skills, and their historic ties to Africa, their unique New World culture, and their

contributions to the American story. Gullah/Geechee people and their culture are an inseparable part of the fabric of what is often thought of as southern culture. Telling a more complete story at these three sites will underscore the contributions and significance of the Gullah/Geechee people to the development of state, regional, and national history and culture. Hampton, Tibwin, and Snee Farm provide many interpretive opportunities relating to early agricultural practices associated with indigo and rice production and processing, production of table crops, and fishing. Additional possibilities for education and interpretation include:

Displays and demonstrations of traditional Gullah crafts, festivals, programs, and concerts;

Educational programs through collaboration with partner organizations;

Production of sweetgrass and other raw materials for basket makers;

Heirloom agriculture and early agricultural methods;

Rice cultivation, both upland and tidal;

Traditional game hunting methods;

Traditional fishing, shrimping, crabbing, and oyster gathering;

Traditional cooking methods;

Water transportation;

Production and interpretation of medicinal herbs;

Visual arts;

Music and rhythms;

Construction and use of traditional percussion instruments; and

Quilting and other textile arts.

This was just the beginning, as will be seen by an overview of the intensive historical research that has been completed and is continually underway throughout the region. As a result of these efforts, fortunately, more and more people have taken the time to read articles and books, tune in to television documentaries, and view films on this subject and are finding it to be fascinating and informative.

Geography in a Nutshell

The Sea Islands, which are the major habitat of the Gullah peoples, lie in an arc from north to south from Georgetown, South Carolina, to Cumberland Island, Georgia. The coastal area from this seashore stretch to some 30 miles inland is considered to be the mainland region of the Gullah/Geechee population, both today and in the past. Studies are not yet conclusive, but there is reason to believe that the coast of northern Florida near Amelia Island was also inhabited by Gullahs, particularly some who were associated for some time with the Seminoles and other Indian tribes. Existing evidence places the islands of South Carolina as the area of greatest concentration of African culture in the Americas, based, in part, on the numbers of people and families who show familiarity with the Gullah language, terms, foods, religion, skills, and other qualities. It is natural that this should be so, considering that Charleston (then called Charles Town), South Carolina, was one of the major ports for slave ships and the market for hundreds of thousands of slaves brought there for sale from West Africa—probably almost half of all the enslaved Africans who reached American shores. There was a period after the Civil War when many of the tiny communities in the Sea Islands were populated almost entirely by former slaves, then freed and on their own, their former white masters and their families having fled to the inland cities of the South and in many cases to the North. Also, the populations of the peoples of African origin remained stable, and even multiplied, because they were resistant to many of the diseases in the area that decimated the white families.

The islands along the southeastern coast are all low-lying and were subject to hurricanes and tropical storms during the summer and fall, just as they are today. This was true also for the mainland strip along the Corridor, referred to as the Low Country, which seldom rises more than 30 feet above sea level and is patterned with tidal creeks, inlets, the surrounding marshlands, and rich tropical and subtropical vegetation. The sandy-loam soil of the Sea Islands is well suited to growing many types of crops, making this region ideal for the plantation economics of rice, indigo, and cotton, all of which increased the need for slave labor. Furthermore, the growing season in this region ranges from 250 to 300 days a year, making it ideal for crop rotation and harvesting. For many years, the freed slaves of Gullah descent were able to transform the lands that they had acquired into small farms and fishing villages, continuing their culture, once the people were free and able to subsist and grow depending upon their individual abilities and goals. But their lives and lifestyles began to undergo changes with increasing rapidity as America's Southeast was "discovered," particularly following World War II and the period of settling back into peace and hoped-for prosperity.

Major Sea Islands

South Carolina

Sea Islands in Charleston County, South Carolina

Bear Island
Bull Island
Daniel Island
Dewees Island
Edisto Island
Folly Island
Isle of Palms
James Island
Johns Island
Kiawah Island
Monis Island
Seabrook Island
Sullivan's Island
Wadmalaw Island

Sea Islands in Beaufort County, South Carolina

Cane Island
Cat Island

Coosaw Island
Dataw Island
Daufuskie Island
Distant Island
Fripp Island
Gibbes Island
Hilton Head Island
Hunting Island
Lady's Island
Morgan Island
Parris Island
Port Royal Island
Pritchards Island
St. Helena Island
St. Phillips Island

Georgia

The Golden Isles of Georgia

Cumberland Island
Jekyll Island
Little St. Simons Island
Ossabaw Island
Sapelo Island
Sea Island
St. Catherines Island
St. Simons Island
Tybee Island

Florida

Amelia Island and Fernandina Beach

An End and a Beginning

The historic city of Charleston, South Carolina, speaks volumes about the arrival in America of Africans made into slaves and their sojourn once they landed in this southern port. Whether it is in its distinctive architecture, its beautiful rivers, its delightful people, or the relics of times past, African Americans who visit this beautiful city can't help but feel a closeness within their souls to their early ancestors who arrived here as slaves from Africa. On Broad Street in the heart of downtown Charleston lies the office built in 1798 that served from 1869 to 1874 as the Freedman's Bank, a national bank for blacks. These banks were created to aid blacks in the Reconstruction efforts following the Civil War and are particularly associated with the promise of "40 acres and a mule," given to freed slaves by the government. On East Bay Street lies the huge Old Exchange and Custom House, built in the 1760s to be used for the selling of slaves, and the Old Slave Mart Museum, the oldest black museum of slave artifacts in America, located on the site where, following the prohibition of selling slaves at the Custom House, slaves were sold. This location, known as Ryan's Mart, was established in 1852 with a black area that consisted of rooms in the auction block that were hidden from public view. African Americans have long referred to Sullivan's Island, across the Ashley River, as their Ellis Island, where a great many of the slaves from Africa were brought into this country.

Among the many Gullah-related locations in Charleston is the noted Emanuel African Methodist Episcopal Church, the oldest A.M.E. church in the South and the second oldest in the world. The original church was destroyed by fire in 1832, its replacement was destroyed by the earthquake of 1886, and the present building was completed in 1892. Charleston is noted also for its "slave quarters," which were formerly servants' quarters, carriage houses, or "dependencies" in the 18th and 19th centuries. Now many of these, attached to the finest homes in the city, are noted as "some of the most expensive real estate properties in the area." Only a few of such, however, are on any of the many Gullah tours of this old city.

Charleston is also noted for the part some of its citizens played in the Underground Railroad, which had little to do with locomotives or trains. The

Underground Railroad was a system of secret locations where runaway slaves could hide out and later be moved, either up north or south into Florida, where there were regions that would harbor them in safety.

Gullah Islands

A typical example of what was occurring in the land of the Gullahs can be seen dramatically in the case of Hilton Head Island, South Carolina, approximately 100 miles south of Charleston, South Carolina, and 50 miles northeast of Savannah, Georgia—two centers of growing interest to vacation travelers from the North. As the *Gullah Special Resource Study* described it, "The great transformation began in 1957 when Charles Frazier launched the construction of Sea Pines Plantation on Hilton Head Island. The availability of air conditioning made the Sea Islands more appealing to affluent people. It was not very long before other developers joined in, and resorts sprang up all over the island. Although only about 20 percent of the island was actually owned by Gullah/Geechee residents, much of the island was owned by absentee landlords who allowed free access to their property. The absentee landlords quickly sold out to developers. Between 1950 and 2000, the population of South Carolina Low Country counties increased by 151 percent, while the national population as a whole increased by only 86 percent."[1]

Before construction of Sea Pines Plantation, Gullah/Geechee residents had been free to hunt and fish all over Hilton Head Island. Suddenly fences and gates blocked much of the land. Residents were cut off from their hunting and fishing grounds as well as their traditional burial grounds. Fences meant that Gullah/Geechee islanders could no longer *"go in duh creek"* to get supper. Today there are only about a dozen truly Gullah neighborhoods that can be reached by visitors on tours, which are being protected by the town, county, and state. Among these are Stoney, referred to now as "the gateway to Hilton Head" but which was once called "downtown," with a post office, grocery store, and even a juke joint; Jonesville, known for its wheelwrights and shoemakers and a small church where rhythmic drumming substantiated connections to African spirituality; Spanish Wells, along the river, where Spanish explorers

were said to have gone ashore to dig wells to replenish their freshwater supplies; Simmons Fishing Camp, where boats docked while bringing supplies
from Savannah and other mainland towns; Union Cemetery, established during the Civil War for Union soldiers and later turned into farmlands when
the soldiers' graves were transferred to the national cemetery at Beaufort; and
Mitchellville, probably the first community established in America for freed
African Americans after the Emancipation Proclamation. Settled in 1862 with

A Time of Transitions

The transition after the Civil War from plantations owned by
wealthy whites to small farms that barely provided subsistence for
former slaves has been documented many times over, in particular by T. J. Woofter Jr., who wrote in the 1920s and 1930s about
the changing South. The following is from one of his documentary
books, ***Black Yeomanry: Life on St. Helena Island:***

The stretch of highway from Charleston to Savannah
cuts the center of the Sea Island area. Formerly the seat of
some of the South's proudest and richest plantations, it now
has only memories of its past glories. A few of the once
gay mansions stand in faded grandeur at the head of wide
avenues of aged moss-hung oaks. Many have passed into
the hands of the outlander as hunting preserves. Still others
are truck farms with an oak-bordered driveway leading to
ruins. The bulk of the land is in woods or fallow fields. Scattered along the highway and tucked away on side roads
are many small farms of Negroes who have been freehold-
ers since emancipation.

Nature and man have conspired to strip the South Carolina tidewater of its glories. First naval stores and timber

brought wealth and were exhausted. Next indigo, rice, and cotton flourished. The fresh water areas along the swamps and rivers teemed with the laborers on the rice plantations. The owners had their own schooners and loaded their product at the plantation wharf for European markets. They were as familiar with London as with New York. But indigo became unprofitable when the bounty was removed and rice was eventually produced at prices below those profitable to the South Carolina planter. Now as the causeways cross the marshes one sees only rotting Hood gates and choked ditches. For many years nature granted to the sea coast a monopoly on silky cotton of superior staple known the world over as "Sea Island."

Prosperity again smiled. In the meantime phosphate mining throve and declined when cheaper phosphates were discovered elsewhere. Nature again brought disaster in the shape of a bug—the weevil—which definitely ruined Sea Island cotton production.

more than 1,500 persons, this was an essential part of the famed Port Royal Experiment, which was mainly a failed attempt of the ill-fated Reconstruction effort in the South.

The Sea Pines story has been repeated on islands all over the study area. A stark example of this is Daufuskie Island, just a few miles from Hilton Head Island and accessible only by boat. It was publicized so often in travel articles, stories, and at least one popular novel that it attracted many visitors—tourists, photographers, artists, nature lovers, hunters, and sport fishermen—and the outcome was inevitable. It has become the faraway site for an isolated, exclusive golf course. Today more than half of the island has been acquired for sports and tourist development, and even some of the most sacrosanct lands of the native islanders have been squeezed into oblivion.

> There are 45,000 people on Hilton Head and upwards of a quarter million in Savannah and you can see both places from Daufuskie. Little wonder developers want Daufuskie for condos and gated communities—plantations, they call them—where you can't go unless you belong. Twenty years ago, developers came like Pharaoh's host in the old Gullah spiritual, two hundred million dollars strong. But the waters came together, rolling over Gucci shoes, and they all went down in a Red Sea of ink—International Paper, Haliburton Oil, and Club Corp. of America, chief among a great drowning of lesser corporations.
>
> Some say marine transportation did them in. Daufuskie is damned inconvenient. Every screw, every nail, every golf ball, T-bone, jug of whiskey, employee, and customer had to be hauled across Calibogue Sound, deep and wide and dangerous as a woman. And then the garbage and customers and employees and money had to be hauled back.[2]

Amen.

Until recently, the town of Bluffton, just to the north of Hilton Head and "off island," was a sleepy little village with a great deal of charm and many sections connected to the Gullah culture. It was originally a King's Grant to one Lord Proprietor Colleton, for whom a nearby river is named. Situated on a bluff (for which it received its name) overlooking the broad May River, it was known as a "summering place" in the early 1800s, where the families of the rice and cotton planters in the region could retreat to escape the heat inland, and where there were many recreations—boating, swimming, crabbing, sailing, and a wealth of tasty seafoods in the nearby bays and inlets. But the town suffered greatly when, in 1863, after South Carolina became the first state to secede from the Union, it was the site of a battle. Union gunboats steamed up the river to attack the rebel troops and blasted away many homes, churches, and public buildings during the ensuing action. Further blows of a different kind have laid waste many of the historical sections during the end of the 20th century and beginning of the 21st as a new breed of destroyers—developers—has turned Bluffton into a small city of housing developments, golf courses, shopping centers, malls, and over-jammed highways. Nevertheless there are enough antebellum homes, churches, museums, and historic Gullah sites to make the community worth a visit for anyone interested in African American or other history.

On the other side of the coin, there are a few Gullah communities that are being preserved because of measures taken by the government and interested individuals and citizen groups to preserve them. One such community is Sapelo Island off the Georgia coast, a 16,500-acre barrier island that is remote, has no bridge connecting it to the mainland, and is reached mainly by a ferry that is operated by the State of Georgia. More than 95 percent of the island is owned and protected by the Georgia Department of Natural Resources. Its major point of interest is Hog Hammock, one of the few intact Geechee settlements along the Georgia coast, which was founded some two decades before the Civil War and named for Sampson Hogg, an enslaved African. The residents, about 70 in all, are descendants of some of the 400 slaves who lived on the plantation in the early 19th century and still speak the Gullah language, as well as English. The island, open to visitors in limited numbers, is ringed by lush salt marsh lands, which are strictly preserved and protected as a national wilderness and salt marsh ecosystem.

As a Georgia guidebook describes this locale, it is typical of many of the small Sea Islands occupied by Gullah/Geechee peoples:

> From the edge of the marsh to higher, drier ground, one will see red cedar, marsh elder, groundsel tree, and yaupon. Maritime forests, identified by a distinct canopy, vary from live oak and palmetto communities, to American holly and laurel oak hardwoods, and pine forests consisting of longleaf, loblolly, slash, and pond pine. Neotropical migrants visit the dense forests, and found nesting here are yellow-throated warblers, parulas, and painted buntings that nest in the oak woodlands in summer. Some young cypresses are re-establishing themselves after significant drainage activities from nineteenth century owners of the island killed the water-loving older trees. Mono-culture pine forests are found in some sections where the island is managed for timber production. An artificial freshwater pond on the north end of the island supports a noisy rookery of egrets and herons in spring and summer, and waterfowl during winter migrations. Alligators are found in the pond, along with southern bullfrogs and leopard frogs and other freshwater-loving reptiles and

amphibians. Bottomland hardwoods such as maples and sweet gum are found near freshwater drainage ditches and sloughs between dune ridges, which serve as breeding sites for frogs and toads, including the green, squirrel, and pine woods tree frogs and southern and narrow-mouth toads. Eastern diamondback rattlesnakes are found on the island, as are cottonmouths, corn snakes, garter snakes, and king snakes. The most common lizard on the island is the green anole.[3]

In her book, *God, Dr. Buzzard, and the Bolito Man*, Cornelia Walker Bailey, a Gullah whose family has lived on Sapelo Island, Georgia, since 1803, has this to say about this place that time has passed by:

Hog Hammock is on the southeast side of Sapelo, not too far from the ocean, and about three miles inland from the Big House. The legend is that Sampson Hogg, Mama's great-great-grandfather, founded Hog Hammock.

When freedom came, black people got to pick their own names for the first time. A lot of people didn't want to take the name of their former slaveholder and some of them named themselves based on the task they did during slavery. According to the story, Sampson Hogg was in charge of raising hogs for the Spalding family. After the war, he used the name *Hogg*, with two g's.

Sampson Hogg and his wife, Sally, lived in Hanging Bull after the war, then they moved to the Bluff, and then they moved down to what became Hog Hammock. There were already black landowners in the area, but somehow the place wound up being called Hog Hammock.

The family kept the name *Hogg* until after Sampson died, but they must not have liked it, even with those two g's. They rowed over to Darien, to the other side, and petitioned the court to change their name to Hall, and that was the end of the Hoggs. They were just Halls from then on.

In 1950, when we moved to Hog Hammock, there were about three hundred and fifty people, all black, living there, and it was the city to me, coming from the North End where there weren't many people. There were at least sixty houses, small wooden houses sitting back from a dirt road that wound through the community.[4]

Another protected area of considerable interest is Sandy Island, located between the Waccamaw and the Great Pee Dee Rivers north of Charleston,

South Carolina. Here, according to the Nature Conservancy, which manages the island's Waccamaw National Wildlife Refuge, there are two small Gullah villages with some 120 residents, most of whom are descended from the slaves of more than 10 rice plantations that flourished there in the 18th and 19th centuries. This was an ideal location because of more than 1,000 acres of wetlands along the river that could be converted to rice plantations. Reached only by small boats, Sandy Island is a particular retreat for nature lovers because of its rare plants, aged longleaf pines, turkey oaks, wildlife, and unusual species of birds, including the red-cockaded woodpecker.

On St. Helena Island, South Carolina, there are a number of vital, ongoing efforts to preserve the Gullah culture. One very important and longtime program, of course, is that of Penn Center, as described in the chapter on Penn School and in other references to this important seat of learning and culture. Another is the organization known as the Gullah/Geechee Sea Island Coalition, founded in 1996 by Marquetta L. Goodwine, a native of St. Helena, which

The South Carolina National Heritage Corridor

This Corridor, running some 240 miles and bounded on the south by the venerable port city of Charleston and on the north by the mountains of the Blue Ridge, contains historical, cultural, and natural resources that tell—separately and jointly—the vibrant story of the Low Country's centuries-long evolution. Much of this history concerns epochs and sites relating to African American and Gullah/Geechee culture. By following the routes designated on the map, travelers can learn about cotton fields, rice and indigo, slaves and freedmen, mill villages and native crafts, railroads and back roads, spiritual and religious life, soul food and cures, ghosts and goblins, and a wealth of information about animals and fish, forests and fields, lakes and streams, and natural wonders of many kinds. The trail is lined with historical preservations, museums, nature sites, state parks, art galleries, and gardens of many sizes.

aims to "promote and participate in the preservation of Gullah and Geechee history, heritage, culture, and language; works toward Sea Island land re-acquisition and maintenance; and celebrates Gullah/Geechee culture through artistic and educational means electronically and via 'grassroots scholarship.'"[5]

Ms. Goodwine has personally been a leading figure for many years working with local land planning groups—both civilian and governmental—to establish zones of protection for Gullah lands and, in some instances, to actually retrieve lands that were questionably, or in many cases illegally, taken away from native peoples without cause. She has also gone to court, as well as to state, county, and city institutions on many occasions—and even to Washington—to speak out on behalf of Gullah and Geechee rights and the means to being self-sustaining.

A Matter of Co-Existence

Unlike the case of the American Indians, whose ancient customs and methods of life are preserved mainly on reservations, the Gullah culture is threaded through the entire area of the Sea Islands. A good example of this is Mitchellville, situated at the northern end of Hilton Head Island, South Carolina, where until recently very little had changed since the days of Reconstruction following the Civil War. Tom Barnwell, one of the island's best-known Gullah personalities, described this site:

> From the historical marker at the junction of Beach City Road, Fish Haul Road, and Dillon Road, you can see St. James Baptist Church, which postdates the foundation of the Mitchellville settlement by a mere 25 years; various scattered dwellings of indeterminate age; and lots and lots of trees. Traveling up nearby Mitchellville Road towards the coast, spears of grass as tall as a man point upwards towards the sky as woodland gives way to swamp. Beyond lies Port Royal Sound, where you can faintly hear the waves lapping on the sandy shore, with nearby Parris Island on the other side, an hour away by road but looking close enough to touch through the binocular viewer fixed to the overlook.
>
> As you drive away in any direction from the historical marker to

where the actual town of Mitchellville developed, family houses dot the landscape. Many of the families who live there today may very well be direct descendants of the original Mitchellville site. Looking on mailboxes you see such names as Jones, Chaplain, Simmons, White, and Rivers—all names that date back to Mitchellville. Further east to the coast, a mere half-mile away, you can see turtles cruise lazily below the surface of the water, and only the shrill cry of the occasional water bird interrupts the perfect tranquility of the scene.

But on November 7, 1861, *tranquil* would have been the last word an observer would use to describe the area. The sound of cannon fire filled the air as the largest fleet ever assembled in North America at the time, comprising 15 Union warships plus a host of steamers, schooners, and frigates, did battle with the Confederate forces.

Mitchellville, named after Union Army General Ormsby M. Mitchell, who made humane efforts to establish living quarters for freed slaves, offered only the most basic necessities for its new residents. As it was described, "The houses were of rough boards, with small windows without glass. The floors were of sand and lime. At one side was an open hearth. In spite of doors and shutters, large cracks let in the bitter winter cold. The older people slept in bunks, the younger on the floor. The cooking utensils usually consisted of a single pot; the food was hominy or peas and salt pork. Long oyster shells were used for spoons, and when the family had scraped the hominy from the pot, the dogs were allowed to clear it for the next meal. Such conditions were little short of those in a savage settlement in the Congo."[6]

Nevertheless, as Barnwell pointed out, one of the reasons why the Gullah culture has persisted to this day all along the Sea Islands and into the Low Country is that enough people like Mitchell had the foresight to believe that "blacks, with guidance, could improve their conditions, build adequate housing, be educated, and become self-sufficient."

Taking a cue from history, and explaining that Mitchellville was able to move from a subsistence to a cash economy and set the tone for land ownership and freedom across the island, Tom Barnwell has been a motivating force in helping to identify and preserve other Gullah neighborhoods on Hilton Head Island, especially the Squire Pope–Gum Tree Road area where he lives, which is perhaps the largest Gullah neighborhood in both population and area on the island. Landmarks there include Mount Calvary Missionary Baptist Church, a fishing cooperative on Skull Creek, and two model housing projects—Cedar Wells and Wild Horse Court, which occupy former watermelon, bean, and cattle fields. Although many of the older dwellings have been replaced, the neighborhood retains the old-time community spirit.

Increasingly, many of the old Gullah villages and neighborhoods have been, or are being, restored and preserved, if not occupied strictly as modern-day communities. One of the finest examples is that of Hobcaw Barony, a 17,500-acre plantation in Georgetown, South Carolina, and one of the few undeveloped tracts on the Waccamaw Neck, between the Winyah Bay and the Atlantic Ocean. The Waccamaw Indians called the land Hobcaw, which meant "between the waters," and it was granted as a barony during the Colonial era by the King of England to settlers who established a number of plantations for the growing of rice. After the slaves who worked at Hobcaw were freed, many of them remained as paid workers until the turn of the 20th century and were residents of a village known as Friendfield until as recently as the early 1950s.

Although Hobcaw no longer classifies as a Gullah community per se, it is important as a preservation project of many of the elements of Gullah life in the past. Now classified as a "research reserve," Hobcaw is used by southern colleges and universities as a site where historians and sociologists can study many aspects of plantation life, including those peoples who lived and worked there during the critical transition period from slavery to freedom.

Of similar importance to an understanding of the Gullah culture is Caw Caw Interpretive Center in Ravenel, South Carolina, situated on a site that is rich in natural, historical, and cultural resources. Once part of a 5,500-acre rice plantation that flourished in the late 18th and early 19th centuries, the land was described as "home to enslaved Africans who applied their technology and skills in agriculture to carve a highly successful series of rice fields out of this cypress swamp." In this respect, it is a tribute to the perseverance, adaptability, and craftsmanship of the Gullah peoples, not to mention their ability to survive under the harshest conditions and yet not lose sight of their culture.

Places with a Past

Few towns were at one time as significant in Gullah history and presence as Beaufort, South Carolina. As *God, Dr. Buzzard, and the Bolito Man* describes the town of more recent days, "Beaufort is a languorous island town of 15,000, exuding a gentility reminiscent of the antebellum South. Breezy, white-columned verandas overlook the sweeping bend of a lazy tidal river, spreading oaks and magnolias filter sunlight that falls into lush and pungent gardens of camellia, honeysuckle, and jasmine. Clock time plays second fiddle to sun time and tide time. Residents sip iced tea in the shade, and the conversation seldom gets beyond a strenuous argument over who is going to get up and bring more. St. Helena Island is two bridges and twelve miles away. It's another world—a Gullah world. The Gullah, grandsons and granddaughters of slaves, unwilling builders of an empire, were given land and freedom by the conquering Yankee Army. They have endured and sometimes nearly prospered. Their musical patois, toothsome cuisine, and unlikely amalgamation of African and Christian religion powerfully spice a unique island reality."[7]

In earlier times, however, when the Civil War was still raging and Laura Towne frequented Beaufort while engaged in recruiting people and soliciting funds to establish Penn School on St. Helena as a haven for teaching freed slaves, many of the freedmen and freedwomen were able to live and even find meager jobs in Beaufort. They did so because of the protective wing of units of the Union Army who were bivouacking there after their victory in the Battle of Port Royal and because most of the plantation owners and their families had fled the area. Today Beaufort (the old part), sometimes referred to as "the Queen of the Carolina Sea Islands" and now a National Historic Landmark, is at the forefront of efforts to recognize and recapture the spirit and substance of Gullah culture, history, and even language. Its annual Gullah Festival has grown and become increasingly popular in the Low Country; its public library has one of the finest collections in the state of literature, records, and art relating to African Americans; and its best shops are replete with native arts and crafts. Interestingly enough, all of this is in a setting where visitors can also find and visit some of the South's most elegant 18th- and early 19th-century homes that have been described as "jewels along the Bay."

The African American Coastal Trail

Throughout the Sea Islands and the Low Country, increasing attention is being paid to preserving knowledge of the Gullah culture and history through tours and historical journeys. One such program is the African American Coastal Trail, which runs along the South Carolina shores and slightly inland, tracing history. As the preface of the guide states, "For more than 300 years, the coastal wetlands and sea shores have been shaped and reshaped by the trials, tribulations, and accomplishments of those who settled the coast. From the very beginning, African Americans have been a part of that history. Nearly every aspect of this area's culture has been defined by African American influence."

From the trail's beginning near the historic town of McClellanville, the first stopping point is Hampton Plantation, built in the mid-1700s and home to more than 320 enslaved Africans. The trail proceeds to many other historic sites, including Boone Hall Plantation, the Charles Pinckney National Historic Site, Forts Sumter and Moultrie, and numerous churches, homes, museums, public buildings, galleries, markets, and other sites that are relevant to the subject at hand.

The Golden Isles of Georgia

Heading south along the coast, beyond the Savannah River, we find rich treasures of Gullah history and culture. William S. Pollitzer, in his classic book, *The Gullah People and Their African Heritage*, sums it up most appropriately:

> Along the Georgia coast are the Golden Isles of Guale, as they were called by the Spanish, so numerous and so separated by rivulets that they made ideal entry points for the smuggling of slaves. The Ogeechee that parallels the Savannah River and opens between Skidaway and Ossabaw islands is said to be the source of the name *Geechee*, the Georgia equivalent of *Gullah*. Below St. Catherines, the Altamaha empties be-

tween Sapelo and St. Simons islands, across from the Marshes of Glynn near Brunswick, made famous by the musical, mystical poem by Sidney Lanier. The Satilla enters St. Andrews Sound between Jekyll and Cumberland islands, and St. Marys separates Georgia from Florida.

Up on the Waccamaw River, in 1526, Spaniards began the first, and unsuccessful, Old World settlement in what is now the United States; in 1566 they established a fort on St. Helena Island. Jean Ribaut and his fellow French Huguenots planted a short-lived colony at Port Royal in 1562. On St. Simons Island, Charles Wesley preached Methodism in the 1730s, and the English actress Fanny Kemble, married to Pierce Butler, wrote her journal, highly critical of slavery on his plantation there in the 1830s. In 1861 the guns that fired on Fort Sumter in Charleston harbor started the Civil War.

Today, although many of these islands contain nature preserves to protect wildlife, almost all are accessible to tourists, and the life of their black inhabitants has been altered. As Emory Campbell, the tall and impressive director of Penn Center on St. Helena Island, expresses it, "We are the endangered species."

Ossabaw Island, the northernmost outpost of the Golden Isles, has a history of occupation and settlement going back more than 4,000 years, and it is noted for its ancient maritime forests, freshwater ponds, abundant salt marshes, stretches of white sand beaches, and shifting dunes. It has been described as being "shaped like a wishbone" and is approximately 25,000 acres—twice the size of Bermuda—with marshes in the center. Classified as a barrier island, it is the second-largest of its type on the Georgia coast and is known for its abundance of floral species. Because it was ideally suited for the planting and harvesting of indigo, which produced a rich dye that was highly popular in the 18th and 19th centuries, it was a natural site for plantations and the importing of hundreds of slaves to labor in the fields. The growing, harvesting, and processing of indigo was an example of the innate skills of the African slaves and their ability to adapt themselves to their work under the harshest circumstances, in the worst kind of bondage, and in a strange environment overseas, thousands of miles from their homeland. In addition to cutting the plants at daybreak before the hot sun could dry the leaves, they had to know exactly how to immerse them in vats, boil the sediment, drain it carefully, and press it into molds to dry and be loaded onto barges for shipment to Savannah. Although many decades have passed since the very last crop of indigo went to market, the skills linger in the minds of present-day Gullahs, passed along from generation to generation and made available by them to people who visit Ossabaw and other Gullah lands and islands.

Another significant locale in Georgia's Golden Isles is St. Simons Island, which lies off the coast not far from Brunswick, where many large plantations, as well as small settlements, flourished. There were 14 plantations in all, of which the four greatest were Cannon's Point, Hamilton, Hampton, and Retreat. Here the planters developed and produced a special, fine, long staple cotton that became known as Sea Island cotton, which thrived in the Georgia soil under the right climatic conditions and was greatly prized in English cotton markets.

St. Simons was a key site visited by researchers and interviewers when the *Drums and Shadows* project was in full swing in the 1930s, when access to the island was a small causeway, and when almost all of the residents were descendants of freed slaves. As recently as the 1960s, the population of African Americans was almost 3,000. By the time that this population had dwindled to less than half that number, a Gullah lady named Amy Roberts decided that she and other dedicated locals should take action to restore and preserve their culture. Together they formed the St. Simons African-American Heritage Coalition, "to maintain a vibrant presence where island ancestors first tasted freedom." One of the major goals has been to achieve designation as historic sites, from both the state and federal governments, of major landmarks on the island, and they have successfully received such recognition from the National Register of Historic Places and the National Trust for Historic Preservation. Another goal has been to obtain tax relief for historic properties that have been handed down from generation to generation—thus far successful, but quite a feat in an area that has become increasingly known as a vacationland and the site of many second homes for the wealthy.

St. Simons was personified in "The Marshes of Glynn," published in 1878 by Georgia's most famous poet, Sidney Lanier, from which some of the most pertinent and pictorial lines are quoted here:

Glooms of the live-oaks, beautiful-braided and woven
With intricate shades of the vines that myriad-cloven
Clamber the forks of the multiform boughs,—
Emerald twilights,—
Virginal shy lights,
Wrought of the leaves to allure to the whisper of vows,
When lovers pace timidly down through the green colonnades
Of the dim sweet woods, of the dear dark woods,
Of the heavenly woods and glades,
That run to the radiant marginal sand-beach within
The wide sea-marshes of Glynn;—

Beautiful glooms, soft dusks in the noon-day fire,—
Wildwood privacies, closets of lone desire,
Chamber from chamber parted with wavering arras of leaves,—
Cells for the passionate pleasure of prayer to the soul that grieves,
Pure with a sense of the passing of saints through the wood,
Cool for the dutiful weighing of ill with good;—

O braided dusks of the oak and woven shades of the vine,
While the riotous noon-day sun of the June-day long did shine
Ye held me fast in your heart and I held you fast in mine;
But now when the noon is no more, and riot is rest,
And the sun is a-wait at the ponderous gate of the West,
And the slant yellow beam down the wood-aisle doth seem
Like a lane into heaven that leads from a dream,—
Ay, now, when my soul all day hath drunken the soul of the oak,
And my heart is at ease from men, and the wearisome sound of the
     stroke
Of the scythe of time and the trowel of trade is low,
And belief overmasters doubt, and I know that I know,
And my spirit is grown to a lordly great compass within,
That the length and the breadth and the sweep of the marshes of
     Glynn

Will work me no fear like the fear they have wrought me of yore
When length was fatigue, and when breadth was but bitterness sore,
And when terror and shrinking and dreary un-namable pain
Drew over me out of the merciless miles of the plain . . .
By a world of marsh that borders a world of sea.[8]

The Golden Isles of Georgia

Sidney Lanier, the noted Georgia-born poet, described the Golden Isles of Georgia as "a world of marsh that borders a world of sea." He was also cognizant of the local color and patois of the Gullah peoples in the Sea Islands, as noted in this poem, written in 1876, echoing the language of a favorite Baptist preacher.

SOLO: *Sin's rooster's crowed, Ole Mahster's riz,*
De sleepin'-time is pas';
Wake up dem lazy Baptissis,

CHORUS: *Dey's mightily in de grass, grass,*
Dey's mightily in de grass.

Ole Mahster's blowed de mornin' horn,
He's blowed a powerful blas';
O Baptis' come, come hoe de corn,
You's mightily in de grass, grass,
You's mightily in de grass.

De Meth'dis team's done hitched; O fool,
De day's a-breakin' fas';
Gear up dat lean ole Baptis' mule,

Dey's mightily in de grass, grass,
Dey's mightily in de grass.

De workmen's few an' mons'rous slow,
De cotton's sheddin' fas';
Whoop, look, jes' look at de Baptis' row,
Hit's mightily in de grass, grass,
Hit's mightily in de grass.

Dey jay-bird squeal to de mockin'-bird: "Stop!
Don' gimme none o' yo' sass;
Better sing one song for de Baptis' crop,
Dey's mightily in de grass, grass,
Dey's mightily in de grass."

And de ole crow croak: "Don' work, no, no;"
But de fiel'-lark say, "Yaas, yaas,
An' I spec' you mighty glad, you debblish crow,
Dat de Baptissis's in de grass, grass,
Dat de Baptissis's in de grass!"

Lord, thunder us up to de plowin'-match,
Lord, peerten de hoein' fas',
Yea, Lord, hab mussy on de Baptis' patch,
Dey's mightily in de grass, grass,
Dey's mightily in de grass.

St. Simons has been heralded in many ways in song, story, and art. One of the most moving stories is that of Ebo Landing, the subject of a book by Ihsan Bracy, an African American of Geechee ancestry who, though raised in the North, passed along stories of the Old South to his children. The central story is described on a Web site for Glynn County, Georgia, history and lore:

> Ebo Landing is a small moment in the historical southern past. The legend that remains is a reminder of a life and the tragedy of slavery. Women and men from the Ebo tribe were brought from southern Nigeria, in the western part of Africa, to Savannah, Georgia, to be auctioned off as slaves. Two families from St. Simons Island, Georgia, purchased these slaves and had them shipped to the Island on a ship named *Morovia*. The captain's own slave was the first to commit suicide by drowning in Dunbar Creek. Then the Ebo chief began chanting, "The Sea brought me and the Sea will bring me home." There was no questioning the chief's decisions. They all began chanting together. Chained one to the other, they came into port and were led toward the dock. But, instead of walking onto the bank into a life of slavery, they all turned and followed their chief into the depths of Dunbar Creek. . . . They say the Ebo tribe still haunts the landing and you can hear the chains and their chants: "The Sea brought me and the Sea will bring me home."

Cumberland Island National Seashore

One of the most cherished historic sites in Georgia is Cumberland Island, located off the coast near the mouth of the St. Marys River. It is really two islands connected by a marsh—the main one, Cumberland Island, largely in the hands of the National Parks Foundation, and the smaller one, Little Cumberland Island. Evidence shows that human occupation of the island occurred as early as 4,000 years ago. Some of the earliest records were those of the Spanish Navy, which explored the Atlantic all along this coast and constructed the Fort of San Pedro in 1566. Later a Franciscan monastery was established to convert the Timucuan Indians to Christianity. But the relationship with the Gullah peoples did not occur until some time after General James Oglethorpe, founder of the British colony of Georgia in 1736, named the island Cumberland in honor of the Duke of Cumberland. Plantations were later established, and with them came the arrival of African slaves. After the Civil War, following the general evacuation of white plantation owners and families, former slaves established Half Moon Bluff, a simple village of basic wood frame dwellings and animal shelters. During the following decades, when the land became more and more divided, African Americans were able to purchase parcels of land and maintain small farms and fishing docks. During this period, some of the homes and religious buildings were constructed of tabby, a cement made of lime, water, and crushed oyster shell, which is found in the remains of many buildings of all kinds that are near the ocean throughout the Gullah Corridor. Most of Cumberland Island is managed as a government wilderness area, and many of the acres that are privately owned were purchased with funds provided by the Mellon Institute and Congress, to preserve the rights of families whose forebears were slaves. The First African Baptist Church, constructed in 1937, is a center of religious and educational life for the community.

Although Cumberland Island, Georgia's largest and southernmost barrier island, where wild horses roam freely along with armadillos and whitetail deer, is open to visitors, their number is limited, and generally advance reservations are required for the ferry services, accommodations, and camping areas. One section, the High Point District, was initially developed as a hotel and resort complex in 1880. It was important to the citizens of nearby Half Moon Bluff because it offered them continuing jobs over the years, both for service and construction.

Most visitors to Cumberland reach it through the docks at St. Marys, a village which in itself is a joy to behold and is sometimes referred to as "the jewel in the crown of the Colonial coast." Hundreds of years ago, the Creek, Guale, and Timucuan Indians, from what is now Florida a few miles to the south, saw it as a land of bountiful fish and game and soil on which crops could grow in abundance all year long. Sixteenth-century French explorers described an abundant land full of havens, rivers, and islands. Visitors today find St. Marys a place of charm, with canopies of centuries-old live oaks draped in Spanish moss and wisteria, magnolias, white picket fences, and a mixed atmosphere of salt air and tropical blossoms. For many years, it was the dwelling place of freed slaves and later African American farmers and fishermen. By the 1930s, however, most were in their 70s and 80s, and few young people were left to carry on the old traditions. An excerpt from *Drums and Shadows* was a prediction of things to come, as reported in an interview with Aunt Hettie Campbell, then 72 and living in a small house near the waterfront amidst a surrounding arbor of flowers and shrubbery. Remarking that there were few young people thereabouts any more, she reminisced about the olden days:

> *I do remembuh the big times we use tuh have wen I wuz young. We does plenty uh dances in does days. Dance roun in a ring. . . . We shouts an sings all night and wen he sun rise, we stahts ta dance. It ain so long since hey stop that back in the woods, but these young people hey does new kines uh dances. . . . Music? They mosly have guitah now, an we use to but we make em frum goad an we beats drums too. We make em frum coon hide stretched ovah hoops.*

Hettie is long since gone, and visitors to St. Marys are not likely to run into any African Americans of the old school. But the Gullah influence lingers and can be found in the town's history, in monuments of the past, in many of the older homes that are sometimes hidden behind clusters of wisteria, draping Spanish moss, and palm, and always in the atmosphere and fragrance of the surroundings along the shore and the fishing docks up and down the rivers and the inlets.

CHAPTER 9

Feasting
the Stomach

Gullah foods, past and present, have become increasingly popular.
These dishes have been the subject of dozens of regional cookbooks not only
in the Sea Islands and Low Country but throughout the eastern United States
and the Midwest. Many recipes specialize according to the origins of the ingredients, such as the garden, the woods, the river, the creeks, the ponds, the
sea, the marshes, and the shore. The seasons come into play as well, as do holidays, festivals, religious dates, and family observances, in both the selection of
foods and the methods of cooking and preparation. As one experienced cook
explains, *"De crop gather time wus alluz big time. Ebrybody bring sum ob duh fus
crop to duh church an we prepeahs a big feas."* We see how recipes were originally
formulated in the villages of West Africa, brought in the minds of the slaves to
America, and transformed into everyday dishes, some of which were similar
to their origins and some of which were transformed because of the absence
of African components or the introduction of ingredients found in the Sea
Islands. Common Gullah foods and recipes include red rice, hoppin' john, okra
soup, shrimp and grits, collard greens, taters, smoked mullet, boiled peanuts,

Baskets like those shown with this street vendor were the ancestors of the famous sweetgrass baskets still seen in coastal areas of South Carolina and Georgia.
COURTESY OF THE COLLECTIONS OF
THE SOUTH CAROLINA HISTORICAL SOCIETY

corn bread, "Smokin Joe" butter beans, Frogmore stew, Low Country boil, and catfish gumbo.

⁂

"Love is one of the best kept secrets and main ingredients in Gullah food," wrote Veronica Davis Gerald in *The Ultimate Gullah Cookbook*. "However, of all the ingredients, it is most difficult to explain and to pass on in a recipe. For this reason, few books on this food culture attempt to include it. Some call it 'cooking from the heart'; others just call it *luv*. Whatever the preference, it is spiritual exchange between the hands and heart of the preparer and the food itself, a spiritual transfer of love from the cook to those who will eat the food prepared."

Ms. Gerald knows whereof she speaks. Of Gullah descent herself, she is a historian and a professor of English who has spent the better part of her life studying and preserving the culture of her people. "Around the Gullah table," she explains, "it is common to hear someone say, '*E put e fot en um dis time*' or '*Dey's a lot of luv in dis food.*' Expressions such as these mean that the cook has put so much of her or his energy and spirit into the preparation of the food that they transfer to the food and on to the recipient."[1]

Any study of the Gullah history and outlook will be enormously enhanced by learning more about the foods and recipes that are inherent in the culture, past and present, in all the regions in which these peoples have lived and frequented. We start with the basic ingredients, such as rice, okra, nuts, beans, fish, and game, and we examine the cooking utensils, most frequently a single large pot. "Gullah food is older than the South and as ancient as the world," says Ms. Gerald. "It is one of the oldest African American traditions being practiced today. The Africans brought to the Carolina colony, beginning in the 1600s, used the similarities between the Lowcountry and the West Coast of Africa to create a food culture that could come to characterize the region."[2] As she points out, it was ironic that rice, the grain that had been the staple in Africa for thousands of years, was the reason for the enslavement of the people associated with it. They were selected as slaves and brought to America for the simple reason that they were the world's greatest specialists in the growing of rice and would thus be valuable to those plantations in the Carolinas and Georgia that came to be known as the "rice plantations."

The descendant of the owner of one such plantation went so far as to say that the slaves were trapped by their own ability and ingenuity. In the 17th and 18th centuries, rice was planted, cultivated, and harvested entirely by hand, involving a crop cycle of one full year, starting each spring with the plowing of the fields by mules and oxen, the digging of trenches for the seeds, and the preparation of the seeds, which had to remain firmly embedded so they would not float to the surface when the fields were flooded.

Rice planting was a tricky business—more so than for most crops—because it necessitated many steps. Flooding, for example, required a "sprout flood" shortly after the seeds were planted, then another for the "first hoeing" (*"da fus hoe"*), and then the most permanent, the "long water" (*"da long waduh"*), which drenched the fields and eliminated insects, weeds, and any other infestations that might later harm the budding crop. As if that were not water enough, yet another partial draining and reflooding took place. In late spring, the water still remaining had to be drained off in order to start "dry cultivation," extensive hoeing, and after that yet another period of complete flooding in such a way that it supported the new plants, now heavy with emerging rice kernels. All along the way, the system required great personal attention on the part of the workers and constant supervision by the "head men," all of whom were slaves and most of whom had come by their skills long ago in Africa. Near the end of the year, essential skills included chopping and drying the rice, sheaving, threshing, winnowing, fanning, pounding, and husking—all to end up with the tiny morsels without breaking their grains.

For slaves, from generation to generation, rice was their work; rice was their sustenance; rice was their goal. Or as the Geechee saying went, "*Es da Geeche got a peck ah rice, dey'll outlive Methusla.*"

Josephine A. Beoku-Betts, who has authored one of the most comprehensive studies of Gullah foodways, cited one sea islander's words to the same effect: "Rice is security. If you have some rice, you'll never starve. It is a bellyful. You should never find a cupboard without it."[3] William S. Pollitzer, perhaps the most notable of all the anthropologists who have studied the Gullah culture in the past, had much to say about native foods, origins, preparation, and cooking.

In his classic book, *The Gullah People and Their African Heritage,* he wrote the following:

What we eat and how we eat it, products of culture, are reflected in the deposits left behind in the dust as archeology again supplements history. Of some dozen sites on the coast of South Carolina and Georgia that have yielded secrets of the past life of African Americans, especially rich are those from Couper's plantation at Cannon's Point on St. Simons Island from 1794 through 1860. Archeology of Barbados and Jamaica also provides important links between Africa, the West Indies, and the Low Country.

The careful analysis of animal remains from the slave quarters of Tidewater plantations shows that blacks supplemented their rations of corn, meal, rice, vegetables, and a little pork with whatever they could catch in the woods or the waterways, for the bones of wild animals and fish outnumber those of domestic animals two to one.

Lead shot, gun flints, and fish hooks in slave cabins give further evidence of this dietary supplement. Although the nutriment of the master class was similar to that of the slaves, the artifacts confirm the historical record of the enormous gap between the luxurious lifestyle of the planters and the poverty of the bondsmen. Both lived better on large plantations than on small ones, and both were better off than slaves on Barbados.

Remains in the earth show that the manner of partaking of food in the New World continued the habits of the Old. In West and Central Africa the starchy main dish of millet or rice or maize (after 1500) is usually boiled in a large jar; a vegetable relish with a little meat or fish added is cooked in a smaller one. The main dish is then served in a large bowl, the relish in smaller ones. Sitting on the ground in a group, native Africans take a ball of the starchy main dish in their hands and dip it into the relish. That this custom is widespread in space and time is borne out by travelers' accounts from Mali in 1352, the Gambia River in 1623, Sierra Leone in 1803, and Angola in 1865, down to the present-day Mossi and the Dukkawa of Nigeria. The communal African style of cooking, eating, and drinking, learned by children from their parents, survived in America. Such techniques may have furnished antecedents for the stewed hominy, potages, pileus, and "Hoppin' John" that sea-island slaves cooked in iron pots and served in ceramic bowls. The spade of the

archeologist confirms the memory of former slaves of Tidewater Georgia in the late 1930s who recalled how the old folks fresh from Africa sat
on the ground and ate with their fingers out of a bowl.

A good black cook created more than a satisfying meal; she also
perpetuated a culture that in effect moved slaves back toward their African roots. African food ways also influenced whites. Many insist that
okra soup doesn't taste right unless it is cooked slowly in an earthenware
vessel, and spices enrich Southern white cooking.[4]

Many of the foods that are familiar today in the South, and that are generally thought of as "American," originally arrived on slave ships from Africa.
Among these are not only the various types of rice, but okra, yams, peas, sorghum, sesame seeds, peanuts, certain kinds of berries, peppers, watermelon,
certain teas, various blends of coffee, and kola nuts, which were originally a
stimulant and then used in recipes for cola drinks. Because of the limited number of available utensils and cooking facilities, the slaves created many of the
single-pot dishes that are favorites among Gullahs today. The first ingredient,
of course, is always rice—whether white, brown, or otherwise—hence the tradition known as "the rice pot," for that treasured (and often antique) vessel in
which just about everything is cooked. Following that, almost anything in the
larder, fresh or otherwise, can follow, such as vegetables, seafood, chicken, ham,
bacon, nuts, and of course a variety of spices.

As Veronica Gerald tells it, in the early days the pots were difficult to clean
because the rice had a tendency to cake and resisted even the strongest soaps,
thus having to be scraped and scrubbed with a lot of elbow grease. The pot itself was considered more important than the recipes for which it was used, and
in between the preparation of more solid foods this vessel was the best recepta-
cle in which to simmer soups, which were often partial leftovers from the main
meal. It was considered to be very poor taste to leave an empty but scummy
rice pot soaking on the stove between meals. "Rather, it should be promptly
washed after each use and be ready, with a clean lid, for cooking at all times." As
a consequence, she says, "stories about the rice pot are a part of Gullah families
around the world."[5] A few of these included strong family disputes over which
child in a family was to be bequeathed a certain pot after the death of a parent
in whose possession it had been.

Over the years, the traditional Gullah cooking has of course been influenced by other cultures along the Gullah Corridor of the Carolinas and Georgia. Chiefly, these have been English, French, and Spanish influences, and in some regions the foods and cooking of American Indian tribes. In this respect we see chili peppers and hot sauces from Spanish speaking peoples who have arrived on American shores from the Caribbean; grits from the Old South cooks in cities such as Charleston and Savannah; corn bread from New Englanders who have escaped from cold winters to migrate southward; shellfish delicacies from cooks who have moved eastward from New Orleans; teas from visiting Asians; pastries from French expatriates; pastas from Italian newcomers; and roasts from the British.

Despite these influences, nothing can match the true Gullah ingredients in the cook pot, since there was very, very little that ever went to waste, whether the sources were field, forest, stream, ocean, or just plain backyard. In this respect, we see recipes that call for what to many are rather unappetizing ingredients, such as ox tails, fish bones, fins, snake livers, and frogs' eggs, in addition to various parts of the pig, including neck bones, hog maws, pigs' feet, jowls, ears, chitlins (intestines), and eyeballs.

A popular dish is neck bones 'n gravy, sometimes called "neck bones divine," made with pork neck bones, bell peppers, onions, rice, and almost anything else the cook wants to throw into the pot. Neck bones, which are almost never on the shopping list of non-Gullah cooks, are best if soaked in water for 30 minutes or so to remove salt, and then simmered for an hour and a half along with the other ingredients. Although there are increasingly numerous cookbooks and cooking articles that claim to provide Gullah recipes, anyone familiar with this specialty advises the reader that no decent Gullah cooks will be confined to a printed recipe. They will always alter the cooking to personal taste, adding or changing by instinct, governed in many ways by what their mothers and grandmothers did before them. Furthermore it is a lesson in frustration to try to associate the common names of recipes with any kind of gustatory rule. The list is almost poetic in nature, and certainly esoteric: *blacken fish, ketch uh da day, limpin' susan, hoppin' john, cracklin' bread, watermelon tea, conch bile, sat'day monin pancakes, fry bread,* and on and on and on.

An unexpected Gullah favorite is chitlins or "chits," whose prime ingredients are chitterlings (small intestines from hogs), a chunk of hog maw, celery, on-ions, peppers, and various spices according to the cook's taste. Only the best of cooks, however, can handle this recipe properly, since the chitterlings and maw have to be processed and cooked separately at the beginning, washed, and refrigerated overnight before they can even get to the mixing and cooking stage. Further boiling, simmering, combining, and flavoring make this dish a compli-cated one, not to be undertaken lightly by inexperienced chefs.

As Veronica Gerald describes in her *Ultimate Gullah Cookbook*, the tra-dition of eating chitlins is one that developed in America. It originated during plantation days when the slave families were given those parts of hogs and oth-er domestic animals that the white families did not want, including not only the intestines but also feet, jowls, ears, tails, maws, and heads. As Gerald explained, "Adaptive and creative cooks learned to clean them and prepare them in the most delectable way so much that the desire for the meat crossed into freedom and remains today an expected and anticipated dish at all big celebrations and occasions." Her comments did not come from a history book but from personal experience in the Sea Islands. "On hog killing days, when we were children, the steam from the chitterlings could be seen like fog in the cold air when they were taken out of the warm bellies of the hogs. Before they made it to the Gullah table, however, there was the long, arduous process of cleaning and preparing them to be cooked." As can be imagined, the initial task of removing, cutting, separating, and cleaning alone was one that few people—even slaves—could face. "Even today," says Veronica, "great respect is given to those who *'kin clean chitlins.'* Most Gullah will not eat chitlins from *'jis anybody.'"*[6]

Transplanted Food Sources

Where did the many foods and food substances associated with the Gullah culture originate? According to the *Low Country Gullah Culture Special Resource Study*,

Africa is home to many life-sustaining crops, including nine cereals,
half a dozen root crops, five oil producing plants, a dozen forage crops,

a dozen vegetables, three fruits and nuts, coffee, sesame, and the ancient and ubiquitous bottle gourd or calabash useful as a drinking cup, float for fishnet, or sound box for music. West Africa alone is the locus of origin of cereals such as Guinea millet, African rice, pearl millet, and sorghum; cowpeas, okra, some species of yam, oil palm, and the akee apple, as well as varieties of cotton.

Valuable plants were also imported into Africa from other continents. When Spanish and Portuguese galleons sailed between the Old World and the New, they carried more than people and treasure; they engaged in the greatest transport of plants and animals the globe has ever known. Among nineteen species from Central and South America transplanted to Africa, none is more important for feeding humanity and has a more colorful history than corn or maize (*Zea mays*). Known from Mexico by 5000 B.C., it extended from Canada to southern Argentina at the time of the European contact with the Americas.

As colonists learned from the Indians how to cultivate this major food crop, it became the bridge by which European civilization gained a foothold in the New World. Brought by the Portuguese and Dutch from Guiana and Brazil, it was known on the coast of West Africa perhaps as early as 1502 and clearly by 1525. Names for maize in local languages correlate with its entrance through trading centers like Port Harcourt in Nigeria. By the seventeenth century, it was an important foodstuff from Uberia to the Niger Delta, especially on the Gold Coast and Dahomey; established as a valuable crop in the Congo Basin and Angola; and significant for provisioning slave ships. Tobacco, peanuts, cacao, and beans, first grown in Latin America, also spread to Africa. Africans brought to South Carolina were thus familiar with cultivation of many useful crops. . . . Of at least nineteen plants introduced by Africans into the Americas, most flourished in the West Indies, including some varieties of yams, the akee apple, the Angola or pigeon pea, broad beans, maroon cucumber, senna, bichy nut, and oil palm. At least six more were also brought into Carolina.

Best known from West Africa is that tasty mucilaginous vegetable, okra or gumbo (*Abelmoschus esculentus*). First domesticated in tropical Africa, it spread widely along the Guinea coast and into the Cameroons by the time of the slave trade and was brought to the Americas in the 1600s. Words for it are found in many African languages. Since "okra" is from *nkruman* in the language of the Gold Coast and "gumbo" is from *tshingombo* in Bantu languages, the popularity of this plant is evident.

Benne seed, from a word in Bambara and Wolof, is also called sesame (*Sesamum indicum*). Probably first domesticated in East Africa, it was widespread on the continent at the time of the slave trade as a valuable source of oil. In 1730 Thomas Lowndes of South Carolina sent samples of oil made from "sesamum" to the Lords of the Treasury. Best known today on cookies or in candies, it was brought with blacks to Carolina, where it was also used in soups and puddings.

The black-eyed or cow pea (*Vigna unguiculata*) is an import from West and Central Africa that found its way to the West Indies and the Low Country. First domesticated at the margin of the forest and savannah in tropical West Africa, its seeds are known from Kintampo in central Ghana as early as 1800 B.C. and at Zimbabwe in southeast Africa by 1000 A.D.; it flourishes especially in Ghana, Benin, and Nigeria today, and names for it are also found in many African languages. Introduced into the New World tropics by the Spanish no later than the seventeenth century to supply towns and missions, it was known in the southern United States by the early eighteenth century.

The circular route of the peanut (*Arachis hypogaea*) is unique. Taken from Brazil to Africa around 1500 by the Portuguese, it established a secondary center in the Congo [and] was widespread in West Africa by 1600. Fed to slaves on ships to Virginia, peanuts spread to South Carolina. Eggplant, originally cultivated in India, was brought by Arabs into Spain and by Persians into Africa before the arrival of Europeans. Widespread from Senegal to Cameroon, it is known not only as a food but also as a medicine and as a symbol of fertility. Watermelon (*Citrullus lanatus*), a native of the dry savannah of east and south Africa, was grown in the Nile valley by 2000 B.C., and brought to Florida by Spanish colonists in the middle of the sixteenth century.[7]

Natural Relationships

Dr. Josephine Beoku-Betts, whose roots are in Sierra Leone in West Africa, is a professor at the University of Georgia in the Department of Sociology and is very conversant with the subject of native foods. The following is an extract from her essay "Connections Between the Natural Environment and Gullah Food Practices."

The value of self-sufficiency in food supply is an integral aspect of the Gullah food system. Men and women of all ages are conversant with hunting, fishing, and gardening as ways to provide food. From an early age, both men and women are socialized into the concept and the practice of self-sufficiency as a primary goal of the food system and are encouraged to participate in the outdoor food-procuring activities of parents and other kin or community members. Velma Moore, a woman in her mid-40s, became sensitive to environmental causes when, as a child, she accompanied both her parents on daily walks in the woods. This experience taught her a variety of survival skills involving the use of the island's natural resources for subsistence and medicine. She learned how and where to collect medicinal herbs, and when and for what purpose they should be used. She also learned various folk remedies that had been passed down in her family for generations, such as life everlasting tea for colds, or leaves of the mullein plant for fever. Velma recollected that when she was a child, her mother kept these herbs on hand in the kitchen and stood over a reluctant patient to make sure every sip of the tea was consumed. Now married and the mother of five children, Velma pointed out that she encourages the practice of these traditions among her sons and daughters.

Grandparents also play an important role in developing children's skills in food self-sufficiency. A typical example was Maisie Gables, a lively and active woman about 70 years of age. When I interviewed Miss Maisie, as she was called, I did not know that our scheduled appointments conflicted with her plans to go fishing with her five-year-old granddaughter, whom she was teaching to fish. Miss Maisie explained later that her granddaughter liked fishing from an early age, so she had decided to cultivate this interest by teaching her the necessary skills, as she had once been taught by her mother. By transmitting these skills, which are part of collective memory, the senior generation of Gullah women fosters and sustains cultural identity inter-generationally, thus broadening the base of cultural knowledge in the community.

While the Gullah depend on their natural surroundings as a reliable source of food, they also have a deep understanding of their coexistence with other living things and believe that the use of these resources should be moderate and non-exploitative. This sense of shared membership in the natural environment stems from Gullah belief systems, which emphasize harmony and social exchange between the human and the natural world. Such a view is influenced by African spiritual beliefs, which are community centered and involve a set of relationships involving God, the ancestors, other human beings (including those yet unborn), and other living and nonliving things. In this complex system of relationships, the well-being of the whole is paramount; individual existence is woven into the whole.

Some aspects of this world view are reflected in my interview with Velma Moore. She describes herself as a self-taught woman, although "self-taught" does not adequately describe her intelligence, strong will, and vast knowledge of Gullah history and culture. During one interview, she revealed that she, like many Gullah women, had been taught to hunt and would do so if necessary. Even so, she considered herself a keen environmentalist, with concern for the protection of nature, and would not engage in such activities for recreation because "it is not sporting to go up and kill animals that can't shoot you back." In other words, although she would rely on these resources for survival, anything beyond that purpose would threaten the harmony with nature.

Jonathan Green, long acknowledged as one of the top-ranking Gullah artists in the Sea Islands, is noted for his vibrant paintings that show a sense of jubilation and cover all aspects of life and backgrounds in the land he loves. An expert in the Gullah traditions of the kitchen, he had this to say about his experience with foods, cooking, and the traditions of native families:

> My community in the late 1950s and early 1960s constituted a small, closely knit, rural African American settlement of people referred to in South Carolina as Gullahs. My community, which was near the Sea Islands, was nestled among the inland marshes. It was in many ways more isolated than the Sea Islands, and the community was quite self-sufficient as well as interdependent.
>
> Farming, hunting, fishing, and raising farm animals were common in all families. The community shared with one another, often through barter. My grandmother would feed anyone who came, often farm laborers and people from the community who were experiencing hardship. Her home served as the community hub, as she was a lay minister in the local church. She practiced many of the oral traditions passed down through the generations and shared folk tales with eager listeners.
>
> Religious life was a strong part of the community. Historical traditions brought from Africa (Angola) such as dream interpretation and

sharing spiritual folk tales were very important. Many of the children, including myself, were expected to meditate for several days and share their dreams with the elders before being baptized in the church. It was only through the interpretation of the dreams that one was determined ready for baptism.

The community had a set of customs and mores that guided social behavior. The church was central to the social activities of community life, such as baptism, marriages, funerals, and worship. It was the sense of community that I experienced through the church, my grandmother, and subsequently my mother that instilled in me a deep belief in the value of self, life, and others—a value that I hope continues to be revealed and communicated through my art, a value that reflects that all people have purpose and meaning, and should always be treated with dignity and respect.

Food and Celebrations

For many years, Gullah foods have been served at Penn Center on St. Helena Island on special occasions, such as the Heritage Days festival, held annually in November. Among the most popular with traditional origins and preparation are hoppin' john, a combination of peas and rice hoe cake, a pan bread made of dough consisting either of corn meal or flour, mixed with salt and water, and cooked in a greased iron skillet that makes the ingredients "hop"; gumbos made with either meats or fish or leftovers of any kind; sweetwater tea, which is basically fresh water sweetened with sugar or molasses; perlo, a one-pot meal of rice with a vegetable and meat, shrimp, or fish; collard greens; and swimp 'n grits, made from shrimp simmered in a brown gravy and mixed with grits. When Penn Center was known as Penn School, which was until its closing at the end of the 1940s, it offered courses in cooking, and many of the classroom recipes and projects have survived to this day, mainly coming to light on special occasions when groups such as Elderhostel hold seminars there or when the public is invited to attend colorful festivals and educational courses, such as the Gullah Studies Summer Institute. In addition to foods and dishes previously mentioned, Penn and a nearby Gullah restaurant in Frogmore, South Carolina, give visitors a taste of such delicacies as jambalaya, panygetta, bops, ratifia pudding, calabash, chicken bog, possum, tipsy pudding, stickies, taters, okra daube, pinebark stew (which has fish but no pinebark), and red horse bread. As the old-time slave quarters cooks used to say about the plantation ladies who were their mistresses, "*White folks vittles aint got no suption*," meaning that they had no flavor.

Subsistence farming and fishing were the most reliable sources of family food and, in some cases, income. It was only natural that the Gullah civilization was highly dependent on fields, forests, rivers, inlets, and bays for native fish and game. The shores of the Sea Islands have readily reached sources of shrimp (*swimp*), oysters, crabs, and other shellfish; the surrounding bays and oceans contain common fish of many species and sizes; the ponds have catfish, turtles, and eels; and the woods, though losing ground to housing developments, are still plentiful sources of quail, venison, 'coon, duck, and shad. For those who prefer liquid refreshment with more of a kick than sweetwater tea, there is dewberry wine, blackberry wine, muscadine sherry, plum beer, rice brew, scuppernong, syllabub, and pokeberry brandy, among other alcoholic beverages. It was interesting to note that during the 1930s and other eras of financial depression in the South, when many white families and whole communities subsisted almost at the starvation level, the Gullah peoples suffered few crises in the matter of foods for their tables. The natural world around them, with its sources of edibles, remained relatively unchanged. Also, all through the Great Depression, the people who suffered most in the surrounding white communities—the aged, the very young, and the disabled—were nourished and protected by the Gullah tradition of close-knit family members caring for each other.

A Gullah Cook's Point of View

If you would like to view the situation from the standpoint of a Gullah cook, here is what has been recorded as "A Slave Recipe for Cooking Rice," recommended by a former slave from Brookgreen Plantation:

Fus ting yo roll up yo sleeves es high es yo kin, en yo tak soap en yo wash yo han clean. Den yo wash yo pot clean. Fill um wid col wata en put on da fia. Now wile yo wait de wata de bile, yo put yo rice een a piggin en yo wash well. Den wen yo dun put salt een yo pot, en bile high. Yo put yo rice een en le um bile till e swell, den yo pour off de wata en yo pot back o de stove, fo steam.

The Old Plantation was painted circa 1790. The two female figures are playing the shegureh, an instrument used by women of the Mende and neighboring tribes in Sierra Leone.

CHAPTER 10

Festivals and Celebrations

Each year more and more events are planned up and down the Gullah Corridor, the Sea Islands, and the Low Country to celebrate the many aspects of the Gullah heritage and history in whole or in part. These range from small gatherings where a few hundred people may come together for a day or two of remembrances about their culture to large celebrations that take several days or a week and host many thousands of visitors of all races and denominations. Other events, such as the Gullah Studies Summer Institute, are more educational in nature, with seminars and lectures about many subjects, including language, customs, religion, health, training, and the environment. Some of the key occasions with large attendances include Heritage Days at Penn Center in November; the Native Islander Gullah Celebration; Black History Month in February, with many different happenings and exhibits; the Gullah Festival in Beaufort; the Georgia Sea Islands Festival; and the Sweetgrass Festival. These occasions often include many of the arts, such as literature, performances, and exhibits, and almost without exception there are plenty of ways for visitors and participants to feast the stomach, as well as the mind, ears, eyes, and heart.

Gullah Celebrations

T he numbers of festivals, feasts, holidays, and other events recognizing the Gullah culture have increased noticeably over just the past two decades in the Sea Islands and Low Country. In addition there have been many proliferations of small businesses and individual engagements devoted exclusively to this culture, including dress and gift boutiques, art galleries, specialized grocery markets, bookstores, language courses, and museums. The origins of a few of these events and establishments can be traced, directly and indirectly, to Penn Center itself—the former school for freed slaves that was founded in 1862 and is today a center of much Gullah activity, especially in the York W. Bailey Museum, with its collections, library, and regular exhibits of Gullah arts and artifacts.

One of the most notable commemorations of the Gullah culture is the Heritage Days celebration, inaugurated in 1982, which is held during five days in November at Penn and which attracts thousands of people. It is always highlighted by a Gullah theme, which changes from year to year. A recent one, for example, was *"De Ole Sheep Done Know de Road! De Young Lamb Mus Find E Way,"* which showcased the history of Penn School and celebrated the abundant cultural legacy of the Gullah people of the Sea Islands. It touted such popular favorites as the Hallelujah Singers, Ron and Natalie Daise, and Aunt Pearlie Sue and her Gullah Kinfolk. On the grounds there are always many other attractions, with authentic presentations of basketry, storytelling, netmaking, braiding, quilting, sculpturing, and bateau (boat) construction. Also featured regularly are old-fashioned prayer services, art exhibits, a cultural symposium, education seminars, fish fries, oyster roasts, blues performances, a fashion show, a student talent show, films, and a traditional crafts fair. Programs run concurrently for all ages, so that family members can enjoy what each one likes without having to sit around waiting their turn. *"Fun Fuh de Chillun"* is a boon for parents who want fun time for themselves as well.

For visitors who want something more remote, a small island off the Carolina shore offers Daufuskie Day, founded in 1976 and usually held in June as a commemoration of folkways, foodways, and other cultural features. For visitors as well as natives, one of the most popular delicacies—on holidays or at any time of the year when in season—is spicy, succulent, home-cooked deviled crab. Daufuskie, the last in the islands that make up Beaufort County, South Carolina, became famous through the noted author Pat Conroy, who wrote a best-selling book, *The Water Is Wide* (later a popular film), about his life as a teacher in the one-room schoolhouse that served as the only source of education for generations of children. Until recently, when much of this small island was unfortunately taken over for golf courses, Daufuskie typified the small, remote, and hard-to-reach islands of the Gullah people, accessible only by small boats. It was the subject of lawsuits against developers who, among other things, were blocking ages-old accesses to some of the graves and religious properties of Gullah families who had lived there since slave days and who were members of the historic and hallowed First Union African Baptist Church.

To the north and on the mainland, the charming old town of Beaufort, South Carolina, has long used the Memorial Day weekend for its particular Gullah Festival, held along the recently refurbished and expanded Henry C. Chambers Waterfront Park, with its boat quay at the north bend of the Beaufort River. The attractions are multitudes of booths with native foods aplenty, folk arts, ceramics, publications, and other commodities, and, on all sides where there are open spaces, plenty of music, dancing, theatrics, and outdoor tables. This celebration in particular was greatly enhanced after the publication of *Daughters of the Dust*, a novel by Julie Dash, a prominent African American writer, producer, and director, which was later made into a film that won the Best Cinematography award at the 1991 Sundance Film Festival. As a result of Dash's works, Beaufort's Gullah Festival has been transformed into something much larger, attracting visitors from far beyond the Sea Islands and Low Country.

All festivals and celebrations include a growing number of performers of traditional Gullah/Geechee music. The National Park Service study reports, "Many of these groups reach out to their audience and create an instinctive performance that enables those in attendance to share in the singing, clapping, and rhythms of the music." Among the most notable of these are the McIntosh County Shouters; the Georgia Sea Island Singers; the Moving Star Hall Singers of Johns Island, South Carolina; the Brotherhood Gospel Singers of Mount Pleasant, South Carolina; and the Plantation Singers of Charleston,

South Carolina. Appreciation of traditional music has increased to the point that some groups such as the Hallelujah Singers, who are not native Gullah/ Geechee people, are now performing the music.

Frankie Quimby, leader of the Georgia Sea Island Singers, says, "I'm a firm believer that you can't know where you're going until you realize where you've come from. We have dedicated our lives to trying to preserve that rich heritage and culture that our ancestors handed down to us. . . . The McIntosh County Shouters of Bolden, Georgia, are among the last active practitioners of one of the most venerable of African American song, rhythm, and movement traditions, the shout, also known as the ring shout. The tradition of the shout itself is actually in the fervor of the hand clapping and audible footwork, rather than in the song."

Arts and Crafts

The most important and best known craft associated with African Americans, and particularly those with strong Gullah backgrounds, is coiled sweetgrass basketry. The skills go back to the 17th century in America, where on southern plantations there was a continuing need for carrying foods and household supplies but very little in the way of cloth or fabric with which to make bags or sacks. The solution came when some unknown person or persons realized that the grasses growing in the marshlands of the Carolinas were sturdy and flexible enough to shape baskets of many sizes and shapes. Not only were these vessels of utilitarian value in the slave quarters and fields, but one type, known as the "fanner basket," became an essential tool in the processing of rice at that stage of its cultivation when it was necessary to separate the ripe kernel from the husk. The workers in the field, equipped with the proper size and shape of sweetgrass basket, simply tossed the rice into the air and caught it cleanly in a basket as the chaff blew away. This was known as "fanning the rice." Some of the baskets, because of their relatively large size, were conveniently used by mothers for carrying their infants!

Traditional baskets that can be found on sale throughout the Southeast are most likely to resemble those that were designed and fashioned in Angola and the Congo, although over the past century or so they have been found in increasingly elaborate and intricate designs—some to such a degree that they are more ornamental than utilitarian. But in many Gullah households and kitchens they are used as serving or storage containers or handbags. One of the problems in the production of these baskets, however, is that the steady disappearance of marshlands and seashore grasslands because of developers has made it increasingly difficult to find stands of sweetgrass. As a result, many basket makers (referred to commonly as "sewers") now combine the grasses with long leaf pine needles, which adds to the products since they incorporate an attractive element of design.

Encyclopedia of Africa: South of the Sahara describes two methods of basketry that slaves carried with them in their minds and experiences to the plantations of the South. The first is the Old World method of plaiting, where braids of wood strips, reeds, grasses, and sometimes roots are twined or twilled into patterns, of which there were many. However, it is from the second method that the Gullah sweetgrass baskets descend. As it is explained, "Sewn basketry, often called coil-sewn, involves a thin continuous foundation, usually of grass, which is sewn spirally on itself, using split palm leaf, raffia, or similar fiber. Some baskets are so tightly sewn that they can be used for containers of liquid, being watertight when the fibers have swelled. Other sewn basketry may have the foundation elements plaited or lying in parallel rows, sewn together, and then sewn to the rest of the basket."[1] Although not common in the Sea Islands, basketry is used occasionally, as it is in Africa, for roof and wall paneling, fish and animal traps, strainers, clothing, hats, and ceremonial dance masks.

Charleston, South Carolina, is one of the major centers of basket making, an outgrowth of the time at the end of the 19th century when this very "southern" city produced almost all of the crafts in the Sea Islands and was a training center for a wide variety of crafts and occupations, including iron making, woodworking, coopering, blacksmithing, stone masonry, maritime carpentry, leather crafting, and shoe making. Charleston's reputation for basketry started around 1916, when a white entrepreneur, Clarence Legerton, formed the Sea Grass Basket Company on King Street and sold the baskets not only in local shops but also in a growing mail-order business. One of the most talented in this art is Jery Bennett-Taylor, a descendant of the West Africans of Sierra Leone, where this unique style of coil basket weaving originated. Born and raised in the town of Mount Pleasant, South Carolina, she learned the weaving art at her grandmother's knee, starting at the age of five. Although she studied medical administration, in which she could have had a successful career, her skills and real interests were in basket weaving, and she is represented in a display at the Smithsonian in Washington, D.C.

A fine example of a celebration of this art is the Sweetgrass Festival at Christ Church Parish in Mount Pleasant, South Carolina. This event focuses almost entirely on the delicate skills of the basket makers, whose legacy is traced back to West Africa, where the technique was developed over many generations. Although baskets and basket makers can be found throughout the Sea Islands, the Mount Pleasant area, to the northwest of Charleston, is the center of the art in America. Few people—even the basket makers themselves—can explain to lay persons how these intricate baskets are designed and woven. The basic patterns begin with a knot or long row, which is gradually extended round and round and upward until the basket reaches its desired size. As for the shape and style, unbelievably graceful in baskets of museum quality, the maneuvering of fingers and grass are mathematically unexplainable, requiring skills that the weavers have developed over many years and etched into their memories, bit by bit, as they moved from the basic steps to increasingly intricate ones. The Sweetgrass Festival is part of Charleston's annual Spoleto celebration, which is traditionally held in June and includes not only arts and crafts but also music, theater, opera, choreography, and other traditional performances.

Another important Gullah center of arts and crafts is the Sea Islands of Georgia, in places such as St. Simons, Yamacraw, Sapelo Island, and Wilmington Island. There have been a number of exciting archaeological digs in places where early civilizations of Gullah people left evidence behind. These included drums made of hollow logs with pegged heads that were probably used for religious music or dancing, carved wooden walking sticks with spirals of snakes, remains of dugout bateaus not unlike American Indian canoes, stone pots, graveyard relics, and other signs of the lost culture.

One of Georgia's enduring riches is its native folk art, the labors of artisans whose skills had been handed down from generations of their antecedents in West Africa. Their works are called traditional and fall into the "folk art" category, but they were largely self-taught, adapting their personal skills and ingenuity to family and community situations that were very different from those of their forebears. During the Civil War period and for many years afterward, the South faced severe limitations of products and supplies that had previously come from northern factories and shops. Handcrafting came to the fore and continued throughout the 1800s, spurred by the fact that most people, especially the Gullahs, lived at the poverty level. The women in these rural communities became experts not only at basket making but also spinning, weaving, and dyeing, using the local indigo plants grown and harvested during slave days and afterward along the coast to produce the typical indigo blue color, as well as black and shades of brown. Quilting was also one of the most common handicrafts of Gullah women in Georgia, transforming assortments of old rags, torn clothing, and sometimes even the more flexible marsh grasses into objects of beauty as well as utility. Many of the more experienced slave quilters were called upon by the mistresses of their plantations to teach them how to make quilts as a hobby, and thus they enjoyed a few more perks than their less-accomplished neighbors.

The male Gullahs of the Georgia coast were noted for their useful home products of clay, stone, and pottery for cooking, serving, and storing. Much of this field of handicrafts originated with slaves making bricks for their masters, forming the bricks in wooden molds and using the familiar red clay of Georgia. Stone working became a part of the culture because of the tradition of making grave markers and other objects connected with religious observances and native cemeteries. Today, in part as a result of this basic "down-to-earth" need, stone masonry and pottery have surfaced, along with baskets, as products much sought after by tourists during festivals and holiday observances.

Woodworking skills are evident in Georgia, as well as all along the Corridor. This skill owes its origins in part to slave days, when male slaves on plantations had to undertake some of the more laborious jobs of repairing plantation homes, building their own family shacks from the crudest wood supplies, chair-making, and constructing small boats for fishing along the bays, creeks, and tidal inlets. As a result, many of the males in each small community became adept as carpenters, and later even as cabinetmakers, and could do wonders with nothing more than a pocket knife and a chunk of yellow pine. In some regions, the whittling of canes became something of a specialty. Along with boat building, many men—and boys as well—became specialists in the knotting and weaving of fishnets and ropes.

Horses and carriages were of prime importance on the plantations of Georgia—as well as in every other region where there were plantations—and the toughest, dirtiest, and most labor-intensive jobs in the stables and fields fell to the lot of the slaves. Those who ascended from the lowest tasks, such as cleaning stables and disposing of slops, undertook assignments to repair, and sometimes make, equipment needed for horses, carriages, and stalls. Thus there evolved a small coterie of slaves who eventually became cobblers, saddlers, harness makers, and even shoemakers, and who handed down these skills and trades to following generations. Along the way, they also became skilled at processing and tanning leather from horses, cows, sheep, and goats. Thus, whenever and wherever there is a true Gullah festival, visitors are likely to find, in one or more stalls, some excellent selections of leather goods.

One of the most colorful and fascinating events along the Corridor is the annual Georgia Sea Islands Festival, sponsored by the St. Simons African-American Heritage Coalition and held appropriately in the early summer on St. Simons Island. Visitors and locals alike can enjoy arts and crafts, blues, jazz, storytellers, dancers, drummers, children's corners, a spiritual/gospel extravaganza, and enough food, merchandise, exhibits, excitement, history, and culture—and even healing—to satisfy them that the Gullah Nation, as it is sometimes referred to, has a great deal to offer.

This event is rivaled by others along the Sea Islands and in the Low Country, one of which is the annual Native Islander Gullah Celebration on Hilton Head Island, South Carolina, which presents many of the same features as those on St. Simons Island. Held in February, a "slow month" for tourism, it is designed largely to help the local population understand and appreciate the rich heritage that exists on the island and to help preserve as many aspects of the old Gullah culture as possible in the midst of a thriving community of tourists, vacationers, and permanent home owners—a far cry from what the island was like in the past. The past is always spoken of as "before the bridge," the days when the island was a strictly rural community, separated from the mainland by a barrier of open water and accessible only by small boats and a somewhat intermittent ferry. One of the vital features of this delightful festival, however, is a serious symposium where panelists and audiences of people from the Sea Islands, the Caribbean, and Africa gather to learn about and share the history of the Gullah culture as it relates to their unique life experiences.

Fine Arts

Even back in the slave days, there was evidence that the ancient tradition of art on the African continent had not been lost in the tragedy and turmoil of the forced journeys to America. Here and there in the Sea Islands, individuals and groups, though in bondage, managed to create crude drawings and later paintings and sculpture that are today recognized for their genius and worth. One of the most unusual African American artists was Bill Traylor, who was born on a plantation in 1856 and who died in 1947. By the end of his long span of life, he was judged to be "one of the most important 20th-century artists the United States has produced."[2] He was described in his 80s as "an imposing presence, a large, quiet, full-bearded man, about six feet, four inches tall, and bald." But the most curious fact of his life and work is that his career did not begin in slave days, but in 1939 when, at the age of 83, he picked up a pencil stub and began drawing pictures of people and animals on scraps of cardboard. A young friend who was an artist became intrigued with his unique style and ability to capture action with little more than dark stick figures and scenes reminiscent of the work of children in kindergarten. From that auspicious day on, he worked full-time, largely on the streets of Montgomery, Alabama, where he chatted amiably with passers-by, many of whom became intrigued by his animated renderings of people, animals, birds, crude buildings, and geometric forms. He confined his art supplies to paper (often very crude), pencils, charcoal, crayons, and snippets of paint, and rarely ever erased or made corrections.

One of the earliest Gullah artists to obtain recognition in the United States was Henry Ossawa Tanner, who was the son of a minister in the African Methodist Episcopal Church. In 1879 he enrolled in the Pennsylvania Academy of Fine Arts, under the tutelage of the noted Thomas Eakins, before moving to Atlanta, Georgia, to try to subsist as a painter. He depicted African Americans as subjects with a dignity that had been lacking in previous art, where they were usually caricatures or overly sentimental figures in great poverty. "Many of the artists who have represented Negro life," he wrote, "have seen only the comic, the ludicrous side of it, and have lacked sympathy with, and appreciation for, the warm big heart that dwells within such a rough exterior."[3] In 1894, in contrast to the usual depiction of banjo players as down-and-outers strumming their lives away in vain, he painted *The Banjo Lesson*, a portrait of a man teaching a youngster that became a classic of love and warmth.

The story of another African American artist, William Henry Johnson, is one of personal tragedy. Born in Florence, South Carolina, in 1901, he grew up in poverty and with little education, doing fieldwork to help keep his mother and siblings from starvation. As a youngster, he began copying comics in the dirt with such skill that one of his teachers gave him supplies and encouraged him to study art, which resulted in his decision to go to New York to attend the National Academy of Design. With financial support and great determination, he did well, winning a number of awards. In the 1930s, although having earned a reputation as a landscape painter, he began to devote more and more time to what he termed a "primitive" style, using bright and contrasting colors and two-dimensional figures to depict African Americans and everyday figures, often of a religious nature. But Johnson was destined to be plagued by bad luck. A fire destroyed much of his work and possessions; his wife died of breast cancer; the beginning of World War II saw a lessening of public interest in his field of art; and to top it all off, he suffered an ever-worsening mental illness that destroyed his ability to paint. Confined and hospitalized after being found wandering and lost in the streets, he never painted again.

The story of Sam Doyle, considered to have been one of the top Gullah artists, is much brighter. As a child in the early 1900s on St. Helena Island, South Carolina, he attended school only until the sixth grade. Having exhibited skills as an artist, he was offered an opportunity to leave his island and go to New York City to study. But he refused out of loyalty to his family's impoverished condition and elected to remain in the location he loved, which became the backdrop for many of his most noted paintings. The isolated rural atmosphere of St. Helena was an ideal blend for his subject matter, which depicts an eclectic mix of historical events, members of the community, and religious imagery.

As a self-taught artist, Doyle began painting not on the characteristic artist's canvas but on wood, sheet metal, cloth, and almost anything handy that would hold paint. His subjects ranged from island characters, such as *Dr. Buzz*, a voodoo practitioner, to *The First Football Game on St. Helena Island* and religious scenes and people. He was well known for his deep commitment to the local community and made it a practice to display his art in the yard around his house, replacing paintings as he sold them and often giving paintings away for charitable purposes.

One of Sam Doyle's special awards was given to Richard Dennis White, an artist and musician and native of Beaufort, South Carolina. Despite his dedication to art, White left it temporarily to enter the military and afterward took on a truck-driving job to pay the rent. When an accident left him unable to do physical work, he returned to his art but found that painting left him unfulfilled. It so happened that his career took a turn for the better when one day, while tossing out some pieces of wood, he spotted a pattern of sorts in the grain. He glued two chunks together, started whittling away, and, lo and behold, had an art object. This was his first wood carving, entitled *Cerebral Island*, showing a mask in the foreground and a painted island, palm tree, and full moon in the background. His wood carvings, including one of the most popular, *Old Man Playing the Guitar*, have received further awards for what one critic terms "the Gullah experience."

Joe Pinckney, who died of kidney failure in 2005, was a Gullah descended from enslaved Africans who came to his art late in life. He did not complete his first Gullah painting until 1970, when he became interested in the subject in discussions with some fellow native islanders. "It was an extraordinary kind of art," explains Emory Campbell, a longtime friend and former Executive Director of Penn Center, "because Joe did such a great job portraying Gullah life and people and all of the traditions of the Gullah culture." Pinckney, a South Carolinian, was always one of the favorite exhibit artists during Heritage Days, the Gullah celebration on the Penn campus each November. His paintings, such as one entitled *Daufuskie Island Road*, tend to have more detail and fewer bright colors than some of the characteristic Gullah palettes. This particular scene is typical of Pinckney, depicting a single-room Gullah house of the early 20th century, on short pilings, with a simple porch, tin roof, and crooked steps, a curving mud road, crude fences, two women working, a live oak, and a background of bushes and smaller trees.

James Denmark, who was born in Winter Haven, Florida, in 1936 into a family of artists, was influenced by Dr. Samella Lewis, who exposed him to the traditions of the African American art movement. He was also influenced by several others in the same school, including Norman Lewis (1909–79), who focused on African American life in Harlem; Romare Bearden (1911–88), a North Carolinian who was noted for book illustrations, costume design, and political cartoons relating to black America; and Ernest Crichlow (1914–2005), who, with Bearden and Lewis, organized what is thought to be the earliest gallery exhibition of black artists. Denmark, who was also a sculptor, was eulogized by a fellow African American, who said of him, "James Denmark has plunged himself heart and soul into his craft, and as a technician he has mastered the difficult medium of collages. However, his importance as an artist reaches far beyond that. His work reveals deep commitment to restoring us to our dignity as human beings and as a race."[4] He exhibited a special skill with collages, watercolors, and woodcuts, and is particularly identified by his improvisational style, brightly handcrafted fabrics, and intermingled objects.

If there is any one artist today who most exemplifies Gullah art and printmaking, it is likely to be Jonathan Green, who not only paints as an artist but also is known for his generosity in donating works to various Gullah causes and programs throughout the Sea Islands. He was born and raised in the small Gullah community of Gardens Corner, South Carolina, a typical farming enclave on the mainland near the historical coastal town of Beaufort. He was raised by his maternal grandmother in a matriarchal society where traditions—especially oral ones—played a basic part in the upbringing of children and young people. Even as a small child, he was continuously curious about the world around him. "I was always interested in things, in how crafts were done," he said in an interview, "who everyone's relatives were and the religious functions of the community. I had all this stuff in my head, but I didn't have a place for it until I started painting. . . . My culture is in me, and my art is connected to the spiritual, mental, and social concerns of the global environment."[5] One of the major objectives in his art has been to translate the Gullah life he knew and appreciated as a youth into aesthetic renderings, which have won many awards in America and are meaningful to viewers regardless of their color or education.

De Aarts Ob We De People X

Despite the colorful, somewhat perplexing name, this is a Gullah organization of talented people who support each other in their common skills, bring their art before the public, and hold regular exhibitions at art centers in the Low Country. The group is sponsored by the Native Business and Community Affairs Association on Hilton Head Island, an African American fraternity of business people who are dedicated to helping their fellow citizens in their professional careers. In addition to several of the previously mentioned artists, *De Aarts Ob We De People X* includes a number of other talented members.

Natalie Daise, already mentioned in this book for her skills as a folk artist and for her Gullah storytelling on national television channels, is skilled at designing and making colorful furniture, ceramics, and other functional pieces in her workshop.

Diane Britton Dunham has been recognized internationally for her depictions of the Low Country culture and is a mixed media artist and instructor known for her brilliant coloring, intricate human and landscape forms, and themes that represent both the Creole history and the Gullah lands and traditions.

Allen Fireall is a native of Savannah, Georgia, who was raised by his Gullah grandparents and speaks the Gullah language fluently. He started to draw and paint at an early age and skillfully used the resources of the public school, art books, and his immediate surroundings for the subjects in his paintings. He is known for contributing his time and talent to helping youngsters who show abilities in any fields relating to art and creativity.

James E. St. Clair has been recognized the world over for his popular series of paintings, which include *Low Country Folktales*, *The Adventures of Geechee Joe and Gullah Girl*, and *The Misadventure of the Chickens*. A clever adapter of materials at hand, he is known for painting with acrylics on a wide assortment of surfaces, including not only traditional canvas but also paper, clayboard, masonite, plywood, natural wood, metal, and even newspaper.

Cassandra M. Gillens, though almost unknown at the turn of the 21st century, has become one of the most recognized Gullah artists in the country. This is particularly significant since she is a self-taught painter who began what would be her career by drawing with chalk on a sidewalk outside her home. Her earliest drawings depicted her childhood years, and thus she has shown a fondness for subjects with young people in various typical activities. This author and his wife are fortunate to own four of her earliest paintings. One day in the spring of 1999 when we were attending meetings at Penn Center on St. Helena Island, South Carolina, we wandered down the road to a shop called Red Piano II, known for its collections of a wide variety of Gullah art, much of it primitive. My wife, who is an artist herself, immediately spotted a wall with half a dozen or so paintings by this then-unknown artist and exclaimed, "These are wonderful! This young lady has real talent." So she bought the four, to the delight of the artist (who later thanked us for "spending so much money to have them framed—I've never been framed before!"). Cassandra has since blossomed into one of the most popular artists in the Sea Islands, using vivid colors and depicting scenes from the culture and people she loves.

Deeper Insights into the Gullah Culture

For those who want to know more about the subject than can be found at festivals and celebrations, there are an increasing number of educational programs open to the public that are planned and delivered by sociologists and historians who are well qualified to teach this subject. One is the Gullah Studies Summer Institute, a two-week program designed to introduce a broad and diverse audience to the Gullah culture with offerings in history, language, music, religion, traditions, and heritage. This program is held each summer on the campus of Penn Center on St. Helena Island, South Carolina, an institution that was originally founded in 1862 to teach freed slaves how to read and write and acquire basic skills in farming, carpentry, quilt making, cooking, metal working, and other subjects necessary to earning a living. Among the subjects covered at the Institute are the origins of slavery in West Africa, cultural legacies, the Gullah language, religious practices, civil rights, music, dance, culinary arts, medicines and healing, oral traditions, genealogy, theater, photography, crafts, art, and the environment.

For more serious students, there is the Sea Islands Institute, hosted by the University of South Carolina Beaufort, which has a new course, Introduction to Gullah Culture, with weekly three-hour sessions. The syllabus states, "This survey course introduces students to the unique culture of African Americans in the coastal regions of South Carolina and Georgia. It covers some of the key components of Gullah life, social structure, and culture from its African roots in contemporary times, combining historical, sociological, anthropological, and psychological perspectives." Among the components are readings from a selective bibliography, lectures, discussion groups, written assignments, musical selections, films, and field trips.

There are, of course, any number of colleges and universities that offer courses in African American subjects, many of which include Gullah culture and history. But for the layperson interested in learning about the subject in an informal and personal manner, there are few that can match Introduction to Gullah Culture from the standpoint of historical accomplishment, dedication, personal sacrifice, perseverance, color, humor, and drama.

A typical group of native Sea Island musicians at the end of the 19th century
COURTESY OF THE COLLECTIONS OF THE SOUTH CAROLINA HISTORICAL SOCIETY

CHAPTER 11

Music, Song, and Dance

The narration opens in Africa, with accounts of the beginnings of music centuries ago and the creation of instruments with which to support singing, dancing, marching, grieving, and religious ceremonies. The most primitive instruments described are drums, rain sticks, rattles, clappers, shakers, kalimbas, bells, rasps, and udus, and then later flutes and stringed instruments, and finally keyboards.

The music of slaves was at first largely vocal and related to religious practices, spirituals, and entertainment. As in other chapters, our account probes into the intrinsic mystery, intriguing and still unsolved, of how it was possible for devastated and ravaged human beings and groups, stripped of all belongings, deprived of even the most basic liberty, and totally severed from family members over the years, to find within themselves the drive and the ability to rejuvenate vital elements of their past existence—whether in creating musical instruments, concocting medications, improvising foods, or pursuing spiritual lives—all totally from scratch. Today it is almost incredible that the Gullah peoples have a reputation for their exuberance, creativity, and diligence in establishing evidence of their roots in their music, entertainment, and rejuvenation of their ancient traditions. The chapter will have examples of this—notably in the Heritage Days festival observed each November at Penn Center on St. Helena Island, South Carolina, which attracts more than 20,000 visitors; a similar festival in the town of Beaufort, South Carolina; Daufuskie Day on a remote island reachable only by small boat; as well as a growing number of other celebrations that, only in the past decade, have evidenced an escalating interest in the Gullah culture, heritage, and history.

⁂

"**M**usic fills the life of the African from birth to death, closely associated with the gods, magic, and healing," reports the expansive *Low Country Gullah Culture Special Resource Study*, published in 2006 by the National Park Service. "A wide variety of native instruments are played there, including drums and fiddles, and the *banjar*, the forerunner of the banjo; but the human voice is the crowning instrument. Even on the slave ships, the memory of African music was kept alive, and in America black mothers passed on melodies to their children. The ring shout, spirituals, and instruments of the Sea Islands can be traced to Africa. Sounds born there came to enrich American music."

As reported by William S. Pollitzer, noted for his research on the Gullah culture, "Music from Africa was retained among the Gullah because it expressed feelings of joy or of grief, promoted physical and spiritual well being, provided escape from drudgery, molded the young, and fostered a sense of community. Slaves speaking different tongues could communicate feelings in this universal language, and music at funerals united the living with the dead. Sacred songs, echoing religion, evolved from the syncretism of Christianity and African belief, and some also contained a veiled cry for freedom." Evidence shows that in some cases, certain songs and chants also contained messages that the slaves could understand but their white masters could not. In extreme cases, these may have been plans for uprisings, secret messages that could lead to escapes, or warnings about situations that were going to make more misery or problems for the slaves. Many of the references to places that sounded fictitious had meanings to the singers but not to their masters. Such names as

"Sweet Canaan," "the Promised Land," "Jordan," and "My Home," for example, were cognomens for places where people could be free if they had the good fortune ever to find their way to them.

Other phrases referred to what is known as the Underground Railroad, a system whereby sympathizers, mainly northerners, helped slaves to escape from their southern bondage to freedom away from the plantations. Thus we find phrases like "wade in the water," which referred to escaping by wading in streams so that dogs being used to hunt runaways could not follow them; "swing low, sweet chariot," referring to carts in which escapees could be hidden under goods and chattels and taken en route to a safe location; or "the Gospel train," whereby slaves were disguised as parishioners on their way to a church meeting.

According to William S. Pollitzer in *The Gullah People and Their American Heritage*:

> Music of the Sea Islands is a group activity, the sharing of a creative experience, an avenue for expressing common sentiments. Call-and-response, noted in preaching, produces antiphony in music, as a phrase is repeated or answered by a chorus or an instrument. The presence of polyphony, however, with two or more independent phrases sung or played simultaneously, is doubtful.
>
> No mere words can ever describe the myriad variations of their music, especially the attributes and techniques of the human voice. It must be heard to be appreciated. The style of the Sea Island singers displays constant overlapping, part crossing, polyrhythms between leader and chorus, clapped accompaniment, improvisation, syncopation, and shifting vocal qualities. In order to appreciate the African origin of these traits it is necessary to tour the music of the land. Music permeates and dominates the African continent and influences people from before birth through the funeral that marks the entrance into the afterlife. The African expresses life in all its aspects through sound; living close to nature he incorporates natural sounds into his music and renders his emotions to their accompaniment. It is the outward, audible manifestation of inward feeling, the support and realization of purpose. Songs begin for the child in the womb and continue at birth, naming, lullabies, puberty, and circumcision. Marriage is marked with song and dance; one learns counting songs, work songs, drinking songs, and political songs, as he

becomes integrated with society. When only three or four years old, he learns to make musical instruments, plays musical games, and imitates the songs and dances of his elders. The vitality of African music, even at a funeral, startles the non-African, but it is an affirmation of life, a transformation into another form of life. Work songs are closely related to the seasons, especially where agricultural labor is required. In the tropical grasslands or savannah, such collective songs are frequently sung to the accompaniment of a small orchestra.

History shows that in America, the spiritual, as we know it today, was fully developed around the time that the Civil War began, born of the revival meetings at the beginning of the 19th century, nurtured by the Bible and the sufferings of the Savior, and developed in camp meetings that were attended in many cases by whites as well as blacks, who readily adapted music that they were hearing for the first time but that appealed to their ears and sensitivities. Many of the songs that had previously been passed along only from mouth to mouth and ear to ear became recorded on paper and later in print as instrumental music. It became evident that "white folk" were increasingly interested in African American music, particularly ring shouts—those chants and songs during religious ceremonies in praise houses—which could be heard so frequently in the villages where there were large populations of freed slaves. Traditionally the songs would start with one person, in the evening, in a corner of the community's small praise house, perhaps in a strong low alto, very soft but rising in a series of cadences, soon to be joined by the rich bass of a male singer, followed by the almost falsetto moans and wails of other members of the congregation, then rising in volume until every person in the room was fully involved and able to continue, almost without letup, into the night and even the early morning hours.

Laura Towne, founder of Penn School on St. Helena Island in 1862, was struck by the soulful singing of the black teachers who worked with her, and by their families and even her young pupils. An important breakthrough in her early days at Penn was the work of Lucy McKim, who published the first songs of a group known as the Port Royal Contrabands. She was captivated by "the wild, sad strains of people who suffered crushed hopes, keen sorrow, and dull daily miseries which covered them as hopelessly as the fog from the rice swamps."

"Work songs were also common on the Sea Islands," reported the *Resource Study*, "whether in rowing boats or thrashing rice sheaves." During slavery and in the years that followed, when former slaves found work on farms and in the forests, workers were allowed to sing on the job. This was practical, as well as a relief from tedium. In the case of a job calling for a crew to work together on tasks like sawing and hauling timber or moving heavy loads, singing in rhythm helped to coordinate the efforts. In cases where outright singing was forbidden, humming—whether individually or in groups—provided relief. Each plantation had its own work songs, and many of those who labored mightily on the job took pride in singing them. Improvisation and rhythm, coupled with the circumstances that triggered the music, were the driving forces behind the patterns of evolving music. Around the turn of the 20th century, W. E. B. Du Bois, one of the nation's most noted educators, put his finger on the situation when he said, "The Negro folk song, the rhythmic cry of the slave, stands today not simply as the sole American music, but as the most beautiful expression of human experience born this side of the seas."[1] In another instance, he wrote, "What are these songs and what do they mean? I know little of music and can say nothing in technical phrase, but I know something of men, and knowing them, I know that these songs are the articulate message of the slave to the world."[2]

In the African tradition, as brought to American shores by the slaves, music and religion are joined as one body. Between the two, there is no separation of sacred and secular music, nor is there any distinction in the matter of vocalization, instruments, or musical scores. Drums play an important role, and down through the ages were evolved in what one report called "sixty varieties, with some orchestras consisting of nothing but percussion instruments that could imitate the human voice through pitch, sending a message understood by one who knows that particular language."[3] In Africa, music also incorporated a profusion of wind instruments, many of them made from bamboo; stringed instruments, some limited to a single string; and horns. In all music, whether in Africa or later in the Gullah islands of America, improvisation was a common denominator, as were body movements, although in religious ceremonies these were likely to be more sinuous and less pronounced than in secular musical presentations, and in the praise houses there were more "call-and-response" patterns of behavior. On the plantations prior to the Civil War, and even on the slave ships, individuals and groups were permitted to indulge in singing and other simple forms of music on the theory that it kept individuals more healthy and able to work longer and harder.

The individual who is considered to have been the key in bringing Gullah music to national attention was Thomas Wentworth Higginson, a white abolitionist who was a colonel in the First South Carolina Volunteers, the first regiment of African Americans to be formed in the Union Army. Writing an article for the *Atlantic Monthly*, he described his experiences one night while returning on horseback to his army camp. He heard groups of freedmen "chanting, often harshly, but always in the most perfect time." He was so impressed that when he reached his tent, he wrote down the words and melodies while they were still fresh in his memory. "Almost all their songs were thoroughly religious in their tone," he commented, indicating "patience for this life—nothing but triumph in the next." From that point on, he began collecting and publishing spirituals, and in most cases commenting on their meaning and nature. One of his early favorites was "I Know Moon-Rise," which had emotional lines such as *"I'll lie in de grave an stretch out my arms."* "Never, it seems to me," he wrote, "since man first lived and suffered, was his infinite longing for peace uttered more plaintively than in that line."[4]

Higginson and others who studied Gullah spirituals and other types of songs again and again realized, too, that they were not always the same but might change in rhythms and structure—even if ever so little—depending upon the people singing, their sorrows and pleasures, their numbers, the location, and other such factors. In the Gullah tradition, it is not uncommon for songs to change in an instant from the somber to the lighthearted, sometimes accompanied by the stamping of feet or the waving of the hands in an uplifting manner.

Multiplying and Identifying

Eventually groups of people who had long histories of singing spirituals and other religious music began to identify themselves with the more popular or inspiring numbers and devote time to appearing in public on special occasions to sing and play the music of their preference. One of the first of these groups was the Fisk Jubilee Singers, composed of young men and women who were, or had been, students at Fisk University. Fisk, located in Nashville, Tennessee, was founded in 1866 as the first sizeable institution in America to provide a college education to African Americans. Since most of the students at Fisk had been slaves, and had many slaves in their own families, the term *jubilee* was most appropriate. In the Old Testament, each 50th Pentecost was followed by a year of jubilee, in which, under Hebrew law, all slaves were set free.

Originally the group was composed of two quartets and a pianist under the direction of George L. White, who was the university's musical director. In 1871 the Singers gave performances to raise much-needed funds for the college and over the next decade set a remarkable record of achievement. Not only did they tour most of the northern states and were widely recognized for an appearance at the White House, but they also toured much of Europe and England, where they performed for Queen Victoria herself. The astonishing success was not only a high point in the history of the Gullah culture but also a real milestone in terms of musical history—the introduction to America and the world at large of what has been referred to as music that celebrates "life, survival, and human victory." This was even more impressive when one considers that, heretofore, the only African American music performed in public was that of white minstrels in blackface, whose performance was largely in the nature of ridicule and certainly not stirring and heartfelt. At first, the Jubilee Singers sang ballads and patriotic anthems, but George White suggested that they would make more of an impact on people and serve their traditions better if they sang "the songs of their ancestors." When they did so, it was reported that the music was not only well received but "often moved audiences to tears." Over the years, among the most popular titles by the Jubilees have been "Swing Low, Sweet Chariot," "Steal Away," "Help Me," "Couldn't Hear Nobody Pray," and "If I Have My Ticket, Can I Ride?" Mark Twain (Samuel Clemens) was an everlasting fan of the group and once commented, "I don't know when anything has moved me so much as the plaintive melodies of the Jubilee Singers."

A fine assessment of the extraordinary success of the group appears in *The Music of Black Americans* by Dr. Eileen Southern, a leading authority in this subject field:

Inevitably, the success of the Fisk and Hampton student singers inspired emulation. So many spurious groups appeared in imitation of the Fisk Singers that Fisk University gave up its promotion of concert tours in 1878. Thereafter, Frederick J. Loudin, a member of the university singers since 1875, took over direction of the now-private group and brought in new singers. In 1884, Loudin's Jubilee Singers embarked upon a six-year tour around the world that brought fame not only to the singers but also to Fisk.

Orpheus McAdoo, like Loudin a former member of the Fisk Singers, formed spin-off groups from the Fisk Singers and took his Jubilee Singers to South America and Australia. Again, audiences confused his groups with the original Fisk Jubilee Singers. In any event, the Negro folk songs were disseminated into far-flung lands; by the end of the nineteenth century there were few places in the world that had not heard black America's spirituals and plantation songs.

Among the groups that began to tour in the 1880s were the Canadian Jubilee Singers of Ontario, Canada, who performed primarily in Great Britain. There were dozens of other groups, of whom the best known were the Wilmington (North Carolina) Jubilee Singers, Slayton's Jubilee Singers, the Sheppard Jubilee Singers, and the MacMillen and Sourbeck Jubilee Singers (which later changed its name to Stinson's Jubilee Singers). One of Stinson's singers, Billy Mills, was the grandfather of four brothers who would later win fame as the Mills Brothers quartet.

In the 1890s, the South saw the appearance of what were called "Christ's Sanctified Holy Churches." These harked back, in part, to the old praise houses of slavery days, with their "shouts," stamping of feet, and hand clapping. Today the church reiterates its adherence to "No Creed but Christ, No Law but Love, No Guide but the Bible" and maintains that, along with preaching and heartfelt praying, its members are urged to engage in "energetic singing."

Gospel Music

The term *gospel music* is used more or less loosely for the religious music that derived from African American churches in the early 1900s. According to the *Wikipedia* encyclopedia:

> The term refers to both black gospel music and to the religious music composed and sung by predominately white southern gospel artists. While the separation between the two styles was never absolute—both drew from the Methodist hymnal and artists in one tradition sometimes sang songs belonging to the other—the sharp division between black and white America, particularly black and white churches, kept the two apart. While those divisions have lessened slightly in the past fifty years, the two traditions are still distinct.
>
> In both traditions, some performers, such as Mahalia Jackson, have limited themselves to appearing in religious contexts only, while others, such as Sister Rosetta Tharpe, the Golden Gate Quartet and Clara Ward, have performed gospel music in secular settings, even night clubs. Many performers, such as The Jordanaires, Al Green, and Solomon Burke, have performed both secular and religious music. It is common for such performers to include gospel songs in otherwise secular performances, although the opposite almost never happens.
>
> Gospel singer, songwriter and guitarist Sister Rosetta Tharpe was the first great star of gospel music, surfacing on the pop music charts in 1938. She remained popular through the 1940s, continuing to hit the charts and drawing tens of thousands of fans to see her perform live in venues across the United States. She lost the support of some of her church fans, now and then, when she performed in secular venues as well, as when she recorded songs not recognized as "Christian." The fans she lost were somewhat forgiving, as she remained true to her faith, for the most part, throughout her recording career, which spanned the remainder of her life.[5]

Although it is questionable which musician, singer, or composer really rates the rank of "first" in the field of gospel music, Thomas Andrew Dorsey has often been referred to as "the father of gospel music," largely because he was the first to compose this kind of music—even to the point of having his kinds of music popularly referred to as "Dorseys." Born in Villa Rica, Georgia, he was originally known as "Georgia Tom," a leading blues pianist, and was the first African American to be elected to the prestigious Nashville Songwriters Hall of Fame. Credited with more than 400 blues and jazz compositions, he began writing and recording what he called "gospel music" (the first to use that term) when his life was abruptly changed by personal tragedy. His wife, Nettie, died in childbirth in 1932, along with his first son. Stricken with grief, he wrote one of the most noted of gospel songs, "Take My Hand, Precious Lord." It was performed by Mahalia Jackson and said to be a favorite of the Reverend Martin Luther King Jr.

Charles Albert Tindley, known as "one of the founding fathers of American gospel music," was another musician and self-taught composer who played a remarkable part in musical history. The son of slaves, he taught himself to read and write while still in his teens. Described as a driven young man, he worked as a janitor and a hod carrier in his home town and earned his divinity degree as a preacher through a correspondence course. Some of his most popular recordings, still sung by thousands of people, were "A Better Day Is Coming By and By," "Christ Is the Way," "Consolation," "Go Wash in the Beautiful Stream," and "I'll Overcome Some Day," which was the basis for the civil rights anthem "We Shall Overcome," remembered by Americans of all colors and ages as a theme song for Martin Luther King Jr. "Tindley used his intellectual ability, eloquence, and spiritual singing," wrote one of his biographers, "to amass a congregation of over 10,000 members. During this time, he worked for civil rights, took care of the poor and disadvantaged, and wrote more than 45 hymns."[6]

Among the other musicians and composers who were of Gullah ancestry and who contributed to this body of music was Harry Thacker Burleigh, who grew up listening to and learning spirituals and other African American songs from his grandfather, a former slave who had been blinded by a savage beating before escaping to the North. He had the good fortune to attend, and graduate from, the Institute of Musical Art, directed by the Czech composer Antonin Dvořák, who was fascinated with the music that had come from the days of slavery, and whose Symphony no. 5, *From the New World*, reflects it so superbly.

Among Burleigh's most recognized works are "Deep River," "Steal Away to Jesus," "Sometimes I Feel Like a Motherless Child," and "Nobody Knows." During his career, he performed internationally before thousands of people from many cultures, including the King of England, President Theodore Roosevelt, and just about everybody in the music world. He was a favorite of Marian

Anderson, who liked to include selections of spirituals in her concerts, many of which were arranged by Burleigh.

Speaking about his genre, Burleigh said:

> The plantation songs known as "spirituals" are the spontaneous outbursts of intense religious fervor, and had their origin chiefly in camp meetings, revivals, and other religious exercises. They were never "composed," but sprang into life, ready made, from the white heat of religious fervor during some protracted meeting in camp or church, as the simple, ecstatic utterance of wholly untutored minds and are practically the only music in America which meets the scientific definition of Folk Songs.
>
> Success in singing these Folk Songs is primarily dependent upon deep spiritual feeling. The voice is not nearly so important as the spirit, and then rhythm, for the Negro's soul is linked with rhythm, and is an essential characteristic of most all Folk Songs. It is a serious misconception of their meaning and value to treat them as "minstrel" songs, or to try to make them funny by a too literal attempt to imitate the manner of the Negro in singing them, by swaying the body, clapping the hands, or striving to make the peculiar inflections of voice that are natural with the colored people. Their worth is weakened unless they are done impressively, for through all these songs there breathes a hope, a faith in the ultimate justice and brotherhood of man. The cadences of sorrow invariably turn to joy, and the message is ever manifest that eventually deliverance from all that hinders and oppresses the soul will come, and man—every man—will be free.

Among the other composers of note who greatly influenced the development of and public interest in spirituals and other genres of African American music were John Rosamond Johnson, Nathaniel Dett, Hall Johnson, Edward Boatner, William Levi Dawson, and Thomas Andrew Dorsey. They were part of a series of "stepping stones" in the Gullah tradition of music, ranging from long before their time in the spontaneous songs, composed on the spot, of the slaves; the spirituals of escape during the Civil War; the "call-and-response" chants in the praise houses and churches; the transition period from the 19th century to the early 20th; the jazz age of the 1920s; the expansion era just before and after World War II; and to the present day.

John Rosamond Johnson was born free in Virginia in 1873 and, unlike many African American composers of his era, had a formal musical education, first at the New England Conservatory and later in London. As a songwriter team with his brother and Bob Cole, he wrote *The Evolution of Ragtime* (1903), two Broadway operettas with casts of black actors, and numerous musicals. But he is probably most notable as the composer of "Lift Every Voice and Sing," which was referred to as "the Black National Anthem." He was also noted as an editor, compiling books of spirituals and shout songs and a folk song anthology.

Nathaniel Dett, who was born in 1882 in Ontario of Canadian and American parents, was known during his lifetime as one of the most successful black composers, noted for his use of folk songs and spirituals for choral and piano compositions in the romantic style. He was gifted enough to be accepted at the Oberlin Conservatory of Music, where he conceived the idea of using spirituals in music normally considered classic in style, and was the first black student to receive a degree at the Conservatory. After serving as a professor at Tennessee's Lane College and the Lincoln Institute in Jefferson City, Missouri, he moved to the Hampton Institute in Virginia, where he was the first black director of music and where he composed many of his most noted works, which were heralded by the *Chicago Evening Post* for their innovation and high-level pianistic skill. Two of his most noted works were *Magnolia* and *In the Bottoms*.

Hall Johnson, born in Athens, Georgia, in 1888, was acclaimed along with Harry Burleigh as "one of the two American composers who elevated the African American spiritual to an art form, comparable in its musical sophistication to the compositions of European Classical composers."[7] As a boy, he taught himself how to play the violin after hearing a violin recital by Joseph Henry Douglass, grandson of the noted Frederick Douglass. Becoming interested in choral music, he formed the Hall Johnson Negro Choir, which was selected by the Department of State to represent the United States at the International Festival of Fine Arts in Berlin, Germany. He was also an excellent teacher, coaching such famous singers as Marian Anderson and Shirley Verrett.

Johnson said the following of the spiritual, one of the most popular forms of African American music and one that has certainly been most prominent in the Gullah culture:

This music was transmitted to us through humble channels, but its source is that of all great art everywhere—the unquenchable, divinely human longing for a perfect realization of life. It traverses every shade of emotion without spilling over in any direction. Its most tragic utterances are without pessimism, and its lightest, brightest moments have nothing to do with frivolity. In its darkest expressions there is always a hope, and in its gayest measures a constant reminder. Born out of the heart-cries of a captive people who still did not forget how to laugh, this music covers an amazing range of mood. Nevertheless, it is always serious music and should be performed seriously, in the spirit of its original conception.

Edward Boatner traveled with his father, an itinerant minister, when he was a young boy, and thus at an early age he came into contact with rural church choirs and learned many of the old hymns. Later, because his parents were determined to have their children well schooled despite the obstacles of money and race, he had the privilege of studying music privately, as well as at two conservatories. He began his career as a concert singer and was for a time associated with Nathaniel Dett, who encouraged him and assisted him in his work. He sang leading roles with the National Negro Opera Company and served as the director of music for the National Baptist Convention for six years, as well as directing community and church choirs. Whenever he had time, he arranged music, and eventually he became known as an accomplished composer. His best known arrangements are "Let Us Break Bread Together," "O What a Beautiful City," "Soon I Will Be Done," "Trampling," and "I Want Jesus to Walk with Me," which he composed for one of the most famous of all African American singers, Marian Anderson. He also composed many other works of music, including *Freedom Suite*, for chorus, narrator, and orchestra; *The Man from Nazareth*, a spiritual musical; and *Julius Sees Her*, a musical comedy.

William Levy Dawson, born in Alabama in 1899, composer, choir director, and teacher, was credited with developing the Tuskegee Institute Choir into an internationally known ensemble, which helped greatly to spread public interest in spirituals and other African American music. He was influenced, too, by the work of Czech composer Antonin Dvořák, who had come to America in the 1890s and composed his famous *New World Symphony* based on native music and rhythms. Dawson's best known works are arrangements on spirituals, one of the most notable being his *Negro Folk Symphony*, which received international applause in 1934 under the direction of one of the era's most prominent figures in the music world, Leopold Stokowski, director of the Philadelphia Orchestra. The symphony's three movements were "The Bond of Africa," "Hope in the Night," and "O Let Me Shine." A highly favorable article in the *New York Times* observed that Dawson had "dramatic feeling, a racial sensuousness and directness of melodic speech, and a barbaric turbulence," and another review praised his work for its "imagination, warmth, drama, and sumptuous orchestration."[8] Dawson, not completely satisfied with his work, flew to West Africa in 1952, where he revised his symphony, infusing it with the spirit of the native music he listened to intently during his visit. He said at the time about African music and its transfer to America, "A link was taken out of a human chain when the first African was taken from the shores of his native land and sent to slavery."[9]

Thomas Andrew Dorsey, a Gullah by birth in his native rural Georgia, often traveled as a boy with his father, an itinerant Baptist preacher (as Edward Boatner had also done), and learned his music through choirs and helping his mother on the church organ. He started his professional career, however, as a blues pianist and songwriter before concentrating on the area that earned him a nickname as "the father of gospel music." In the late 1920s, he promoted his gospel songs from one church to another not only in the South but also in the Midwest. There is no doubt that he had a great deal to offer on every subject imaginable in the religious world; he composed at least 800 songs during his career.

Hallelujah!

Ever growing in popularity, the old spirituals and gospel music favorites have steadily regained their place in America, and most especially throughout the Low Country and Sea Islands of the South. Among the most active are the Hallelujah Singers, who embody the Gullah culture in every way, song, word, manner, and dress. This ensemble was formed by Marlena Smalls, herself of Gullah lineage, in 1990 in the enchanting and historic town of Beaufort, South Carolina, where this African American culture is alive and strong. Speaking about the Singers and what the group means to all of them, she says that getting involved has not only helped people to understand her culture but has given her new insights about herself and where she stands in life and what she can contribute to it.

The group combines singing with storytelling, helping to explain in a uniquely historic and personable manner who the Gullah are, where they originated, and what influence they have on today's culture. "Before we learned about this culture," explains Smalls, "the African was just a former slave. But understanding Gullah is the key to humanizing our race and showing that our ancestors came to this country with their own history, rituals, and customs." The Hallelujah Singers are noted for the inventive way in which they can interweave music with narration, present miniature dramatizations of many of the unique personages, rituals, and ceremonies that have played a vital role in shaping their culture, and stimulate their audiences to become participants rather than just listeners. As a result the group has earned much recognition and many awards. It has performed in concerts not only in the South but also at the Kennedy Center and across America and abroad. It has appeared often on television, with performances on *Good Morning America*, the *Today* show, and the *Crook & Chase* show, and was in the award-winning film *Forrest Gump*, with Smalls playing the part of Bubba's mama. It achieved special recognition to represent the state of South Carolina in the bicentennial celebration of the Library of Congress with a concert for preservation in the Library's Folklife Center.

The Georgia Sea Island Singers have been preserving the Gullah culture and traditions for more than a quarter of a century and have toured the world, including performances at the Olympic Games in Mexico and Lillehammer, Norway. They have performed before many types of audiences besides the general ones, including those at universities, schools, conventions, conferences, and museums, as well as on radio and television shows and before presidents and royalty. They continue a tradition of singing that was begun more than a century ago on St. Simons Island, Georgia, for the purpose of preserving the rich reservoir of African American culture and Gullah/Geechee language spoken in the isolated Sea Islands of the Georgia coast. Frankie Sullivan Quimby, the leader of the group, was born and raised in these islands in a family that was able to trace its roots squarely back to Africa, to the Foulah tribe, which came from the town of Kianhah in the District of Temourah in the Kingdom of Massina on the Niger River. The oldest of 13 children, she is descended from slaves on the Hopeton and Altama Plantations in Glynn County, Georgia. Many of her relatives still live on St. Simons and in the Brunswick area. As she likes to say, "We are a strong people who know how to survive, and we want everyone to know where we came from. You can't know where you are going until you realize where you came from. So we have dedicated our lives to trying to preserve that rich heritage and culture that our ancestors handed down to us."

Frankie's husband, Doug, was born in Baconton, Georgia, where his family members were sharecroppers who sometimes earned less than $10 in cash for a year's work, and he has been singing since the age of four. His grandfather spoke only Gullah, and to this day there are isolated pockets on small islands along the coast where Gullah and Geechee are used more often than English. He began his professional career in 1963, joining the Sensational Friendly Stars, a well-known gospel group, and six years later he became a member of the Georgia Sea Island Singers. He is best known for his very deep bass voice, especially when singing sea chanteys and call-and-response songs, in which the audience participates. One of his most powerful songs is "Freedom, Freedom over Me," which recounts the very tragic and moving story of Ebo Landing on St. Simons Island, where 18 Geechee men chose death over servitude.

The Singers are known for their versatility and range of presentations. These include several ways of demonstrating the Gullah language to their audiences, the rice dance, work songs of the Sea Islands, gospel music, call-and-response, hand clapping, sailors' chanteys, the "shout," which originated in religious services in the praise houses on the old plantations, and "slave games," in which the human body (the "hambone") is used as a percussion instrument. As demonstrated most effectively by Doug, it is a memorable performance in which his hands, lightning quick, use his body as a "drum," producing an astonishing variety of sounds by beating on his thighs, chest, and other parts of the body. Customarily the performer chants, "Hambone, hambone, where you been?" Known also as "the Juba dance," this action is often performed by groups jiving together around in circles, clockwise and then counter-clockwise, all in rhythm with stomping, patting the body, and slapping, and ending with a step called "the long dog scratch." Although dancing groups are generally mixed, male and female, the men were more likely to take delight in it because they could exert more bombastic noise and demonstrate bodily calisthenics, all the time chanting:

Hambone, hambone,
Where you been?
Round the corner
An' back agin.
Hambone, hambone,
Where's your wife?
In the kitchen
Cookin rice!

Although slaves were generally not permitted to have musical instruments or drums (in part because it was discovered that slaves were very clever in using them as signals or secret messages) and had to suffice with these bodily "drums" and hand clapping, when they were freed they began devising many kinds of instruments, based on what they and their ancestors had known and used in Africa. Today groups such as the Singers specialize in rhythmic demonstrations with the *jimbay* drum, talking drum, and stick box drum, which were traditionally made from hollowed out logs or tree trunks, the skins of antelopes or goats, and bamboo. Bells of all kinds and sizes were also common, played with different kinds of sticks or metal spoons to vary the tones, and were often coordinated with rattles and maracas made from gourds, shells, nuts, and woven baskets. The banjo was also popular, originating with the *banjar* in West Africa, and today can be found in Gullah bands in many varieties and designs—often things of real beauty as well as musical quality.

The McIntosh County Shouters

This noted group of singers and dancers is the principal, and possibly the last, active practitioner of one of the most venerable of African song-and-movement traditions, the "shout," also known as the "ring shout." This song-and-dance in the Sea Islands and Low Country is probably the oldest surviving African American performance tradition on the North American continent. According to *The New Georgia Encyclopedia*:

> It continues to be performed in a black community in McIntosh County on Georgia's coast. This compelling fusion of counterclockwise dance-like movement, call-and-response singing, and percussion of hand clapping and a stick beating a drum-like rhythm on a wooden floor is clearly African in its origins and most salient features. The ring shout affirms oneness with the Spirit and ancestors as well as community cohesiveness.
>
> As the tradition developed in slavery times, strong elements of Christian belief were grafted onto it. The ring shout was first described in detail during the Civil War by outside observers in South Carolina and Georgia. Its practice continued in those areas well into the twentieth century, even as its influence was resounding in later forms like spiritual, jubilee, and gospel music, and elements of jazz. By the last quarter of the twentieth century, however, the ring shout itself was presumed to have died out until its rediscovery in 1980 in McIntosh County.
>
> To this day, the shouters of Bolden or "Briar Patch," a community near Eulonia, perform the ring shout at the Mt. Calvary Baptist Church on Watch Night, or New Year's Eve, to welcome in the New Year. In earlier times the shout, often criticized by white missionaries and some black clergy, occurred in the church after the formal worship, or in "praise houses" in the woods, or even in homes or barns. . . .
>
> A "songster" will "set" or begin a song, slowly at first, then accelerating to an appropriate tempo. These lines will be answered by a group of singers called "basers" in call-and-response pattern. The stick-man, sitting next to the leader, will beat a simple rhythm with a broom or other wood stick, and the basers will add rhythm with hand clapping and foot patting. The songs are special shout songs, at one time called "running spirituals." For the most part they form a separate repertoire from spirituals, jubilees, and later gospel songs. Ranging from light-spirited to apocalyptic, at times they carry coded references to slavery. Sometimes participants pantomime the meaning of the verses being sung—for example, extending their arms in the "eagle wing" gesture to evoke friends urging a slave, Daniel, to fly from the master's whip.

. . . Today's shouters differentiate between the singers and the shouters, the latter referring to those who move counterclockwise in the ring. . . . The shout movement is a forward hitching shuffle in which the feet never cross; the practitioners of the tradition maintain that crossing the feet would be unholy dancing, whereas the shout is in the service of the Lord.

When the living ring shout tradition in Bolden became known to outsiders in 1980, a performing group from the community was organized, calling themselves the McIntosh County Shouters. Under the leadership of elder songster Lawrence McKiver, they endeavored to present on stage faithful re-creations of their community tradition that had been passed on from their slave forebears, especially London and Amy Jenkins, grandparents of the current group's elder shouters. From their first appearance at the Sea Island Festival on St. Simons Island, the group went on to such venues as the National Folk Festival at Wolf Trap Farm in Virginia, Atlanta's Black Arts Festival, and New York's Lincoln Center. They were featured in a Georgia Public Television documentary and on a Folkways LP. In 1993 the group was awarded the prestigious National Heritage Fellowship from the National Endowment for the Arts.

Ron and Natalie Daise are among the most popular singers, storytellers, and authors in the Gullah world today. They present inspirational love songs in a blend of jazz, gospel, pop, and other genres. As Natalie says:

> You probably know me as "Miss Natalie" on *Gullah Gullah Island*—the mother who, with a song on my lips and a smile on my face, solves all the problems and loves all the children. Well, actually, that's not all that far from the truth. I am a mother. Sara and Simeon, who play themselves on our show, are Ron's and my real children. I do sing a lot. Everybody in our house does. As a matter of fact, I grew up in a house that was full of music. My dad sang baritone, my mom contralto, my great-grandmother had a strong lead voice, and my two brothers and I filled in the spaces. And yes, I do smile a lot. . . . As far as loving children goes, that's true, too. In real life, though, I don't have quite as much time for daylong games, elaborate decorations, and wacky snacks. And as for problem solving? I do my best. I'm not nearly as good or as calm about it as my character is on TV (sometimes I'm downright grouchy), but what can I say? That's

TV for you! Everything neat and tidy and wrapped in 23 minutes. But I'm sure you knew there was more to our lives than what you've seen on television. . . . I moved to the Low Country of South Carolina in 1983 and fell in love with the stories, the water, and the salt-scented air, and of course, Ron. We married in 1985 and have been singing and working together ever since. Together we have told stories, sung songs, done theater, given lectures, and visited schools, libraries, museums, theaters, convention centers, festivals, all over the country. For the most part, it has been a lot of fun. It's also been a challenge to live by our talents. We realize that many people never have that opportunity. When I was a little girl dreaming of what I would be when I grew up, it never occurred to me that I could tell stories for a living. Or that the things that made me unique (my imagination, love of music, passion for words) would create and shape the life I would lead as an adult. Now I know that the very best thing that anyone can do, regardless of their age, is to be themselves to the best of their ability. If I can pass that on to my children, along with a deep trust in God, it will be my greatest accomplishment.

Ron Daise is a fourth-generation Gullah, the youngest of nine children born in the Cedar Grove community of St. Helena Island, South Carolina. When he was growing up, however, he says that he and his family were not proud of their origins. But later that all changed as they learned more and more about their background and its significance. "I'm glad that my wife and I have been helpful in changing this outlook among other people of Gullah heritage," he says. "The songs, the stories, the speech, the crafts, the superstitions, and the dietary practices of the Gullah people have influenced the world culture. And the Gullah communities were the gateway for most Africans who were brought to America during the slave trade. We're a group of independent, persevering, spiritually minded people, and I'm proud of my heritage. . . . A Gullah expression is 'Wha fa ya, fa ya.' 'If something's going to be, it will.' I've learned to put my best foot forward at all times. For me, it's a way of life."

And for many thousands of others with Gullah heritages, this recognition has become increasingly strong.

"Swing Low, Sweet Chariot"

English Version

Swing low, sweet chariot,
Coming for to carry me home.
Swing low, sweet chariot,
Coming for to carry me home.

I looked over Jordan, and what
  did I see,
Coming for to carry me home?
A band of angels coming after
  me,
Coming for to carry me home.

Swing low, sweet chariot,
Coming for to carry me home.
Swing low, sweet chariot,
Coming for to carry me home.

If you get there before I do,
Coming for to carry me home,
Tell all my friends I'm coming too,
Coming for to carry me home.

Swing low, sweet chariot,
Coming for to carry me home.
Swing low, sweet chariot,
Coming for to carry me home.

Gullah Version

When dat ar ole chariot comes,
I'm gwine to lebe you,
I'm boun' for de promised land,
Frien's, I'm gwine to lebe you.

I'm sorry, frien's, to lebe you,
Farewell! oh, farewell!
But I'll meet you in de mornin',
Farewell! oh, farewell!

I'll meet you in de mornin',
When you reach de promised
  land;
On de oder side of Jordan,
For I'm boun' for de promised
  land.

Note: This is a typical example
of a "call-and-response" chant as
practiced most often in churches,
with the preacher singing one line
and the congregation, in unison,
responding with the next line. The
"response" is often the same from
verse to verse, as in the case of the
top version: "Coming for to carry
me home."

This photograph shows a large group of slaves standing in front of buildings on Smith's Plantation, Beaufort, South Carolina, circa 1862.
COURTESY OF THE LIBRARY OF CONGRESS

Chapter 12

Roots

This chapter chronicles the impassioned journey of the small band of African Americans of Gullah descent returning to Africa in 1989, as well as a second trip in 1997 and a third trip in 2005. The focus is also on Fourah Bay College in Freetown, Sierra Leone, in West Africa, founded by the Church Missionary Society of London in 1827 as a constituent arm of the University of Sierra Leone. Following this recap, we particularly look at the work of the many efforts that have been made and are pending to establish and present important segments of information about the Gullah peoples—their origins as well as events and activities in today's world—that reflect the vital meaning of the Gullah/Geechee culture and heritage and their place in America in the 21st century.

Back to the Beginning

When American historian Joseph Opala began to investigate Gullah origins in West Africa in the 1970s, very little was known about the subject in the public domain. Most people's impressions at the time were based on the best-selling book *Roots*, published in that period by author Alex Haley, which, while presenting some authentic historical accounts, turned out to have many fictional elements.

But now a completely different story of African Americans finding their roots emerged. In a three-page interview in *West Africa* magazine in 1986 titled "The Gullah Connection," Joseph Opala, after very extensive research right on the spot, reported, "I have found that, during the second half of the eighteenth century, there was a significant slave trade connection between Sierra Leone and South Carolina. During that period, South Carolina's prosperous economy was based largely on rice agriculture, and local planters were willing to pay higher prices for slaves from the rice-growing region of West Africa— what they called the 'Rice Coast'—and particularly from Sierra Leone."[1] He explained that the European colonists who settled the Low Country had no experience with rice farming, but the slaves brought from the Rice Coast were experts at cultivating this difficult crop.

Opala was building on the work of pioneering scholars who came before him, especially the linguist Lorenzo Turner and the historian Peter Wood. Turner's book *Africanisms in the Gullah Dialect* (1949) showed that the Gullah people have preserved thousands of African words and names in their everyday speech, and that it is possible to determine the specific origins in Africa of many of these items. Wood's *Black Majority* (1974) showed that South Carolina rice planters had a strong preference for slaves brought from the Rice Coast of West Africa, the region extending between what is now Senegal and Gambia in the north to Sierra Leone and Liberia in the south. Wood proved that Africans from that area brought the knowledge and skills that made the rice industry in the Low Country a tremendous economic success.

Following in the footsteps of these earlier scholars, Opala did two things that no one had ever done before. First, he went to the Rice Coast and lived there for almost 20 years, researching that region's links to the Gullah people from the *other* side of the Atlantic. From that vantage point, he was able to see that while all the modern nations of the Rice Coast are important for an understanding of Gullah history and culture, Sierra Leone is by far the most important. Sierra Leone's links to the Gullah run in *two* directions; not only were many slaves taken from Sierra Leone to the Low Country, but Gullahs also returned to Sierra Leone after the American Revolution and made an important impact on the course of Sierra Leone's history.

Second, Opala played the role of public historian for many years, making documentary films, giving public lectures, and providing interviews to newspapers and broadcast journalists in both Africa and the United States. He brought the news about what he and other scholars were learning about Gullah history home to Gullahs and West Africans. More than that, Opala encouraged Africans and Gullahs to direct the course of his research. As his findings got more and more public attention, Sierra Leoneans and Gullahs came to him frequently to say what *they* wanted to know about their links to family on the other side of the Atlantic. Both sides wanted to know more and more "specific" connections, provable links between individuals and families. Opala shaped his research to find out what Africans and Gullahs themselves wanted to know about their past.

With his many years of experience in West Africa, including a stint in the Peace Corps working with Sierra Leonean rice farmers in a rural village, and with six years as a lecturer at Sierra Leone's Fourah Bay College in the capital city, Opala was able to zero in on Sierra Leone's many links to the Gullah people. He focused much of his research on Bunce Island, a British slave castle on a small island in the Sierra Leone River, a vast estuary forming the largest harbor on the African continent. Bunce Island is located about 20 miles upriver from what is now Freetown, the capital of Sierra Leone. Interest in this unique site goes back to 1948, when M. C. F. Easmon, a Sierra Leonean medical doctor and amateur historian, led a small expedition to clear the vegetation and map and photograph the ruins for the first time. But for more than two decades thereafter, the site remained forgotten and unvisited.

Opala began research on Bunce Island back in 1976. He cleared the vegetation from the ruins, mapped and photographed the walls, and collected artifacts in the two middens, or rubbish heaps, where the slave traders and their African workers tossed their rubbish. He examined the ruins closely, looking for clues in the walls that indicated where verandahs and wooden stairwells long decayed were originally attached. He concluded that the "factory house," the castle's main building, looked like a Low Country rice planter's mansion.

Opala also went by canoe to the neighboring islands and interviewed African elders, who told him their oral traditions about the time the British slave traders were buying captives at Bunce Island and exiling them to places unknown on the big ships that took them out of the great harbor into the endless ocean.

Later Opala did historical research in libraries and archives in Sierra Leone, the United States, and Great Britain. He discovered that between about 1750 and 1800, Bunce Island was the largest British slave trading operation between Senegambia and the Gold Coast, exporting as many as 7,000 slaves per year. It is estimated that about 30,000 African slaves passed through Bunce Island, and that many of them were shipped to Charleston and Savannah and sold to rice planters. In Charleston the business agent for Bunce Island's London-based owners was Henry Laurens, a wealthy slave trader who would later become president of the Continental Congress during the American Revolutionary War. Laurens is still well known in South Carolina as that state's most distinguished Revolutionary War patriot. One of South Carolina's counties is named after Laurens, and many of its cities and towns have streets named in his honor.

As a result of his painstaking research on both sides of the Atlantic, Opala has documented an important part of the origin and development of the Gullah people in the Low Country and Sea Islands. But Opala went beyond just doing research. He brought Gullah people to West Africa to see for themselves the historical and family connections that he and other scholars were uncovering. He organized three historic homecomings to Sierra Leone: the Gullah Homecoming (1988), the Moran Family Homecoming (1997), and Priscilla's Homecoming (2005). The documentary films based on these events—*Family Across the Sea*, *The Language You Cry In*, and *Priscilla's Homecoming* (in preparation)—have been seen by thousands on both sides of the Atlantic and have helped restore family ties severed in the slave trade more than two centuries ago.

When Gullahs came to Sierra Leone, they met people with very common local names, such as Sorie, Sanie, and Salifu for men and Kadiatu, Isatu, and Fatu for women. Learning from Opala that these names were recorded by Lorenzo Turner in the Low Country 60 years ago, they understood more clearly that they had come home, or at least to one of the principal homes where their ancestors originated. Meeting people of the Loko, Kono, Soso, and Kisi tribes in Sierra Leone, they were also astounded to learn that these were common Gullah names when their own grandparents were young. Opala also showed the Gullah visitors *shukublay* baskets made with the same coil technique as the sweetgrass baskets so typical of Gullah culture, and "country cloth" blankets made of long strips sewn together just like traditional Gullah strip quilts.

For many years Opala has been determined to establish a permanent memorial at Bunce Island to the suffering of the Africans exiled from that slave castle and to the enduring family ties between West Africans and Gullahs. He has worked for years with the Sierra Leone government on this project. Opala accompanied a team of U.S. National Park Service experts who surveyed the castle in 1989. One of the team members said that he had "never seen a site so important for U.S. history in such desperate need of preservation." Three years later Opala took Colin Powell, then chairman of the U.S. Joint Chiefs of Staff, to Bunce Island while he was on an official visit to West Africa. Deeply moved by his experience, Powell said at his departure from Sierra Leone, "I am an American. But today, I am something more. . . . I am an African, too. . . . I feel my roots here in this continent."

This kind of historical research and preservation has become increasingly important to the Gullahs of today, particularly because of the long, dark period before the Civil War for which genealogical and cultural records are missing and, in many cases, were even actually suppressed. As an article in *West Africa* magazine noted, most of the records of African Americans have vanished or been destroyed, but "the Gullah people [of the Carolinas and Georgia] have retained far more of their African cultural heritage than any other black Americans, due to geographical and social isolation. South Carolina had a black majority for much of its history, allowing the slave communities there to develop in relative isolation. Those Gullahs living on the Sea Islands were particularly isolated. There were few bridges built, and as late as the 1940s some islanders had never visited the mainland."[2]

Numerous studies have pointed out that this isolation helped to preserve family, spiritual, and cultural values their ancestors brought from Africa. "Gullah people are complex," reported the U.S. Park Service's *Low Country Gullah Culture Special Resource Study*. "They have many characteristics that illustrate the perseverance of African cultural traits which have shaped their world view and value system. For much of history, Gullah life was lived and governed in accordance with nature, seasons, climate, and the tide. What remains as the most important aspects of Gullah life are religion, kinship and family, community, and culture. The extended family is the most important social unit within Gullah culture. Many aspects of life are shared within the larger kinship network, including child-rearing, monetary and food resources, labor, and decision-making. Gullah families who have not yet lost their land to development and tourism still live in compounds, within which many generations live in close proximity to one another."

Gullah/Geechee people are survivors. Their survival instincts are strong because at the time of the slave trade people who lived on the west coast of Africa were hard-working and knowledgeable agriculturalists, like rural West African farmers today. They were accustomed to physical labor and to growing crops successfully in a variety of different environmental settings. They also knew how to fish, use nets, and navigate creeks, bays, and waterways. They were intimately familiar with the natural vegetation and could utilize it to its full extent. They were skilled at all kinds of game hunting in the fields and forests. Most important, the organization and fulfillment of their work was based on each and every member of the family doing his or her part. What set the Gullahs' ancestors apart from European settlers in the Low Country was their knowledge of tropical environments. They had thousands of years of background in adapting to conditions that Europeans found utterly baffling. For Africans from the Rice Coast, the Low Country looked like home.

So when the slaves came to America naked and in chains and with no physical possessions, even in servitude and with only rudimentary clothing and housing, they brought their skills, habits, values, and upbringing with them. Although the plantation owners used the Gullah people only as a means to enrich themselves, they never severed or altered the primordial Gullah family structure as a way of life.

Dr. Emory Shaw Campbell, the former Executive Director of Penn Center and himself a distinguished Gullah, has spent his life combining his work in the social sciences with an interest in African American affairs, specifically in the histories and genealogies of the Gullah peoples. He was one of the leaders of the first homecoming to Sierra Leone, and he has been involved along with

Joseph Opala in the arrangements for the trips that followed. One of Campbell's favorite quotes, whenever he talks about the benefits that come to people who seek out their roots, is *"Ef oona ent know weh oona da gwine, oona fa know weh oona come from"* ("If you don't know where you are going, you should know where you come from"). Not surprisingly the same proverb is often quoted in Sierra Leone: *"If yu noh no usai yu dey go, yu foh no usai yu kohmoht."*

As founder of Gullah Heritage Consulting Services and cofounder of Gullah Heritage Trail Tours, Campbell is thoroughly familiar with the Gullah outlook on land, property rights, and related matters. "Although the use of the land is changing," he says of the Low Country and Sea Islands, "and more and more people are working away from the land, we still have many who raise part of their own food, who fish the waters, who hunt in the forests, and who do so using the methods of their forebears rather than modern-day equipment and techniques. In some places there is still a 19th-century aura, with evenly rowed farms, dense forests of palmetto, pine, and live oak, dusty roads overhung with trees where no tall trucks can pass, and trails where only mules and marsh tackies can navigate—relics of a laid-back era that all of us strive to protect. Keeping one's land in the family provides that sense of place so central to holding our families together. We treasure what you might call the 'family compound,' whereby there is a physical, as well as an emotional and often spiritual, connection among family members that is so vital to our culture."[3]

"People cannot maintain their cultural heritage without a land base," explains Campbell. "One of the reasons that sea islanders have preserved their cultural heritage is because they had an early opportunity to own land and stabilize their families."[4] Much of his personal mission in his professional life as an educator, Executive Director of Penn Center, and founder of several small businesses in the Low Country has been not only to seek out and consider the values of one's roots, but to establish continuing dialogues between people of different races and callings.

This has been particularly important in the matter of land ownership and development. "We need a continuing dialogue between residents and property owners, real estate developers, government officials, and newcomers interested in establishing new roots in our region. Unless we get all of these people in communication with each other, to recognize the values inherent in our culture, then the destructive elements and relationships will foster continuing problems. When people tend to believe that mainstream American culture is the only culture of value—when our outlook is one-dimensional—then the other cultures—and the roots of the other cultures—become dormant."[5]

Campbell places great emphasis on "the human connection—the value of a child getting to know his or her heritage—of finding self-worth, of putting more value in the family and its members, not only where they live, but where they came from. The connection requires an educational focus both on this side of the sea, here in America, and that side of the sea, in our case, Africa. We must work to ensure that our own children, and the adults, understand their culture and heritage."[6]

John Tibbetts, editor of *Coastal Heritage*, a quarterly publication of the South Carolina Sea Grant Consortium, which conducts research studies in this field, explains what happens when people lose touch with their roots. "It's the oldest American story," he says. "For generations, an ethnic or religious clan, tightly knit by language and religion, huddles in a New World rural enclave or urban ghetto, enduring prejudice and poverty. Then abruptly ancient bonds fray. Strangers move in and disrupt local traditions, elders complain about their heritage's neglect and exploitation by outsiders, while young people leave home in droves to gain better jobs and education."[7]

We are well familiar with the saddening immigrant records that described the downtrodden plights of Irish Catholics in Boston, Russian Jews in New York, and the Chinese in San Francisco. "But over the last 50 years," notes Tibbetts, "groups with centuries-old roots in America also have been dragged into the mainstream, including the Cajuns in Louisiana, highlanders in Appalachia, Native Americans in every state, and the Gullah people of coastal South Carolina."[8]

"Yet down through centuries, the Gullah people managed to retain extensive African sources in their speech and folklore. The grammar of Gullah is African, and many aspects of Gullah culture—religious beliefs, arts and crafts, stories, songs, and proverbs—were derived from African sources. The Gullah people have preserved more of their African cultural history than any other large group of blacks in the United States," noted the late William S. Pollitzer, professor emeritus of anatomy and anthropology at the University of North

Carolina at Chapel Hill, in a 1999 book. "So many Africanisms survived in Gullah culture," said Pollitzer, "to some degree, it was a re-creation of Africa within the New World."[9]

The Gullah language is unique, the only lasting English-based Creole in North America. Nothing like it survives in other places in the United States. Similar Creole languages may have been spoken outside of coastal South Carolina in the slavery era, but they disappeared quickly. By the early 19th century, there was little evidence that other Creole languages existed in the Chesapeake region and North Carolina, where slaves adapted to standard English. This is remarkable when one considers that the Gullah people are descendants of many ethnic groups, including the Ibo, Fante, Fula, Mandingo, Yoruba, Ashanti, Bakongo, and others, and that in the English-speaking colonies they developed what is the Gullah language, now more and more often appearing in print as well as in verbal communication. Despite the circumstances that have led to the current state of communication, it is important—in fact, vital—that there be no slipping backward.

As Tibbetts warned, "Like all oral societies, Gullah is fragile. Without a written language, the passing of knowledge within a culture can quickly break down. In many of today's endangered oral cultures, children are not interested in learning the old ways, which disappear as elders, the repositories of knowledge, die out. An oral culture is transmitted primarily through families, and when there is a break—even of just 30 years or so—the loss often cannot be regained."[10]

Emory Campbell has echoed this opinion many times, particularly when he was Executive Director of Penn Center, which has become a rallying place for individuals and groups who want to preserve the Gullah culture and language, and when he was working as a volunteer for more than two decades helping to produce the translation of the New Testament into the Gullah language. And Marquetta L. Goodwine, founder of the Gullah/Geechee Sea Island Coalition, addressing the issue in a completely different medium and approach, has been effective in bringing the language and culture to the Internet, where it is exposed to many thousands of interested readers and viewers.

When reviewing ways in which the Gullah language has been nurtured by the community over the years, we must remember that *the way of life* plays a significant role in the preservation of the culture. The Gullah have a culture of persistence and perseverance not unlike old school New Englanders, who like to think of their ancestors and what they had to cope with in Colonial days.

An interesting example of this culture of persistence is provided by an islander named George Hamilton, 73, who survived an experience that might have meant death for someone not brought up in the Gullah tradition. Born into the steady hands of a Gullah midwife in the Spanish Wells section of Hilton Head Island, South Carolina, he was indoctrinated early on into the native ways. By the age of six, he had learned how to row a handmade wooden boat, and within a few more years he was adept at pulling fat blue crabs from long drop lines baited with ham skin and earning his keep on a job with the local fishery.

"We had to learn what we had to do and make do with what we had," Hamilton said of his childhood, explaining how he and his siblings and neighbor friends taught each other and learned through success and failure. They knew where to get berries and certain kinds of barks that would cure toothaches and stomach ailments; they knew the waters and the tides; they could foretell weather conditions by changing winds; they gained respect for the marshes and waters around them and knew what dangers to avoid and what animals and other wildlife to respect.[11]

So it was in the spring of 2006 that, by accident, when his 16-foot wooden hulled boat broke loose while he was picking oysters and drifted away from him in a strong current, he found himself stranded on uninhabited and isolated Turtle Island, far off the cruising waters between Daufuskie Island and Savannah. Not too concerned at first, he expected that family members and friends would come looking for him, or that he would spot one of the nature tour boats that occasionally ventured far from the usual courses. But one day faded into the next and the next, and it was nine days before he was found.

How did an elderly gentleman survive and remain in such good health? As one account detailed it, he survived on dew and plant juices. He ate cactus scraped open with oyster shells. He ate the soft, salty-sweet roots of marsh grasses. He sucked on tiny flowers and blooms and pine needles that were moist and dripping at sunrise. Water was made available when he found a cache of a dozen carelessly discarded water bottles. They were empty, but he turned them upside down in the grass at night with the caps slightly loose, and by early morning each one had half an inch of water that had condensed inside. During the day, he stuffed the bottles with shaved cactus plants and placed them in the sun, where the heat drained moisture from them. He was also able to open a few oysters and small mussels laboriously with the only metal implement he had in his pockets—a key ring.

Shelter was a problem because the nighttime temperature dropped into the 50s, and he was wearing only jeans and a T-shirt. But he found a small hillock that sheltered him from the wind, where he made a lean-to from a small pine tree and palmetto fronds, with a bed of pine straw.

During the day, some of his most agonizing moments were when he saw U.S. Coast Guard helicopters off in the distance, rising and falling and lowering divers at a spot where he later learned his boat had been found capsized. No amount of waving with his T-shirt on a long stick got any attention, and his efforts served only to exhaust and dishearten him for several hours. After his eventual rescue, he learned that the Coast Guard had given him up for dead, believing him drowned and swept away in the often strong currents between the islands. On about the third or fourth day, he spotted a fishing boat offshore, but it vanished past the far end of the island, and in his haste to get attention by waving he slipped and bloodied himself from head to toe on the sharp oyster beds that rimmed the shore lines. When he was finally able to get back up, the boat had vanished. Fearing, from long experience as a striker on a shrimp boat, not only the injury itself but the infection that can come from oyster cuts, he splashed salt water over every affected part of his body, even though the pain of the salt on the sores was almost unbearable. Then he sat in the sun to bake away the saline.

"The mosquitoes were thick like bees," he later recalled. "You ask God for strength, help, and understanding. As the time rolled on and rolled by, I was getting weaker. But there was strongness in my belief, and I knew in my mind that somebody would come to find me. I knew I was going to make it."[12]

His savior, on the ninth day of Hamilton's playing Robinson Crusoe, was a charter boat captain who spotted him waving his shirt as the captain navigated his boat past the island with three anglers going after redfish. Because he could not land on the treacherous oyster banks, the captain radioed the Coast Guard for help. Hamilton spent three days in the hospital recuperating and getting treatments for his cuts, bruises, insect bites, and lack of food and water. During that time he reiterated again and again to visitors that God and his Gullah upbringing had saved his life.

An African Look at the Gullahs in America

In December 2006, Daufuskie Island, the subject of so many references in this book, became a source of particular interest to two filmmakers from West Africa, Thomas Akodjinou and Felix Yao Eklu, on a three-state tour to gather research for a documentary titled *Children . . . the Artists of the World*. The film traces what happened to the last ship that transported slaves from Africa to the New World, sifting hundreds of details from sources such as the Civil Rights Museum in Selma, Alabama, the Gullah Gallery in Charleston, South Carolina, and local historical societies in the Sea Islands.

"Everybody doesn't know about this history, because sometimes it is not easy for them to talk about it or write about," Akodjinou explained. "But now we think it is necessary to show this history. To present this history. To learn this history . . . I think it is necessary for the children to know what it was like in the past and how we are living now and how we want to build the future world."[13]

The two men learned about Daufuskie and its Gullah history from Diane Cameron, who met them while working as an artist-in-residence in Africa, and who, since then, had gone to Charleston, South Carolina, to establish a nonprofit organization called Seed 2 Seed, which serves as a cultural bridge between Africa and the American South. Cameron acted as their guide and introduced them to students in the Daufuskie Elementary School. She explained, "What we've come to find out is that until now many Africans did not know what really happened to their ancestors once they were placed on that slave ship and sailed to America." As she further explained, Thomas and Felix were doing their research and producing a film to take back to Africa so they could tell people exactly what had taken place and what had happened to the slaves and their descendants once they had finally been freed.

Few people other than professional sociologists can appreciate the problems Diane Cameron and these young African filmmakers dealt with when they studied the Gullahs and other people with family roots in Africa. As Victor E. Dike, CEO of the Center for Social Justice and Human Development, wrote, "For many African parents, raising their children in Diaspora (particularly in the U.S.) is a very daunting and challenging task. The reasons are many, including the culture of the society, which gives enormous powers to the child. Torn between two cultures, African parents are therefore in a dilemma as to where to raise their children. Those who have the infrastructure and courage to send their children back home to Africa (in the care of their relatives) to get familiarized with the African culture have many things to be thankful for. While completing their high school education, some of them seize the opportunity to know their uncles, cousins, nieces, nephews and grandparents, and to grow up in an environment where morality and good character education are relatively regarded. But a few of the misinformed African parents in Diaspora who have argued that those who ship their children home are callous and selfish seem to forget that there is no substitute for a good education anchored on progressive traditional African values. It is difficult, if not impossible, for an African child to acquire a good western education with a blend of African cultural and traditional values in Diaspora. Because the system lacks the tools to teach African culture and tradition and virtues such as obedience and respect for the elders/ higher authorities, to care for parents at old age (not dumping them in old folks' homes), community orientation, and good moral character and behavior, among others. Common sense shows that if the culture and tradition of a people perish, the group also perishes."[14]

It is a step in the right direction to review the work of the two young African filmmakers who, along with Diane Cameron, are tackling this intricate and difficult situation.

Another person who was helpful to the filmmakers was Yvonne Wilson, a fifth-generation Daufuskian who shared her own story about how her family came to live on this little island, explaining that many of the original islanders gradually left as the outsiders and developers arrived and the cost of living, combined with rising taxes, made it impossible for most to continue in the old ways inherited from their parents and grandparents. According to her story, her great-great-grandmother Rosetta Frazier came to Daufuskie as a slave from Sierra Leone but eventually found freedom and made a home of her own there. She explained that the family was able to remain intact because her grandfather Samuel Holmes was for some time the only carpenter on the island. And the family has held on still. Among the only 12 African American natives still in residence, her grandson, Qur'an Greene, is one of the few remaining students at the Daufuskie Elementary School.

Before leaving, Thomas and Felix were given a tour of what was left of the island the slaves from Africa might have known. But tragically the relics that remain are few—a shabby ruin of a fireplace from an old slave house, a praise house outside the First Union African Baptist Church, an old graveyard, now half-destroyed to make way for a golf course, and some almost indistinguishable jumbles of sun-blanched wood probably once a fishing shack. Thomas Akodjinou and Felix Eklu were greatly moved by their experience, and when they eventually left to return to Africa they were convinced that their research had, indeed, been helpful in its aim: to find a link from the past to the present, bridging an enormous historical gap.

The Past As Prelude to the Future

Where does the Gullah culture go from here? Few people can predict it more persuasively than Emory Campbell, who has contributed so much to this book and in so many ways to the Low Country community in which he lives:

> While growing up on Hilton Head Island, South Carolina, in the 1940s and 1950s among a total population of about 1,500 Gullah people, Gullah cultural traditions shaped our entire world. And similar situations existed among native families in the coastal regions from roughly Wilmington, North Carolina, south to Jacksonville, Florida. As is still the case today, 10 simple neighborhoods held the Gullah culture on Hilton Head Island.
>
> Yet, strangely, I never heard the word Gullah used to describe us, although scholars applied the term in their research of the population. The term Geechee was used sneeringly by ordinary outsiders to describe

the cultural mystique defined mainly by our love of rice with our meal, coiled baskets as household utilities, spiritual beliefs, and particularly our vernacular. Having been rebuffed because of these derisive outsider opinions for many years, members of the culture submerged their expressions and actions in order to assimilate into mainstream America.

But thanks largely to curious scholars like those cited earlier in this book, who dedicated extensive research to studies of this culture, we have become delightfully aware of who we really are in relation to our African origin. These scholarly research efforts have resulted in a body of new information. No longer do we Gullah/Geechee people hesitate to express our love of rice dishes, weave a basket as a commemorative piece of art, or share a folktale in the Gullah vernacular.

A renaissance of widespread interest and acceptance of Gullah/ Geechee culture is manifested in a number of cultural art forms as well as economic ventures. These art forms are portrayed in annual vibrant cultural celebrations along the Sea Islands and Low Country of Georgia and the Carolinas. The Penn Center Heritage Celebration on St. Helena Island climaxes these events every November, as do an increasing number of other festivals in the Gullah Corridor. Many fine arts depicting Gullah life adorn local galleries in this region. The art of Jonathan Green, perhaps the most renowned Gullah artist, has achieved international acclaim. *Gullah Gullah Island*, a Nickelodeon TV series depicting the life of a young Gullah family, rivaled other popular TV programs for children in the 1990s. And the Hallelujah Singers have achieved international fame with their performance of songs rooted in the Gullah culture. Furthermore, cultural tourism has not escaped the cultural renaissance. More than 10 tour companies throughout the Sea Islands routinely highlight our enduring culture as their main attraction.

Perhaps the most widely accepted Gullah cultural asset is food. Culinary anthropologists have popularized fish 'n grits, shrimp 'n grits, gumbos, and rice dishes in mainstream restaurants as well as in Gullah restaurants. Several recently published cookbooks containing traditional Gullah recipes and food ways have achieved best-seller status, and have not only boosted the economy but promoted the transfer of these dishes to other cultures.

Ever since the American Bible Society published the New Testament in the Gullah language (which by the way far exceeded the most optimistic expectations in sales), readers of this extensive work have enthusiastically taken advantage of opportunities to begin pressing through the barriers to Gullah speech. Equally significant, the language is being widely *read* for the first time in history, a marked divergence from its basically oral tradition.

The future of the Gullah culture is bright not only because of its current popularity but also because of the increasing efforts to preserve its vital elements. The publication of the *Special Resource Study* by the National Park Service, described in detail earlier in this book, has provided a very solid access to the public for accurate information about the culture and the boundaries of the Gullah Corridor.

Knowing that Gullah, like other cultures, is influenced by interaction with one another and the natural environment, we are confident that the Gullah heritage will continue its course as a distinct, valued function in American culture. [15]

Although Campbell sometimes belittles the part he played in it, one of the important turning points in bringing the Gullah heritage to light was the program for studying the importance of the West African origins of the Gullah people, highlighted by the series of trips recounted earlier in this book. These occasions were another important point in the turn-around that saw the Gullah culture rise from obscurity. Before that the important research works by Turner and Wood were just sitting on the shelves of academic libraries, unknown to the public. Another step in the right direction was the previously mentioned production of the film *Family Across the Sea*, which sparked widespread interest in the origins of the Gullah culture and served, in a sense, to bring some of the scholarly research studies back off the shelf.

As both Campbell and Opala have emphasized in their research, their findings, and their evaluation, the Gullah culture is not only here to stay but will steadily become more and more of a vital part of the entire American scene.

Notes

Chapter 1

1. Edward Ball, *Slaves in the Family* (New York: Farrar, Strauss, and Giroux, 1998).
2. Ibid.
3. Herb Frazier, "Sierra Leone Homecoming," *Post and Courier*, July 24, 2005, 1F–2F.
4. Philip D. Morgan, *Slave Counterpoint* (Chapel Hill: University of North Carolina Press, 1998).
5. John H. Tibbetts, "Living Soul of Gullah," *Coastal Heritage* 14, no. 4 (Spring 2000).
6. Ibid.
7. Ibid.
8. Ibid.
9. Ibid.
10. Marquetta L. Goodwine, ed., *The Legacy of Ibo Landing: Gullah Roots of African American Culture* (Atlanta: Clarity Press, 1998).
11. Tibbetts, "Living Soul of Gullah."

Chapter 2

1. Willie Lee Nichols Rose, *Rehearsal for Reconstruction: The Port Royal Experiment* (New York: Vintage Books, 1964).
2. Rupert Sargent Holland, ed., *Letters and Diary of Laura M. Towne Written from the Sea Islands of South Carolina, 1862–1884* (New York: Negro University Press, 1912, 1969).
3. Ibid.
4. Ibid.
5. Ibid.
6. Ibid.
7. Ibid.
8. Ibid.

9. Ibid.
10. Ibid.
11. Ibid.

Chapter 3

1. Michael C. Wolfe, *The Abundant Life Prevails* (Waco, TX: Baylor University Press, 2000).
2. Margaret W. Creel, *A Peculiar People* (New York: New York University Press, 1988).
3. Wolfe, *Abundant Life*.
4. Ibid.
5. Ibid.
6. Ibid.
7. Interview by author with Emory Campbell.
8. Unpublished papers in the historical archives at Penn Center, St. Helena Island, SC.
9. Ibid.
10. Ibid.
11. Ibid.
12. Ibid.
13. Ibid.
14. National Park Service, *Low Country Gullah Culture Special Resource Study* (Atlanta: NPS Southeast Regional Office, 2005), F-20.

Chapter 4

1. Correspondence by author with Dr. Joseph Opala.
2. Ibid.
3. Don McKinney, "Family Ties: A Visit with the Campbells of Hilton Head Island," *Sandlapper*, February 7, 2006.
4. Ibid.
5. Ibid.
6. Ibid.
7. Ibid.
8. Ibid.

9. Cornelia Walker Bailey, *God, Dr. Buzzard, and the Bolito Man* (New York: Anchor Books, 2000).

10. Ibid.

11. Ibid.

12. Ibid.

13. Ibid.

14. Ibid.

15. Ibid.

16. Cathy Harley, "Making a Name for Herself," *Beaufort* (SC) *Gazette*, December 5, 2006.

17. Ibid.

18. Ibid.

19. Undated news release from Gallery Chuma of Charleston, SC, 2006.

20. Ibid.

21. Ibid.

22. Ibid.

23. Ibid.

24. Undated news release from Gullah Heritage Trail Tours, Charleston, SC, 2007.

25. Interview by author with Robert Lee, Executive Director of Seabrook retirement community, Hilton Head Island, SC, May 2006.

26. Ibid.

27. John Tibbetts, "Gullah's Radiant Light," *Coastal Heritage* 19, no. 3 (Winter 2004–5).

28. Ibid.

29. Ibid.

30. Ibid.

31. Ibid.

32. Ibid.

33. Thomas Jackson Woofter, *Black Yeomanry: Life on St. Helena Island* (New York: Henry Holt and Company, 1930).

34. Ibid.

35. Jannette Hypes, "Gullah: A Language, a Life, a Living History," *Associated Content*, http://www.associatedcontent.com/article/43638/gullah_a_

language_a_life_a_living_history.html.

36. Joseph Opala, *The Gullah: Rice, Slavery, and the Sierra Leone–American Connection* (Freetown, Sierra Leone: USIS, 1987).

37. National Park Service, *Low Country Gullah Culture*, F-20.

38. Ibid.

Chapter 5

1. National Park Service, *Low Country Gullah Culture*, F-20.

2. Patricia Jones-Jackson, *When Roots Die: Endangered Traditions on the Sea Islands* (Athens: University of Georgia Press, 1987).

3. Woofter, *Black Yeomanry*.

4. Ibid.

5. Elizabeth Jacoway, *Yankee Missionaries in the South* (Baton Rouge: Louisiana State University Press, 1980).

6. The Spirituals Project, www.spiritualsproject.org.

7. Roger Pinckney, *Blue Roots: African-American Folk Magic of the Gullah People* (St. Paul, MN: Llewellyn Publishers, 1998).

8. Ibid.

9. Wolfe, *Abundant Life*.

10. Susan Hayes Ward, *George H. Hepworth: Preacher, Journalist, Friend of the People* (New York: Dutton, 1903).

11. The Spirituals Project, www.spiritualsproject.org.

12. William Francis Allen, *Slave Songs of the United States* (New York: A. Simpson & Co., 1867).

13. Woofter, *Black Yeomanry*.

14. Bailey, *God, Dr. Buzzard, and the Bolito Man*.

15. Dennis Adams, *Gullah Language and Sea Island Culture*, Beaufort County Library, part of an ongoing library series, in-house and on the Web.

16. Pinckney, *Blue Roots*.

17. National Park Service, *Low Country Gullah Culture*, 81.

18. *De Nyew Testament in Gullah* (New York: American Bible Society, 2005).

19. Interviews by author with Emory Campbell.

20. Ibid.

21. Ibid.

Chapter 6

1. Pinckney, *Blue Roots.*
2. Faith Mitchell, *Hoodoo Medicine: Gullah Herbal Remedies* (Columbia, SC: Summerhouse Press, 1999).
3. Vennie Deas-Moore, "Home Remedies, Herb Doctors, and Granny Midwives," *World & I Journal* online, www.worldandi.com.
4. Unpublished account in the archives at Penn Center, St. Helena Island, SC.
5. National Park Service, *Low Country Gullah Culture*, D-18.
6. Pinckney, *Blue Roots.*
7. Ibid.
8. Bailey, *God, Dr. Buzzard, and the Bolito Man.*
9. Ibid.
10. Mary Granger, ed., *Drums and Shadows* (Georgia Writers' Project, under the Works Progress Administration, 1940).
11. Ibid.
12. National Park Service, *Low Country Gullah Culture.*
13. Mitchell, *Hoodoo Medicine.*
14. Granger, *Drums and Shadows.*
15. Ibid.
16. James Mooney, *Myths of the Cherokee and Sacred Formulas of the Cherokees* (Nashville, TN: Charles and Randy Elders, 1982).

Chapter 7

1. David Moltke-Hanson, Arthur Harvey Shaffer papers (faculty papers), Thomas Jefferson Library, University of Missouri–St. Louis.
2. William Edward Burghardt Du Bois, *Souls of Black Folk* (Chicago: McClurg, 1904).
3. Interviews by author with Emory Campbell, a Gullah by birth and one of the foremost Gullah historians, authors, lecturers, and tour directors.
4. NPR News, National Public Radio, series on African Americans and the Gullah culture.
5. Charles Joyner, *Down by the Riverside* (Chicago: University of Illinois

Press, 1984).

6. Jones-Jackson, *When Roots Die*.
7. *West Africa* magazine (April 28–May 4, 1997), 678–79.
8. Julian D. Mason Jr., ed., *The Poems of Phillis Wheatley* (Chapel Hill: University of North Carolina Press, 1966).
9. *Poems of Paul Laurence Dunbar*, in the archives of Wright State University, Dayton, Ohio.

Chapter 8

1. National Park Service, *Low Country Gullah Culture*, F-38.
2. Pinckney, *Blue Roots*.
3. "Sapelo Island," Sherpa Guides Web site, http://www.sherpaguides.com/georgia/coast/central_coast/sapelo_island.html.
4. Bailey, *God, Dr. Buzzard, and the Bolito Man*.
5. National Park Service, *Low Country Gullah Culture*, 95.
6. Interview by author with Tom Barnwell.
7. Bailey, *God, Dr. Buzzard, and the Bolito Man*.
8. Sidney Lanier, *Hymns of the Marshes* (New Haven, CT: Yale University Press, 1912).

Chapter 9

1. Jesse Edward Gantt Jr. and Veronica Davis Gerald, *The Ultimate Gullah Cookbook: A Taste of Food, History and Culture from the Gullah People* (Atlanta: Sands Publishing, 2002).
2. Ibid.
3. Josephine A. Beoku-Betts, "We Got Our Way of Cooking Things," *Gender & Society* 9, no. 5 (October 1995).
4. William S. Pollitzer, *The Gullah People and Their African Heritage* (Athens: University of Georgia Press, 1999).
5. Gantt and Gerald, *Ultimate Gullah Cookbook*.
6. Ibid.
7. National Park Service, *Low Country Gullah Culture*.

Chapter 10

1. John Middleton, ed., *Encyclopedia of Africa: South of the Sahara* (New York: Charles Scribner's Sons, 1997).
2. N. F. Karlins, "Bill Traylor," *Raw Vision* 15 (Summer 1996), http://www.raw vision.com/articles/15/traylor/traylor.html.
3. "Henry Ossawa Tanner," www.artchive.com/artchive/T/tanner.html.
4. News release from Gallery Chuma of Charleston, SC, February 17, 2007.
5. Ibid.

Chapter 11

1. Du Bois, *Souls of Black Folk*.
2. Ibid.
3. *Africa Guide* newsletter, www.africaguide.com (date unknown).
4. Thomas Wentworth Higginson, "Negro Spirituals," *Atlantic Monthly* (June 1867).
5. "Rosetta Tharpe," *Wikipedia* encyclopedia, http://en.wikipedia.org/wiki/Main_Page.
6. "Charles Albert Tindley," The Cyber Hymnal, http://www.cyberhymnal.org/ bio/t/i/tindley_ca.htm.
7. "Hall Johnson," Afrocentric Voices, www.afrovoices.com/hjohnson.html.
8. "William L. Dawson Tribute," Tuskegee University, www.tuskegee.edu/Global/story.asp?S=1199940.
9. Ibid.

Chapter 12

1. From author's interview with Dr. Joseph Opala citing his quote in *West Africa* magazine.
2. Joseph Opala, "The Gullah Connection," *West Africa* (May 19, 1986).
3. Interviews and correspondence by author with Emory Campbell.
4. Ibid.
5. Ibid.
6. Maureen Simpson, editorial, *Island Packet* (Hilton Head Island, SC), December 24, 2006.
7. Tibbetts, "Living Soul of Gullah."
8. Ibid.

9. Pollitzer, *The Gullah People*.

10. Tibbetts, "Living Soul of Gullah."

11. George Hamilton, editorial, *Island Packet* (Hilton Head Island, SC), April 23, 2006.

12. Ibid.

13. Maureen Simpson, editorial, *Island Packet* (Hilton Head Island, SC), December 24, 2006.

14. Ibid.

15. Interviews and correspondence by author with Dr. Emory Campbell.

Bibliography

Books

Bailey, Cornelia Walker. *God, Dr. Buzzard, and the Bolito Man*. New York: Anchor Books, 2000. A "saltwater Geechee" talks about life on Sapelo Island, Georgia, and various methods of living and healing in native cultures.

Ball, Edward. *Slaves in the Family*. New York: Farrar, Strauss, and Giroux, 1998. The story of a family of plantation owners in South Carolina and how blacks and whites lived together during 300 years of American history.

Bebey, Francis. *African Music: A People's Art*. New York: Lawrence Hill & Co., 1975. Recounts how music in America developed.

Bennett, John. *Doctor to the Dead: Grotesque Legends and Folk Tales of Old Charleston*. New York: Rinehart, 1946.

Black, James Gary. *My Friend the Gullah*. Beaufort, SC: Beaufort Book Company, 1974. A collection of personal experiences.

Botkin, A. *Lay My Burden Down*. Chicago: University of Chicago Press, 1945. A folk history of slavery.

Bottume, Elizabeth Hyde. *First Days Among the Contrabands*. Boston: Lee and Shephard, 1893. Young teachers from the North and their experiences in the Sea Islands shortly after the Civil War, living among and teaching freed slaves.

Branch, Muriel Miller. *The Water Brought Us*. New York: Dutton, 1995. A book for young people about the story of the Gullah-speaking people.

Brockington, Lee G. *Plantation Between the Waters*. Charleston: History Press, 2006. The story of Hobcaw Barony, a noted plantation in the Sea Islands that has been preserved for posterity.

Burchard, Peter. *Charlotte Forten: A Black Teacher in the Civil War*. New York: Crown, 1995. The story of a Penn Center teacher shortly after the Civil War.

Burlin, Natalie Curtis. *Negro Folk Songs*. New York and Boston: G. Schirmer,

1918–19. A series of music from the Hampton Institute.

Burn, Billie. *An Island Named Daufuskie.* Spartanburg, SC: Reprint Company, 1991. Illustrated with black-and-white photographs, prints, and maps. Covers history, topography, plantation life, culture, industry, family records, Gullah vocabulary, and stories.

Campbell, Emory S. *Gullah Cultural Legacies.* Hilton Head Island, SC: Gullah Heritage Consulting Services, 2002. An introduction to the Gullah culture, with a sampling of language and information about traditions, beliefs, art, and history.

Christensen, Abigail. *Afro-American Folk Lore Told Round Cabin Fires on the Sea Islands of South Carolina.* New York: Negro University Press, 1969. Stories in the Gullah language.

Conroy. Pat. *The Water Is Wide.* Boston: Houghton Mifflin, 1972. A best-selling memoir with many authentic references to life in the Sea Islands in days gone by.

Cooley, Rossa B. *Homes of the Freed.* New York: New Republic, 1926. The story of living and teaching at Penn School on St. Helena Island, by a former director of the school.

Creel, Margaret W. *A Peculiar People.* New York: New York University Press, 1988. Slave religion and community culture among the Gullahs.

————. *School Acres: An Adventure in Rural Education.* New Haven: Yale University Press, 1930.

Dabbs, Edith M. *Face of an Island: Leigh Richmond Miner's Photographs of Saint Helena Island.* New York: Grossman Publishers, 1970. A collection of large, clear black-and-white photographs of people, buildings, artifacts, and scenery of St. Helena with informative captions.

Dabbs, James McBride. *Haunted by God.* Richmond: John Knox Press, 1972. The cultural, religious, and spiritual experience of the South.

Daise, Ronald. *Reminiscences of Sea Island Heritage.* Orangeburg, SC: Sandlapper Publishing, 1986. A photographic essay of St. Helena Island with recollections by the people themselves.

Dash, Julie. *Daughters of the Dust.* New York: Dutton, 1997. Expands the story from the award-winning film of the same title.

Dillard, J. L. *Black English: Its History and Usage in the United States.* New York:

Random House, 1972.

Du Bois, William Edward Burghardt. *Souls of Black Folk*. Chicago: McClurg, 1904. A searching study by one of the most noted African Americans of his day.

Forten, Charlotte. *The Journal of Charlotte L. Forten*. New York: Dryden Press, 1953. The personal story of a free black and teacher in the South.

Franklin, John Hope. *From Slavery to Freedom*. New York: Knopf, 1988. A history of African Americans and their struggles to gain independence.

Fulop, Timothy E., and Albert J. Raboteau. *African-American Religion: Interpretive Essays in History and Culture*. London: Routledge. 1996. How events shaped beliefs and faiths and how religion impacted important events.

Gantt, Jesse Edward, Jr., with Veronica Davis Gerald. *The Ultimate Gullah Cookbook*. Beaufort, SC: Sands Publishing, 2003. An authentic Gullah cookbook with pertinent historical and cultural comments.

Gates, Henry Louis, Jr., et al. *Unchained Memories*. New York: Bullfinch Press, 2002. Readings from the slave narratives, as presented in the HBO documentary of the same name.

Georgia Writers' Project. *Drums and Shadows: Survival Studies Among the Georgia Coastal Negroes*. Works Project Administration (WPA), 1940. A compilation of interviews with many African Americans, conducted by the government, with tape recordings and notations.

Geraty, Virginia Mixon. *Gullah fuh Oonuh: A Guide to the Gullah Language*. Orangeburg, SC: Sandlapper Publishing, 1997.

Gonzales, Ambrose E. *Black Border* series. Columbia, SC: State Company, 1922. Gullah stories of the South Carolina coast.

———. *With Aesop Along the Black Border*. New York: Negro University Press, 1969. Stories told in the Gullah language.

Goodwine, Marquetta L., ed. *The Legacy of Ibo Landing: Gullah Roots of African American Culture*. Atlanta: Clarity Press, 1998. A collection of topics related to Gullah history, culture, art, language, religion, and fiction.

Green, Jonathan. *Gullah Images: The Art of Jonathan Green*. Columbia: University of South Carolina Press, 1996. A collection of large color plates of Green's paintings, with biographical information on the artist.

Grosvenor, Vertamae. *Vertamae Cooks in the Americas' Family Kitchen*.

San Francisco: KQED Books, 1996. A profusely illustrated cookbook with many commentaries about Gullah foods and personalities.

———. *Vibration Cooking, or the Travel Notes of a Geechee Girl.* New York: Doubleday, 1970.

Guthrie, Patricia. *Catching Sense.* Westport, CT: Bergin & Garvey, 1996. African American communities on a South Carolina island.

Harper, Michael S., and Anthony Walton. *The Vintage Book of African American Poetry.* New York: Random House, 2000. Two hundred years of "Vision, Struggle, Power, Beauty, and Triumph, from 50 Outstanding Poets," from the late 18th century to the present.

Holland, Rupert Sargent, ed. *Letters and Diary of Laura M. Towne Written from the Sea Islands of South Carolina, 1862–1884.* New York: Negro University Press, 1912, 1969.

Holloway, Joseph E., and Winifred K. Vass. *The African Heritage of American English.* Bloomington: Indiana University Press, 1993. A compilation of African derivatives in American English, including place names, folklore, food culture, and religion.

———. *Africanisms in American Culture.* Bloomington: Indiana University Press, 1990.

Jacoway, Elizabeth. *Yankee Missionaries in the South.* Baton Rouge: Louisiana State University Press, 1980. The Penn School experiment and the education of freed slaves in the Sea Islands.

Johnson, Guion Griffis. *A Social History of the Sea Islands, with Special Reference to St. Helena Island, South Carolina.* Chapel Hill: University of North Carolina Press, 1930. Covers the labor culture of cotton, rice, and indigo and the effects of the Civil War.

Johnson, Guy B. *Folk Culture on St. Helena Island, South Carolina.* Chapel Hill: University of North Carolina Press, 1930. Language, customs, religion, and other aspects of life in Gullah communities.

Jones, Bessie. *For the Ancestors: Autobiographical Memories Collected and Edited by John Stewart.* Urbana: University of Illinois Press, 1983. Told by the last active member of the original Georgia Sea Island Singers, who recounts her life as a sharecropper, farmhand, migrant worker, domestic servant, railroad camp cook, and cannery worker.

Jones, Charles Colcock. *Gullah Folk Tales from the Georgia Coast*. Athens: University of Georgia Press, 2000. Tales told in the Gullah language.

Jones-Jackson, Patricia. *When Roots Die: Endangered Traditions on the Sea Islands*. Athens: University of Georgia Press, 1987. Covers social history, personalities, folk literature, texts, and language, with a map showing the South Carolina Sea Islands. Includes a touching memorial tribute to Jones-Jackson, who was killed doing National Geographic research on Johns Island, South Carolina.

Joyner, Charles. *Down by the Riverside*. Chicago: University of Illinois Press, 1984. A cultural history and study of slave existence within the enslaved community.

———. *Folk Song in South Carolina*. Columbia: University of South Carolina Press, 1971. Explores the significance of folk music, ballads, religious songs, and secular music, with data on where they were collected and by whom.

———. *Shared Traditions: Southern History and Folk Culture*. Urbana: University of Illinois Press, 1999. Essays on the relation between history and culture in the South, with a reflection on the future of folk culture.

Kiser, Clyde Vernon. *Sea Island to City*. New York: Columbia University Press, 1932. A study of St. Helena, South Carolina, islanders who moved to urban centers in the North.

Kuyk, Betty M. *African Voices in the African American Heritage*. Indianapolis: Indiana University Press, 2003. The survival of African belief systems and social structures in contemporary African American culture.

Longsworth, Polly I. *Charlotte Forten, Black and Free*. New York: Thomas Y. Crowell, 1920. Biography of the free black woman from a noted Philadelphia family who taught at Penn School on St. Helena Island and kept a journal of the events.

McTeer, J. E. *Adventures in the Woods and Waters of the Low Country*. Beaufort, SC: Beaufort Book Company, 1972.

———. *Fifty Years as a Lowcountry Witch Doctor*. Beaufort, SC: Beaufort Book Company, 1976. How a root doctor traded spells with Dr. Buzzard, the most famed—and feared—root doctor of them all.

Mitchell, Faith. *Hoodoo Medicine: Gullah Herbal Remedies*. Columbia, SC: Summerhouse Press, 1999. History of the Sea Islands, with a directory of various herbs and roots used for healing and pain relief. Includes line drawings of plants.

Montgomery, Michael. *The Crucible of Carolina*. Athens: University of Georgia Press, 1994. Essays concerning the development of the Gullah culture and language.

Moutoussamy-Ashe, Jeanne. *Daufuskie Island: A Photographic Essay*. Columbia: University of South Carolina Press, 1982. With a foreword by Alex Haley commenting on the end of a way of life on this small island.

Opala, Joseph. *The Gullah: Rice, Slavery, and the Sierra Leone–American Connection*. Freetown, Sierra Leone: USIS, 1987. History and culture of the Gullah people, emphasizing the rice connection to West Africa.

Parrish, Lydia. *Slave Songs of the Georgia Sea Islands*. New York: Farrar, Straus, 1942.

Pinckney, Roger. *Blue Roots: African-American Folk Magic of the Gullah People*. St. Paul, MN: Llewellyn Publishers, 1998. History and culture of the Gullah people with a concentration on root workers.

Pollitzer, William S. *The Gullah People and Their African Heritage*. Athens: University of Georgia Press, 1999. Detailed work by one of the top scholars on the history and culture of the Gullahs, in five segments. Contains many maps, tables, black-and-white photographs, and an extensive bibliography and index.

Rawley, James. *The Transatlantic Slave Trade*. New York: Norton, 1981.

Robinson, Randall. *The Debt: What America Owes to Blacks*. New York: Dutton, 2000.

Robinson, Sallie Ann. *Gullah Home Cooking the Daufuskie Way*. Chapel Hill: University of North Carolina Press, 2003. In addition to recipes from a native islander, the book reminisces about the author's interesting life and background as a Gullah.

Rose, Willie Lee Nichols. *Rehearsal for Reconstruction: The Port Royal Experiment*. New York: Vintage Books, 1964. Examines the failed federal program intended to help freed slaves lead a more normal American life after the Civil War.

Sea Island Translation Team. *De Good Nyews Bout Jedus Christ Wa Luke Write:*

The Gospel According to Luke. New York: American Bible Society, 1994. In Gullah Sea Island Creole with marginal texts of the King James Version.

———. *De Nyew Testament.* New York: American Bible Society, 2005. The New Testament in the Gullah language, with English translations in side panels on each page.

Stoddard, Albert Henry. *Gullah Animal Tales from Daufuskie Island, South Carolina.* Hilton Head Island, SC: Push Button Publishing Company, 1995. Stories told in the Gullah language.

Turner, Lorenzo Dow. *Africanisms in the Gullah Dialect.* Chicago: University of Chicago Press, 1949. Regarded as the most important pioneering study by one of the leading scholars of Africanisms and the Gullah language and culture. The author was a longtime student and researcher in this field who personally visited almost every source of potential data in Africa and the Americas. This work includes phonetics, syntax, sounds, morphology, intonation, texts, African and Gullah names, maps of Gullah areas and the west coast of Africa, and many detailed references.

Twining, Mary Arnold, and Keith E. Baird. *Sea Island Roots: African Presence in the Carolinas and Georgia.* Trenton, NJ: Africa World Press, 1991. Thirteen essays by various authors, with a 14th by Twining that is regarded as a valuable tool, describing many sources, books, and other published works on the Sea Islands and islanders.

Weir, Robert M. *Colonial South Carolina.* Columbia: University of South Carolina Press, 1997. A history of the state, with segments on the evolution of African Americans from slaves to freedmen.

Whaley, Marcellus S. *The Old Types Pass: Gullah Sketches of the Carolina Sea Islands.* Boston: Christopher Publishing House, 1925. Illustrated by Edna Reed Whaley. Covers the influence of African Americans on their communities and people. Includes 25 Gullah recollections in what at the time was a modified Gullah dialect.

Wolfe, Michael C. *The Abundant Life Prevails.* Waco, TX: Baylor University Press, 2000. Religious traditions and concepts on St. Helena Island.

Wood, Peter. *Black Majority.* New York: Knopf, 1974. The story of blacks in South Carolina from 1670 through the Stono Rebellion.

Woofter, Thomas Jackson. *Black Yeomanry: Life on St. Helena Island.* New York: Henry Holt and Company, 1930. Life on the Sea Islands, and particularly on St. Helena and at Penn School.

Yetman, Norman, ed. *Voices from Slavery.* Mineola, NY: Dover Publications, 1972. Authentic slave narratives as recorded and published.

Films and Video Recordings

Amistad. The story of the slave ship and the slaves who revolted and took over the vessel, eventually finding freedom in the New World. A reproduction of the *Amistad*, based at Mystic Seaport in Connecticut, makes regular voyages to many ports where visitors can observe what slaves had to endure while being transported from Africa to American ports in both the North and the South. A full-length film of 152 minutes.

Conrack. The engaging story of a young white teacher assigned to an isolated Sea Island populated largely by poor black families. Working with young children who are illiterate, he finds a way to spark their lagging interest in being educated, guiding them to knowledge about reading, writing, and arithmetic that will help them in later life. This film is the story of noted author Pat Conroy and his personal experience on remote Daufuskie Island, South Carolina. 111 minutes.

Daughters of the Dust. A hauntingly lovely story set in the Sea Islands off the Georgia coast a century ago, the film portrays the unique culture of the Gullah people by focusing on a typical local family as its members struggle with the option of leaving their island and heading north. The climax comes when on the eve of their intended departure memories of their ancient history and roots appear in highly dramatic visions. The film was created by Julie Dash, a noted director, as a tribute to her Gullah ancestors. 113 minutes.

Fah de Chillun: Gullah Traditions. A music video that teaches children about the Gullah culture in a lively manner that they can understand and appreciate. The Hallelujah Singers, wearing traditional costumes and with colorful set designs as backdrops, perform Gullah songs and skits, interacting with each other and the young audience. 27 minutes.

Family across the Sea. A vivid story of the ways in which the Gullah people have retained their ties to their homeland in West Africa despite centuries of oppression and hardship. This film chronicles the journey of a small band of Gullah people from South Carolina, Georgia, Florida, and Oklahoma to Sierra Leone, West Africa, in 1989, with the goal of tracing their roots. 56 minutes.

Free at Last. The detailed stories of civil rights heroes and events that are of historical importance. 90 minutes.

Garden of Gold. This film is a brief presentation about the "Rice Kingdom" in the days of the large plantations in the Sea Islands, where rice was one of the major crops. It explores the agricultural methods used to grow rice and examines how many slaves were imported from West Africa because of their proficiency in the planting, growing, and processing of rice. The film was produced in conjunction with the establishment of the Georgetown County, South Carolina, Rice Museum and includes a short history of that institution as well. 17 minutes.

God's Gonna Trouble the Water. Who are the Gullah? What binds these peoples together? This story is told through spirituals and remembrances featuring the renowned Hallelujah Singers, the Gullah Praise House Shouters, and local sea islanders. The film features rare vintage footage, old audio recordings, and vivid commentary. 55 minutes.

Gullah Tales. The story opens with Maum Nancy, an elderly slave woman, telling stories to children, both black and white, on a Georgia plantation in the 1830s. Then it shifts to a dramatization of two typical Gullah animal and human "trickster" tales, in which the actors try to outsmart each other. In all, the sequences also provide an authentic depiction of Gullah culture and language. 28 minutes.

The Language You Cry In. This award-winning "Story of a Mende Song" is a remarkable "detective tale" based on native music and reaching across hundreds of years and thousands of miles from 18th-century Sierra Leone in West Africa to the Gullah people of the present-day Sea Islands of the Carolinas and Georgia. The film also recounts the remarkable story of how the Gullahs of today have retained strong links with their African past. 52 minutes.

My Name Ain't Eve. This film explores the way that African Americans name their children traditionally or through more contemporary methods. 60 minutes.

Palmetto Places: St. Helena Island. This film celebrates the Gullah culture as it exists today on one of the largest Sea Islands in the Carolinas. Viewers are taken on a trip around the island, visiting key points, such as the ruins of an old chapel, a Gullah museum, a Gullah restaurant, and Penn Center, once Penn School, founded in 1862. 28 minutes.

Penn Center. A history of Penn School, founded in 1862 and still in existence as Penn Center, situated on St. Helena Island, South Carolina, and dedicated to the history and preservation of the Gullah language, culture, and heritage. 50 minutes.

Remnants of Mitchellville. A documentary film focusing on the history of Mitchellville, a village established on Hilton Head Island, South Carolina, in 1862 by the Union commander to provide homes for some 1,500 freed slaves, with the idea that they could live there and earn a living largely as wage-earning laborers for the occupying Union forces on the island. Today, this is a historic site visited on Gullah tours.

Robert Smalls: A Patriot's Journey from Slavery to Capitol Hill. The story of a little-known hero who commandeered a Confederate ship during the Civil War and delivered it to the Union fleet. Smalls eventually became the first African American to serve in Congress.

Saving Sandy Island. How the Gullah residents of a small island in South Carolina took very positive and successful steps to preserve the isolation and natural wonders of their environment and protect it from the encroachments of civilization, even to the extent of blocking the efforts of mainland citizens to plan a bridge to the island.

The Story of English: Part V, Black on White. An examination of black English, or Gullah, and its influence on American speech in the South. The film traces the origins of this language from West Africa to modern times and characterizes the people who spoke it along an old slave-trade route. It also uses traditional music and song to explain the powerful influence of the Gullah culture on the people of the Sea Islands. 58 minutes.

The Strength of These Arms: White Rice, Black Labor. The life of Gullah slaves as

seen from an archaeological perspective, starting with the excavation of slave
quarters at Middleburg Plantation in South Carolina. The film shows how
slaves from West Africa brought their skills to the southern plantations and
includes some rare footage of Gullah descendants of slaves working in rice
fields in the 1940s. 27 minutes.

Tales of the Land of Gullah for Kids. An educational presentation that focuses
on both the plight and accomplishments of the first African slaves who
landed on the shores of the Carolinas. The film is enlivened by fables, songs,
and stories that are shared by viewers. 44 minutes.

Tales of the Unknown South. This title is actually a reference to three separate
films about the Carolinas: (1) *The Half-Pint Flask*, the impressive and startling story of a man who disturbs a Gullah grave in order to acquire a souve-
nir for a collection but fails to reckon with something horrible in the grave;
(2) the tale of a woman from the deep backwoods whose home is threatened
when a developer starts purchasing the Gullah lands in her neighborhood;
and (3) an incident in which a black girl enrolls in a previously all-white
school and faces unknown personal danger.

Unchained Memories. Readings from the slave narratives, based on the Federal
Writers' Project of the Works Progress Association (WPA) in the 1930s,
which was commissioned during the Great Depression to interview members of the last living generation of African Americans born into slavery
and compile their memories of bygone years. An HBO documentary film
described as "in their words, our shared history." 75 minutes.

Voices of Color film series. An on-going initiative designed to highlight the range
and depth of the African American experience, giving voice to this subject
area. It was launched on the 20th anniversary of the noted award-winning
film *The Color Purple.*

When Rice Was King. How rice cultivation made the southern colonies among
the richest in America in the 18th and 19th centuries and made possible the
lavish homes and lifestyles of the planters in these regions. Although the
Gullah connections are minimal, the film includes many examples of Gullah
language and work songs and succeeds in explaining the nature and extent
of rice cultivation and the making of the "Rice Kingdom."

Will to Survive: The Story of the Gullah/Geechee Nation. An hour-long TV documentary in celebration of Black History Month, this film documents the ways in which the Gullah peoples have established homes and communities in America and have continued the traditions of their African ancestors. The setting is Sapelo Island, Georgia, one of the last-remaining Gullah communities that is still intact. 60 minutes.

Yonder Come Day. This film documents the efforts of Bessie Jones, the last active member of the Georgia Sea Island Singers, to pass on the songs, games, and traditions of the Gullah past to new generations. Born in 1902, Jones learned many of the songs from her grandfather, who had been brought to America from Africa and died at age 105. 28 minutes.

Sound Recordings

Avery Research Center. *Spiritual Society Concerts.* Fifty-six spirituals performed by three generations of the amateur Spiritual Society between 1936 and 1995.

———. *Spiritual Society Field Recordings.* Nineteen spirituals performed by African American congregations in the Carolina Low Country between 1936 and 1939. Six of these also include performances by the champion "street criers" at the 1936 Azalea Festival.

———. *Spirituals of the Carolina Low Country.* The music and Gullah lyrics of 49 spirituals that were recorded by the Society for the Preservation of Spirituals between 1922 and 1931. Also available is a guide to all of the spirituals collected by the Society, describing where to find them and the form in which they are available.

Daise, Ron. *De Gullah Storybook.* Narrated by Ron and Natalie Daise. A counting book with English and Gullah poems. GOG Enterprises.

———. *Little Muddy Waters.* Compact disk narrated by Ron and Natalie Daise. A story based on Gullah folk tales, which also includes a Gullah song, "Respec Yo Eldas." GOG Enterprises.

———. *Sleep Tight: Night Songs and Stories.* From the *Gullah, Gullah Island* series. GOG Enterprises.

———. *We'll Stand the Storm and Other Spirituals*. Beaufort, SC, collection. Folkway Records.

———. *Johns Island, South Carolina: Its People and Songs*. A collection of field recordings that includes secular and religious songs of the Gullah culture.

Goodwine, Marquetta ("Queen Quet"). *Hunnah Chillun*. A collection of native recordings of traditional Gullah/Geechee spirituals, stories, history, and dance music.

———. *Hunnah Hafa Shout Sumtines*. Gullah Roots Productions.

Hallelujah Singers. *Songs of Hope, Faith, and Freedom*. The first of many recordings by this noted group, including "Carry Me Home," featuring Gullah melodies that span the period of history between the 1860s and the birth of the blues in the 1920s.

Jones, Bessie. *Put Your Hand on Your Hip, and Let Your Backbone Slip*. Songs and games from the Georgia Sea Islands. A compact disk with 31 songs sung by Jones, accompanied by tambourine and various adult and children singers.

———. *So Glad I'm Here and Step It Down*. An album intended to preserve the rich Gullah heritage.

Jones, Bessie, with John Davie and Bobby Leecan. *Georgia Sea Island Songs*. Local performers sing a variety of chants resembling African counterparts, as well as more modern selections. Compact disk. New World Records.

Klein, Thomas, in conjunction with Georgia Southern University. Recordings titled *Lorenzo Dow Turner: Man and Mission*. Covers his work as a key pioneer in studying the Gullah language in the 1920s and 1930s. This project comprises some 18 hours of oral history recordings of Gullah and Geechee residents of the Sea Islands during 1932 and 1933. The subjects cover just about every phase of living, working, and the arts, and although the tapes are primitive, sometimes with high levels of interference, they have been described as "unique, invaluable, and irreplaceable documents of American and world history."

Lomax, Alan. A selection of the most important works arranged by this noted and exceptional collector is now housed in the American Folklife Center in the Library of Congress. The numerous works related to African American and Gullah music include *Southern Journey*, a 13-volume series of original recordings of blues, ballads, hymns, spirituals, reels, shouts, chanteys, and work songs. These selections, recorded by Lomax in extensive travels throughout the southern states, evoke the musical world of the rural South in an era before radio, movies, and television. Notable volumes include *Georgia Sea Islands—Biblical Songs and Spirituals; Earliest Times—Georgia Sea Island Songs for Everybody; Velvet Voices: African-American Music of the Eastern Shores;* and *Brethren, We Meet Again.*

Magee, Richard, and Mary Magee. *Ride With Me, South Carolina.* RMW Associates. A specified objective is "to hear the ancient language of the Sea Islands."

McIntosh County Shouters. *Slave Songs from the Coast of Georgia.* One of a number of recordings made by this popular group, using all of the techniques and accompaniment of the southeastern ring shout, which has been described as "the oldest surviving African American performance tradition on the North American continent," and is pretty much localized to McIntosh County on the Georgia coast.

Moving Star Hall Singers. "Been in the Storm So Long," "Remember Me," "Reborn Again," "See God's Ark A-Moving," and other numbers that have been popular on Johns Island, South Carolina, one of the oldest American communities.

Plantation Singers. "Feelin' Good," "This Little Light of Mine," and other songs particularly oriented to the preservation of the spiritual and sacred music of the Low Country.

Smalls, Marlene. *Heritage, Not Hate: Discovering Gullah and Finding Myself.* A combination of narrated personal history and songs from Smalls and the Hallelujah Singers.

Gullah Web Sites

Providing Web sites in a book or any other publication with a shelf life of more than two months can be an exercise in frustration because sites change periodically or go off the Internet without notice. For a reader of this book who may be seeking such sources, the most practical route is to go to your favorite search engine (Google, Yahoo, or whatever it may be) and simply type in the search bar "Gullah Web Sites." In all likelihood, you will get some references that you do not want and others that are only partly on the mark, but at least you will be in the right field.

Having given this caution, here is a list of Gullah sites that provide excellent information and are more or less permanent.

Low Country Gullah Culture Special Resource Study. This is, far and away, the most comprehensive, up-to-date, and accurate resource available. It is the result of research by the National Park Service over a period of more than five years in the Southeast. On the Web site, the sections are well organized and classified so that different parts can be easily and quickly downloaded for review. The overall study is so comprehensive that it would take several hundred pages just to download from its site. http:www.nps.gov/sero/planning/gg_srs/gg_process.htm.

Abridged Gullah Dictionary. A lengthy glossary of Gullah words derived from *The Black Border* by Ambrose E. Gonzales. http://www.gullahtours.com/gullah_dictionary.html.

The Penn Center: A Link to the Past and a Bridge to the Future. This historical institution was founded in 1862 as a school to teach freed slaves and is now a center for the study of the Gullah culture and language. Located on St. Helena Island, one of the largest Sea Islands, it plays host each summer to the Gullah Institute and holds a Gullah Festival in November, as well as many other African American and Gullah-related events during the course of each year. http://www.penncenter.com/.

Avery Research Center. Located in Charleston, South Carolina, this institution has a mission "to collect, preserve, and document the history of African Americans (including Gullah/Geechee peoples) in Charleston and the Carolina Lowcountry." http://www.cofc.edu/aver/.

Beaufort County, SC, Library. The main county library in the historic town of Beaufort has one of the South's largest collections of materials on the Gullah language and the Sea Island culture, including many illustrations and documents. http://www.co.beaufort.sc.us/bftlib/gullah.htm.

South Carolina State Museum. A key department of the museum is devoted to African American culture and research, including major entries on the Gullah language and history in the South. http://www.museum.state.sc.us/culturalhistory/AfricGullah.htm.

Africana Heritage Project. The mission of this organization is to rediscover records relating to the names and lives of former slaves, their locations, and their descendants in order to share information with individuals and families of African American and Gullah lineage. http://www.africanaheritage.com.

Oxford African American Studies Center. The center uses a system of combining the authority of reference works with technology to access detailed information about the lives and events that have shaped African American history and culture over many years. It includes many references to the Gullah culture and its history, language, and heritage. Reaching this site enables users to trace Gullah roots in great detail. http://www.oxfordaasc.com/public/about.jsp.

Marquetta Goodwine: The African Soul. Goodwine, commonly known as "Queen of the Gullah Geechee Nation," has developed a popular Web site with many offerings to users, such as books, music, recipes, and historical data, and does much to expand interest in the subject. She says, "I founded this organization as a means to connect all of the people of the Sea Islands with other people around the world who are interested in assisting my people with the preservation and continuation of our native culture." http://www.answers.com/topic/marquetta-goodwine.

African American Studies Programs in the United States. A listing of some 35 such programs and Web sites across the United States to which viewers can turn for detailed information. http://www.princeton.edu/ ~aasprog/aasps.htm.

Index

CPSIA information can be obtained
at www.ICGtesting.com
Printed in the USA
LVHW04s2130280718
585266LV00001B/1/P